50% OFF Online NCE Prep (

Dear Customer,

We consider it an honor and a privilege that you chose our NCE Study Guide. As a way of showing our appreciation and to help us better serve you, we have partnered with Mometrix Test Preparation to offer you **50% off their online NCE Prep Course**. Many NCE courses cost hundreds of dollars. With their course, you get access to the best NCE prep material, and **you only pay half price**.

Mometrix has structured their online course to perfectly complement your printed study guide. The NCE Prep Course contains **in-depth lessons** that cover all the most important topics, **30+ video reviews** that explain difficult concepts, **over 1,650 practice questions** to ensure you feel prepared, and **over 500 digital flashcards**, so you can study while you're on the go.

Online NCE Prep Course

Topics Covered:
- Professional Practice and Ethics
- Intake, Assessment, and Diagnosis
- Areas of Clinical Focus
- Treatment Planning
- Counseling Skills and Interventions
- Core Counseling Attributes

Course Features:
- NCE Study Guide
  - Get content that complements our best-selling study guide.
- 7 Full-Length Practice Tests
  - With over 1,650 practice questions, you can test yourself again and again.
- Mobile Friendly
  - If you need to study on the go, the course is easily accessible from your mobile device.
- NCE Flashcards
  - Their course includes a flashcard mode consisting of over 500 content cards to help you study.

To receive this discount, visit https://www.mometrix.com/university/nce or scan the QR code with your phone. At the checkout page, enter the discount code: **BONUS50**

If you have any questions or concerns, please contact Mometrix at support@mometrix.com.

Sincerely,

Webster's Test Prep in partnership with

FREE Test Taking Tips Video/DVD Offer

To better serve you, we created videos covering test taking tips that we want to give you for FREE. **These videos cover world-class tips that will help you succeed on your test.**

We just ask that you send us feedback about this product. Please let us know what you thought about it—whether good, bad, or indifferent.

To get your **FREE videos**, you can use the QR code below or email freevideos@studyguideteam.com with "Free Videos" in the subject line and the following information in the body of the email:

> a. The title of your product
>
> b. Your product rating on a scale of 1-5, with 5 being the highest
>
> c. Your feedback about the product

If you have any questions or concerns, please don't hesitate to contact us at info@studyguideteam.com.

Thank you!

NCE Exam Prep 2025-2026

5 Practice Tests and NCE Study Guide Book
[Includes Audiobook]

A. T. Segura

Interested in buying more than 10 copies of our product? Contact us about bulk discounts:
bulkorders@studyguideteam.com

ISBN 13: 9781637757208

Table of Contents

Welcome

Dear Reader,

Welcome to your new Test Prep Books study guide! We are pleased that you chose us to help you prepare for your exam. There are many study options to choose from, and we appreciate you choosing us. Studying can be a daunting task, but we have designed a smart, effective study guide to help prepare you for what lies ahead.

Whether you're a parent helping your child learn and grow, a high school student working hard to get into your dream college, or a nursing student studying for a complex exam, we want to help give you the tools you need to succeed. We hope this study guide gives you the skills and the confidence to thrive, and we can't thank you enough for allowing us to be part of your journey.

In an effort to continue to improve our products, we welcome feedback from our customers. We look forward to hearing from you. Suggestions, success stories, and criticisms can all be communicated by emailing us at info@studyguideteam.com.

Sincerely,
Test Prep Books Team

FREE Videos/DVD OFFER

Doing well on your exam requires both knowing the test content and understanding how to use that knowledge to do well on the test. We offer completely FREE test taking tip videos. **These videos cover world-class tips that you can use to succeed on your test.**

To get your **FREE videos**, you can use the QR code below or email freevideos@studyguideteam.com with "Free Videos" in the subject line and the following information in the body of the email:

      a. The title of your product
      b. Your product rating on a scale of 1-5, with 5 being the highest
      c. Your feedback about the product

If you have any questions or concerns, please don't hesitate to contact us at info@studyguideteam.com.

Scan Here

Quick Overview

As you draw closer to taking your exam, effective preparation becomes more and more important. Thankfully, you have this study guide to help you get ready. Use this guide to help keep your studying on track and refer to it often.

This study guide contains several key sections that will help you be successful on your exam. The guide contains tips for what you should do the night before and the day of the test. Also included are test-taking tips. Knowing the right information is not always enough. Many well-prepared test takers struggle with exams. These tips will help equip you to accurately read, assess, and answer test questions.

A large part of the guide is devoted to showing you what content to expect on the exam and to helping you better understand that content. In this guide are practice test questions so that you can see how well you have grasped the content. Then, answer explanations are provided so that you can understand why you missed certain questions.

Don't try to cram the night before you take your exam. This is not a wise strategy for a few reasons. First, your retention of the information will be low. Your time would be better used by reviewing information you already know rather than trying to learn a lot of new information. Second, you will likely become stressed as you try to gain a large amount of knowledge in a short amount of time. Third, you will be depriving yourself of sleep. So be sure to go to bed at a reasonable time the night before. Being well-rested helps you focus and remain calm.

Be sure to eat a substantial breakfast the morning of the exam. If you are taking the exam in the afternoon, be sure to have a good lunch as well. Being hungry is distracting and can make it difficult to focus. You have hopefully spent lots of time preparing for the exam. Don't let an empty stomach get in the way of success!

When travelling to the testing center, leave earlier than needed. That way, you have a buffer in case you experience any delays. This will help you remain calm and will keep you from missing your appointment time at the testing center.

Be sure to pace yourself during the exam. Don't try to rush through the exam. There is no need to risk performing poorly on the exam just so you can leave the testing center early. Allow yourself to use all of the allotted time if needed.

Remain positive while taking the exam even if you feel like you are performing poorly. Thinking about the content you should have mastered will not help you perform better on the exam.

Once the exam is complete, take some time to relax. Even if you feel that you need to take the exam again, you will be well served by some down time before you begin studying again. It's often easier to convince yourself to study if you know that it will come with a reward!

Test-Taking Strategies

1. Predicting the Answer

When you feel confident in your preparation for a multiple-choice test, try predicting the answer before reading the answer choices. This is especially useful on questions that test objective factual knowledge. By predicting the answer before reading the available choices, you eliminate the possibility that you will be distracted or led astray by an incorrect answer choice. You will feel more confident in your selection if you read the question, predict the answer, and then find your prediction among the answer choices. After using this strategy, be sure to still read all of the answer choices carefully and completely. If you feel unprepared, you should not attempt to predict the answers. This would be a waste of time and an opportunity for your mind to wander in the wrong direction.

2. Reading the Whole Question

Too often, test takers scan a multiple-choice question, recognize a few familiar words, and immediately jump to the answer choices. Test authors are aware of this common impatience, and they will sometimes prey upon it. For instance, a test author might subtly turn the question into a negative, or he or she might redirect the focus of the question right at the end. The only way to avoid falling into these traps is to read the entirety of the question carefully before reading the answer choices.

3. Looking for Wrong Answers

Long and complicated multiple-choice questions can be intimidating. One way to simplify a difficult multiple-choice question is to eliminate all of the answer choices that are clearly wrong. In most sets of answers, there will be at least one selection that can be dismissed right away. If the test is administered on paper, the test taker could draw a line through it to indicate that it may be ignored; otherwise, the test taker will have to perform this operation mentally or on scratch paper. In either case, once the obviously incorrect answers have been eliminated, the remaining choices may be considered. Sometimes identifying the clearly wrong answers will give the test taker some information about the correct answer. For instance, if one of the remaining answer choices is a direct opposite of one of the eliminated answer choices, it may well be the correct answer. The opposite of obviously wrong is obviously right! Of course, this is not always the case. Some answers are obviously incorrect simply because they are irrelevant to the question being asked. Still, identifying and eliminating some incorrect answer choices is a good way to simplify a multiple-choice question.

4. Don't Overanalyze

Anxious test takers often overanalyze questions. When you are nervous, your brain will often run wild, causing you to make associations and discover clues that don't actually exist. If you feel that this may be a problem for you, do whatever you can to slow down during the test. Try taking a deep breath or counting to ten. As you read and consider the question, restrict yourself to the particular words used by the author. Avoid thought tangents about what the author *really* meant, or what he or she was *trying* to say. The only things that matter on a multiple-choice test are the words that are actually in the question. You must avoid reading too much into a multiple-choice question, or supposing that the writer meant something other than what he or she wrote.

5. No Need for Panic

It is wise to learn as many strategies as possible before taking a multiple-choice test, but it is likely that you will come across a few questions for which you simply don't know the answer. In this situation, avoid panicking. Because most multiple-choice tests include dozens of questions, the relative value of a single wrong answer is small. As much as possible, you should compartmentalize each question on a multiple-choice test. In other words, you should not allow your feelings about one question to affect your success on the others. When you find a question that you either don't understand or don't know how to answer, just take a deep breath and do your best. Read the entire question slowly and carefully. Try rephrasing the question a couple of different ways. Then, read all of the answer choices carefully. After eliminating obviously wrong answers, make a selection and move on to the next question.

6. Confusing Answer Choices

When working on a difficult multiple-choice question, there may be a tendency to focus on the answer choices that are the easiest to understand. Many people, whether consciously or not, gravitate to the answer choices that require the least concentration, knowledge, and memory. This is a mistake. When you come across an answer choice that is confusing, you should give it extra attention. A question might be confusing because you do not know the subject matter to which it refers. If this is the case,

don't eliminate the answer before you have affirmatively settled on another. When you come across an answer choice of this type, set it aside as you look at the remaining choices. If you can confidently assert that one of the other choices is correct, you can leave the confusing answer aside. Otherwise, you will need to take a moment to try to better understand the confusing answer choice. Rephrasing is one way to tease out the sense of a confusing answer choice.

7. Your First Instinct

Many people struggle with multiple-choice tests because they overthink the questions. If you have studied sufficiently for the test, you should be prepared to trust your first instinct once you have carefully and completely read the question and all of the answer choices. There is a great deal of research suggesting that the mind can come to the correct conclusion very quickly once it has obtained all of the relevant information. At times, it may seem to you as if your intuition is working faster even than your reasoning mind. This may in fact be true. The knowledge you obtain while studying may be retrieved from your subconscious before you have a chance to work out the associations that support it. Verify your instinct by working out the reasons that it should be trusted.

8. Key Words

Many test takers struggle with multiple-choice questions because they have poor reading comprehension skills. Quickly reading and understanding a multiple-choice question requires a mixture of skill and experience. To help with this, try jotting down a few key words and phrases on a piece of scrap paper. Doing this concentrates the process of reading and forces the mind to weigh the relative importance of the question's parts. In selecting words and phrases to write down, the test taker thinks about the question more deeply and carefully. This is especially true for multiple-choice questions that are preceded by a long prompt.

9. Subtle Negatives

One of the oldest tricks in the multiple-choice test writer's book is to subtly reverse the meaning of a question with a word like *not* or *except*. If you are not paying attention to each word in the question, you can easily be led astray by this trick. For instance, a common question format is, "Which of the following is...?" Obviously, if the question instead is, "Which of the following is not...?," then the answer will be quite different. Even worse, the test makers are aware of the potential for this mistake and will include one answer choice that would be correct if the question were not negated or reversed. A test taker who misses the reversal will find what he or she believes to be a correct answer and will be so confident that he or she will fail to reread the question and discover the original error. The only way to avoid this is to practice a wide variety of multiple-choice questions and to pay close attention to each and every word.

10. Reading Every Answer Choice

It may seem obvious, but you should always read every one of the answer choices! Too many test takers fall into the habit of scanning the question and assuming that they understand the question because they recognize a few key words. From there, they pick the first answer choice that answers the question they believe they have read. Test takers who read all of the answer choices might discover that one of the latter answer choices is actually *more* correct. Moreover, reading all of the answer choices can remind you of facts related to the question that can help you arrive at the correct answer. Sometimes, a misstatement or incorrect detail in one of the latter answer choices will trigger your memory of the subject and will enable you to find the right answer. Failing to read all of the answer choices is like not reading all of the items on a restaurant menu: you might miss out on the perfect choice.

11. Spot the Hedges

One of the keys to success on multiple-choice tests is paying close attention to every word. This is never truer than with words like *almost, most, some,* and *sometimes*. These words are called "hedges" because they indicate that a statement is not totally true or not true in every place and time. An absolute statement will contain no hedges, but in many subjects, the answers are not always straightforward or absolute. There are always exceptions to the rules in these subjects. For this reason,

you should favor those multiple-choice questions that contain hedging language. The presence of qualifying words indicates that the author is taking special care with his or her words, which is certainly important when composing the right answer. After all, there are many ways to be wrong, but there is only one way to be right! For this reason, it is wise to avoid answers that are absolute when taking a multiple-choice test. An absolute answer is one that says things are either all one way or all another. They often include words like *every, always, best,* and *never*. If you are taking a multiple-choice test in a subject that doesn't lend itself to absolute answers, be on your guard if you see any of these words.

12. Long Answers

In many subject areas, the answers are not simple. As already mentioned, the right answer often requires hedges. Another common feature of the answers to a complex or subjective question are qualifying clauses, which are groups of words that subtly modify the meaning of the sentence. If the question or answer choice describes a rule to which there are exceptions or the subject matter is complicated, ambiguous, or confusing, the correct answer will require many words in order to be expressed clearly and accurately. In essence, you should not be deterred by answer choices that seem excessively long. Oftentimes, the author of the text will not be able to write the correct answer without offering some qualifications and modifications. Your job is to read the answer choices thoroughly and completely and to select the one that most accurately and precisely answers the question.

13. Restating to Understand

Sometimes, a question on a multiple-choice test is difficult not because of what it asks but because of how it is written. If this is the case, restate the question or answer choice in different words. This process serves a couple of important purposes. First, it forces you to concentrate on the core of the question. In order to rephrase the question accurately, you have to understand it well. Rephrasing the question will concentrate your mind on the key words and ideas. Second, it will present the information to your mind in a fresh way. This process may trigger your memory and render some useful scrap of information picked up while studying.

14. True Statements

Sometimes an answer choice will be true in itself, but it does not answer the question. This is one of the main reasons why it is essential to read the question carefully and completely before proceeding to the answer choices. Too often, test takers skip ahead to the answer choices and look for true statements. Having found one of these, they are content to select it without reference to the question above. The savvy test taker will always read the entire question before turning to the answer choices. Then, having settled on a correct answer choice, he or she will refer to the original question and ensure that the selected answer is relevant. The mistake of choosing a correct-but-irrelevant answer choice is especially common on questions related to specific pieces of objective knowledge.

15. No Patterns

One of the more dangerous ideas that circulates about multiple-choice tests is that the correct answers tend to fall into patterns. These erroneous ideas range from a belief that B and C are the most common right answers, to the idea that an unprepared test-taker should answer "A-B-A-C-A-D-A-B-A." It cannot be emphasized enough that pattern-seeking of this type is exactly the WRONG way to approach a multiple-choice test. To begin with, it is highly unlikely that the test maker will plot the correct answers according to some predetermined pattern. The questions are scrambled and delivered in a random order. Furthermore, even if the test maker was following a pattern in the assignation of correct answers, there is no reason why the test taker would know which pattern he or she was using. Any attempt to discern a pattern in the answer choices is a waste of time and a distraction from the real work of taking the test. A test taker would be much better served by extra preparation before the test than by reliance on a pattern in the answers.

6

Bonus Content & Audiobook Access

We host multiple bonus items online, including all five practice tests and access to the audiobook version of this study guide. Scan the QR code or go to this link to access this content:

studyguideteam.com/bonus/nce

If you have any issues, please email support@testprepbooks.com.

7

Introduction to the NCE

Function of the Test

The National Counselor Examination for Licensure and Certification (NCE) is used in many states as well as military health systems. It is one of the two exams that can be taken for National Certified Counselor (NCC) certification. The test was first introduced in 1983 and is reviewed regularly to ensure validity and new research, and it reflects current practices in counseling. This test is for recent college graduates hoping to become certified as counselors and is also used by professional counselors wishing to gain national certification.

The National Board for Certified Counselors (NBCC) has now credentialed counselors in over forty countries. Now over 68,000 counselors have received national counselor certification. The NBCC is internationally recognized for counselor certification exams. All fifty states as well as Puerto Rico, Guam, the District of Columbia, and the U.S. Virgin Islands administer these tests.

The NBCC has a reputation of excellence. The NBCC and its affiliate, the Center for Credentialing and Education (CCE), oversee examination processes across the United States and abroad.

Test Administration

The NCE is offered for 5-week intervals during both spring and fall. To reserve a seat for the NCE, an individual must register online through their ProCounselor account. After receiving an email approving the application, the time and date for the exam can be scheduled by phone or online. The exam will be administered at a Pearson VUE test center for individuals who want to take the test in-person. There is also the option of taking the test online at home through OnVUE. Proper identification is required for both options. Individuals are asked to arrive early but can arrive up to 15 minutes late. If taking the exam at home through OnVUE, individuals can check in 30 minutes before the scheduled exam time and no later than 15 minutes after. The test is computer based, and individuals are given up to 3 hours and 45 minutes to finish the test. If special accommodations are required, they should be requested when submitting the registration. The candidate handbook contains guidelines and documentation requirements when submitting a request for special accommodations. The request will be reviewed for approval by the National Board for Certified Counselors (NBCC).

Retesting can be done the next season that the test is offered. Individuals have two years to retest if necessary, and they can take the exam up to three times per NCC application. A reregistration fee is mandatory each time an individual registers to retest. States differ in what additional tests may need to be taken for state licensure in counseling. Therefore, taking and passing the NCE does not automatically qualify an individual for certification. An individual must check with their state to identify if any other tests are required for certification.

Test Format

The National Counselors Examination is divided into six categories: Professional Practice and Ethics; Intake, Assessment, and Diagnosis; Areas of Clinical Focus; Treatment Planning; Counseling Skills and Interventions; and Core Counseling Attributes. There are 200 multiple choice questions on the test,

8

but only 160 questions count toward the score. The other 40 questions aren't scored and are only used for statistical purposes.

The chart below outlines the areas of the NCE test and the number of questions for each.

NCE Test Subject Areas	# of Questions
Professional Practice and Ethics	24
Intake, Assessment, and Diagnosis	24
Areas of Clinical Focus	58
Treatment Planning	18
Counseling Skills and Interventions	60
Core Counseling Attributes	16
Total	200

These categories and test questions will be aligned with the following eight areas: Professional Counseling Orientation and Ethical Practice, Social and Cultural Diversity, Human Growth and Development, Career Development, Counseling and Helping Relationships, Group Counseling and Group Work, Assessment and Testing, and Research and Program Evaluation.

Scoring

Experts in the counseling field review the test to decide on a passing score. A total score will be provided when the test is complete. The examination score will appear in the individual's ProCounselor account within six weeks. The maximum score a candidate can achieve is 160. If a candidate does not pass, they can retake the test up to three times in a two-year period. Exam scores can be sent to a third party by ordering a score verification request.

Recent/Future Developments

The National Counselor Exam is changed for each administration. Questions are drawn from a pool. All questions undergo review and validity testing. Out of the 200 questions, only 160 are scored and the remaining 40 are used for statistics for future exams. Even though exam questions are changed, the format remains the same.

Study Prep Plan for the NCE

1   **Schedule** - Use one of our study schedules below or come up with one of your own.

2   **Relax** - Test anxiety can hurt even the best students. There are many ways to reduce stress. Find the one that works best for you.

3   **Execute** - Once you have a good plan in place, be sure to stick to it.

One Week Study Schedule

Day 1	Professional Practice and Ethics
Day 2	Intake, Assessment, and Diagnosis
Day 3	Areas of Clinical Focus
Day 4	Treatment Planning
Day 5	Core Counseling Attributes
Day 6	NCE Practice Test #1
Day 7	Take Your Exam!

Two Week Study Schedule

Day 1	Professional Practice and Ethics	Day 8	Addressing Cultural Considerations
Day 2	Counseling Processes, Procedures, Risks...	Day 9	Facilitating Systemic Change
Day 3	Intake, Assessment, and Diagnosis	Day 10	Core Counseling Attributes
Day 4	Selection, Use, and Interpret of...	Day 11	NCE Practice Test #1
Day 5	Areas of Clinical Focus	Day 12	NCE Practice Test #2
Day 6	Religious Values Conflict	Day 13	NCE Practice Test #3
Day 7	Treatment Planning	Day 14	Take Your Exam!

One Month Study Schedule							
Day 1	Professional Practice and Ethics	Day 11	Religious Values Conflict	Day 21	Fostering the Emergence of Group Therapeutic...
Day 2	Legal and Ethical Counseling	Day 12	Adoption Issues	Day 22	NCE Practice Test #1
Day 3	Counseling Processes, Procedures, Risks...	Day 13	Treatment Planning	Day 23	Answer Explanations #1
Day 4	Competency to Provide Informed...	Day 14	Reviewing and Revising the Treatment Plan	Day 24	NCE Practice Test #2
Day 5	Intake, Assessment, and Diagnosis	Day 15	Counseling Skills and Interventions	Day 25	Answer Explanations #2
Day 6	Initial Interview	Day 16	Addressing Cultural Considerations	Day 26	NCE Practice Test #3
Day 7	Selection, Use, and Interpret...	Day 17	Guiding Clients in the Development of Skills...	Day 27	Answer Explanations #3
Day 8	Ongoing Assessment for At-Risk Behaviors	Day 18	Facilitating Systemic Change	Day 28	NCE Practice Test #4
Day 9	Areas of Clinical Focus	Day 19	Exploring the Influence of Family of Origin...	Day 29	NCE Practice Test #5
Day 10	Loneliness/Attachment	Day 20	Core Counseling Attributes	Day 30	Take Your Exam!

Build your own prep plan by visiting:

testprepbooks.com/prep

As you study for your test, we'd like to take the opportunity to remind you that you are capable of great things! With the right tools and dedication, you truly can do anything you set your mind to. The fact that you are holding this book right now shows how committed you are. In case no one has told you lately, you've got this! Our intention behind including this coloring page is to give you the chance to take some time to engage your creative side when you need a little brain-break from studying. As a company, we want to encourage people like you to achieve their dreams by providing good quality study materials for the tests and certifications that improve careers and change lives. As individuals, many of us have taken such tests in our careers, and we know how challenging this process can be. While we can't come alongside you and cheer you on personally, we can offer you the space to recall your purpose, reconnect with your passion, and refresh your brain through an artistic practice. We wish you every success, and happy studying!

Professional Practice and Ethics

Counselor Competency to Work with Specific Clients

Licensed professional counselors are required to work within the scope of their competence. This means that all counselors must have specialized academic training and receive clinical supervision during their practicum and internship. Counselors can also receive additional training through **Continuing Education Units (CEUs)** or other certifications that qualify them to use certain techniques and methods. For example, a counselor is working with a military veteran suffering from PTSD. The client experiences angry, emotional outbursts with his family, uses substances to cope with the intrusive images he witnessed while in the military, and he has not been able to maintain employment since his discharge. The counselor believes that **Eye Movement Desensitization and Reprocessing (EMDR)** would be the best treatment approach. However, prior to treating a client with EMDR, the counselor must have received specialized training and supervised clinical experience. If the counselor does not have such training, they need to refer the client to a clinician who specializes in EMDR. Otherwise, they could use an alternative treatment method for which they are properly trained.

Statistical Concepts and Methods in Research

Simply defined, **research** means to systematically investigate an experience either to understand what causes it or to develop a theory about how that experience can cause a future event. Systematic investigation can occur through a number of different scientific methods. **Deductive research** focuses on a specific theory and then establishes hypotheses to methodically test the theory in order to support or discredit it. Deductive research often involves setting up experiments, trials, or data collection surveys to collect information related to the theory. **Inductive research** examines information that's already available (such as established datasets like the U.S. Census Report) to highlight data trends and make inferences and/or projections from those patterns. **Research designs** determine how to structure a study based on factors such as variables being tested, the level to which the researcher is manipulating a variable in the study, the types of subjects in the study, what the study is testing or looking for, the frequency and duration of data collection, and whether the data collected is qualitative or quantitative in nature. These concepts will be examined further in the following sections.

Non-Experimental Quantitative Research

Quantitative research utilizes logical, empirical methods of collecting information. This information is called data and is often analyzed using statistics. **Non-experimental quantitative research** includes forms of data collection where the researcher collects data that's already available in some form. They then analyze this dataset to describe the relationship between pre-determined variables. The researcher does not set up a novel system of trials to produce new data, and they can't randomize any data collected. The researcher has no part in manipulating any variables or establishing a separate control group to which they can compare collected data. The lack of a control group, lack of variable manipulation by the researcher, and lack of randomization are often seen as weaknesses in non-experimental quantitative research studies. Some examples of non-experimental quantitative research designs are depicted below.

Survey Designs

These can be conducted through telephone or face-to-face interviews. They can also be conducted through paper or electronic questionnaires (either at an external facility or at the study participant's home). **Survey designs** are generally used when research about a particular topic is limited so that more information can be gathered to better shape the research question or topic. Surveys are easy (and usually cost-efficient) to administer, but they can also result in low or biased participant response rates.

Correlational Designs

These analyze the strength of the relationship between two variables in one group. One unique type of correlational design is found in ex post facto studies. The researcher examines two existing groups and analyzes the correlation between the variables of interest. Another unique type of **correlational design** is found in prediction studies, where the researcher determines a correlation between variables and then uses it to predict other correlations, related events, or future events. The strength and description of the correlation is indicated by the correlation coefficient (r), which falls between -1 and 1. If $r = 0$, it indicates there's no relationship between the two variables, while $r = 1$ indicates a direct, perfect correlation. If r equals a negative value, it indicates an inverse relationship between the two variables. If r equals a positive value, it indicates a direct relationship between the two variables. Regardless of how strong the correlation is between two variables, it doesn't indicate that one causes the other. It simply indicates that these two variables tend to occur (or not occur) together to some degree.

Comparative Designs

These examine data trends to determine a relationship in two groups or datasets that have already been established.

Qualitative Research

Qualitative research is commonly employed in social sciences, including the field of counseling. It typically focuses on the analysis of a group of people (which is sometimes biased) to understand different aspects of human behavior, relationships, and social interactions. The researcher does not manipulate variables when conducting qualitative research. Qualitative research is primarily conducted without rigid structures in place. Data is collected through the following:

Case Studies

These are detailed and documented examples of the topic of interest. They can be real or hypothetical situations. **Case studies** often record data over a period of time to examine a specific variable of interest. They can examine a situation involving one individual, a family, a larger community of people, or an organization. Case studies frequently look at how people relate to one another and/or to their physical or emotional environment.

Focus Groups

These bring together a relatively small group of individuals. The group can be diverse in nature or have many similar interests. A facilitator guides a discussion within the group to discern information about individual or collective viewpoints about a specific issue.

Interviews

These are typically more personal in nature. **Interviews** can be conducted in person, over the telephone, or via e-mail or regular mail. The interviewer asks the individual or group a series of meaningful questions related to the research topic. The interview can be structured with the

16

interviewer having pre-set questions to ask, or it can be unstructured with the interviewer asking questions based on the flow of conversation and the answers given by the interviewee(s).

Observation

In an **observation**, the researcher simply watches the individual or group of interest. However, a number of additional factors usually shapes the development of the observation study. The researcher can observe the participant(s) in a specific situation or highly controlled context, or the researcher can observe the participant(s) in their day-to-day routine. The participant(s) may or may not know that they are being observed for specific behaviors. The researcher can involve themselves in the context and become part of the observation study. The researcher can also freely write down data from the observations, or use a pre-made scale or data sheet to document specific behaviors.

Experimental and Quasi-Experimental Quantitative Research

Experimental quantitative research employs highly controlled processes with the hope of determining a causal relationship between one or more input (independent) variables and one or more outcome (dependent) variables. It uses random sampling and assignment methods to make inferences for larger populations. Typically, it compares a control group (serving as a baseline) to a test group. Ideally, experimental studies or experiments should be able to be replicated numerous times with the same results. The ultimate goal of a well-designed experiment is to declare that a particular variable is responsible for a particular outcome and that, without that variable, the associated outcome wouldn't occur.

Quasi-experimental quantitative research employs many of these same qualities, but it often doesn't use random sampling or assignment in its studies or experiments. Consequently, quasi-experimental research produces results that often don't apply to the population at large. They do, however, often provide meaningful results for certain subgroups of the population.

External Validity

External validity illustrates how well inferences from a sample set can predict similar inferences in a larger population (i.e., can results in a controlled lab setting hold true when replicated in the real world). A sample set with strong external validity allows the researcher to generalize or, in other words, to make strongly supported assumptions about a larger group. For a sample to have strong external validity, it needs to have similar characteristics and context to the larger population about which the researcher is hoping to make inferences. A researcher typically wants to generalize three areas:

- Population: Can inferences from the sample set hold true to a larger group of people beyond the specific people in the sample?

- Environment: Can inferences from the sample set hold true in settings beyond the specific one used in the study?

- Time: Can inferences from the sample set hold true in any season or temporal period?

If results from the sample set can't hold true across these three areas, the external validity of the study is considered threatened or weak. External validity is strengthened by the number of study replications the researcher is able to successfully complete for multiple settings, groups, and contexts. External validity can also be strengthened by ensuring the sample set is as randomized as possible.

17

Internal Validity

Internal validity illustrates the integrity of the results obtained from a sample set and indicates how reliably a specific study or intervention was conducted. Strong internal validity allows the researcher to confidently link a specific variable or process of the study to the results or outcomes. The strength of a study's internal validity can be threatened by the presence of many independent variables. This can result in confounding, where it's difficult to pinpoint exactly what is causing the changes in the dependent variables. The internal validity can also be threatened by biases (sampling bias, researcher bias, or participant bias) as well as historical, personal, and/or contextual influences outside the researcher's control (natural disasters, political unrest, participant death, or relocation). Internal validity can be strengthened by designing highly controlled study or experiment settings that limit these threats.

Sampling

Sampling is the method of collecting participants for a study. It's a crucial component of the research design and study process. There are a number of different ways to select samples, and each method has pros, cons, and situations where it's the most appropriate one to use.

Simple Random Sampling

For this type of probability sampling, the participants are taken directly from a larger population with the characteristics of interest. Each individual in the larger population has the same chance of being selected for the sample.

- Pros: closely represents the target population, thus allowing for results that are the highest in validity

- Cons: obtaining the sample can be time consuming

- Use When: a highly controlled experiment setting is necessary

Stratified Random Sampling

For this type of probability sampling, the researchers first examine the traits of the larger population, which are often demographic or social traits like age, education status, marital status, and household income. They then divide the population into groups (or strata) based on these traits. Members of the population are only included in one stratum. Researchers then randomly sample across each stratum to create the final sample set for the study.

- Pros: closely represents the target population, which allows for results that are highest in validity. Since the sampling method is so specific, researchers are able to use smaller samples.

- Cons: obtaining the sample can be tedious. Researchers may first need to compile and become acutely knowledgeable about the demographic characteristics of the target population before selecting a representative sample.

- Use When: a highly controlled experiment setting is necessary; demographic, social, and/or economic characteristics of the target population are of special interest in the study; or researchers are studying relationships or interactions between two subsets within the larger population

18

Systematic Random Sampling

For this type of probability sampling, researchers pick a random integer (n), and then select every *n*th person from the target population for the research sample.

- Pros: a simple, cost-effective sampling technique that generally provides a random sample for the researchers. It ensures that sampling occurs evenly throughout an entire target population.

- Cons: researchers need to ensure that their original target population (from which the sample is selected) is randomized and that every individual has an equal probability of being selected. Researchers need to be familiar with the demographics of the target population to ensure that certain trends don't appear across the selected participants and skew the results.

- Use When: a highly controlled experiment setting is necessary; researchers are short on time or funding and need a quick, cost-efficient method to create a random sample

Convenience Sampling

This is a type of non-probability sampling where researchers select participants who are easily accessible due to factors like location, expense, or volunteer recruitment.

- Pros: saves time and is cost-effective since researchers can create their sample based on what permits the easiest and fastest recruiting of participants

- Cons: highly prone to bias. It's difficult to generalize the results for the population at large since the sample selection is not random.

- Use When: conducting initial trials of a new study, when researchers are simply looking for basic information about the larger population (i.e., to create a more detailed hypothesis for future research)

Ad Hoc Sample

For this type of non-probability sampling, researchers must meet a set quota for a certain characteristic and can recruit any participant as long as they have the desired characteristics.

- Pros: allows for greater inclusion of a population that might not otherwise be represented

- Cons: results won't be indicative of the actual population in an area

- Use When: it's necessary that a group within the larger population needs a set level of representation within the study

Purposive Sampling

Another non-probability sampling method used when researchers have a precise purpose or target population in mind.

- Pros: helps increase recruitment numbers in otherwise hard-to-access populations

- Cons: usually unable to generalize the results to larger populations beyond the sample's specific subset

- Use When: researchers have a precise purpose for the study, or a specific group of participants is required that isn't easy to select through probability sampling methods

Levels of Measurement

Levels of measurement describe the type of data collected during a study or experiment.

- **Nominal**: This measurement describes variables that are categories (e.g., gender, dominant hand, height).

- **Ordinal**: This measurement describes variables that can be ranked (e.g., Likert scales, 1 to 10 rating scales).

- **Interval**: This measurement describes variables that use equally spaced intervals (e.g., number of minutes, temperature).

- **Ratio**: This measurement describes anything that has a true "zero" point available (e.g., angles, dollars, cents).

Independent and Dependent Variables and Type I and Type II Errors

A **variable** is one factor in a study or experiment. An **independent variable** is controlled by the researcher and usually influences the dependent variable (the factor that's typically measured and recorded by the researcher).

In experiments, the researcher declares a hypothesis that a relationship doesn't exist between two variables, groups, or tangible instances. This hypothesis is referred to as the **null hypothesis**. Errors can be made in accepting or rejecting the null hypothesis based on the outcomes of the experiment. If the researcher rejects the null hypothesis when it's actually true, this is known as a **type I error**. A type I error indicates that a relationship between two variable exists when, in reality, it doesn't. If the researcher fails to reject the null hypothesis when it's actually false, this is known as a **type II error**. A type II error indicates that a relationship between two variables doesn't exist when, in reality, it does. These errors typically result when the experiment or study has weak internal validity.

T-Test

A **t-test** is a statistical testing method used to determine the probability that, when comparing two separate sample sets with different means, the difference in the means is statistically significant. In other words, researchers can infer that the same difference will be found between the same two groups in the target population as opposed to only being found between the two specific sample sets. Usually the t-test is only used when the data sets have normal distributions and low standard deviations. The calculated t-test statistic corresponds to a table of probability values. These values indicate the likelihood that the difference between groups is simply due to chance. Traditionally, if the t-test statistic corresponds with less than a 5% probability that the differences between the two data sets are by chance, then researchers can assume that there's a statistically significant difference between the two sample sets.

Forms of Hypothesis

A hypothesis typically takes one of two forms:

- **Null Hypothesis**: declares there is no relationship between two variables

- **Alternative Hypothesis**: declares a specific relationship between two variables, or simply states that the null hypothesis is rejected

Analyses of Variance

Variance tests examine the means of two or more sample sets to detect statistically significant differences in the samples. **Analyses of variance tests** (commonly referred to as ANOVA tests) are more efficient and accurate than t-tests when there are more than two sample sets. There are multiple types of ANOVA tests. One-way ANOVA tests are used when there's only one factor of influence across the sample sets. Consequently, two- and three-way ANOVA tests exist and are used in the case of additional factors. ANOVA tests can also analyze differences in sample sets where there are multiple dependent and independent variables.

ANOVA tests work by creating ratios of variances between and within the sample sets to determine whether the differences are statistically significant. Calculating these ratios is fairly tedious, and researchers generally use statistical software packages such as SPSS, SAS, or Minitab to input the data sets and run the calculations. SPSS stands for Statistical Package for the Social Science and is one of the most popular packages that performs complex data manipulation with easy instructions. **SAS** stands for **Statistical Analysis System** and is a software developed for advanced analytics, data management, business intelligence, multivariate analyses, and predictive analytics. **Minitab** is an all-purpose statistical software created for simple interactive use.

Analyses of Covariance

This analysis is a type of ANOVA. This analysis is used to control for potential confounding variables and is commonly referred to as **ANCOVA**. Say a researcher is testing the effect of classical music on elementary students' ability to solve math problems. If the students being tested are in varying grades, then their grade level must be taken into account. This is because math ability generally increases with grade level. ANCOVA provides a way to measure and remove the skewing effects of grade level in order to better understand the correlation that's being tested.

Chi-Square and Bivariate Tabular Analysis

Similar to statistical testing methods like t-tests and ANOVA tests, a chi-square test analyzes data between independent groups. However, **chi-square tests** focus on variables that have categorical data rather than numerical data. They can only be run on data with whole integer tallies or counts, and they're typically used when a researcher has large, normally distributed, and unpaired sample sets.

Bivariate tabular analysis is a basic form of analysis used when the value of an independent variable is known to predict an exact value for the dependent variable. This is most commonly illustrated by a traditional XY plot graph that marks independent variable (X) values across the horizontal axis, and marks dependent variable (Y) values along the vertical axis. Once all of the values are plotted, a relationship (or lack thereof) can be seen between the independent and dependent variables.

Post Hoc and Nonparametric Tests

Post hoc tests are usually performed after running other tests (e.g., t-tests or ANOVA tests) where it's been determined that statistically significant differences exist between two or more sample sets. At this point, researchers can pick and choose specific groups between which to analyze similarities or

21

differences. Some common post hoc tests are the Least Significant Difference test, Tukey's test, and confidence interval tests, which are often similar to running multiple t-tests. Post hoc tests can be complex and time-consuming to calculate by hand or with simple software, so they often must be completed using sophisticated statistical software packages.

Nonparametric tests are typically used when datasets don't have pre-set parameters, are skewed in distribution, include outliers, or are unconventional in some other way. As a result, nonparametric tests are less likely to be valid in showing strong relationships, similarities, or when differences between groups exist. It's also easier to make a type II error when running nonparametric tests. Some common nonparametric tests include the Mood's Median test, the Kruskal-Wallis test, and the Mann-Whitney test.

Legal and Ethical Counseling

Counseling maintains a person-focused perspective that stipulates that the profession strives to "meet people where they are," not forcing ideals and decisions onto those in need, but instead using their own values to empower them to make changes.

In general, counselors follow basic ethical guidelines to do no physical or psychological harm to their clients or to society and to provide fair, honest, and compassionate service to their clients and society when making professional decisions. The **ACA Code of Ethics** exists as a resource to provide clear guidelines for counselors to practice by and as a resource for counselors to consult when facing an ethical decision that they're unsure of making. This Code supports the mission of the counseling profession as established by the ACA.

Ethical dilemmas occur when three different conditions are met in a situation. The first is that the counselor must make a decision. If the situation does not require that a decision be made, then there isn't an ethical dilemma. The second is that there are different decisions that could be made or different actions one could take. The third condition is that an ethical ideal will be conceded no matter what decision is made.

One type of ethical dilemma occurs when you have a situation in which two ethical principles are conflicting. This is a **pure ethical dilemma** because either choice of action involves conceding one of these principles, and there is no way to keep both principles intact. Another type of ethical dilemma occurs when ethical principles conflict with values and/or laws. In these types of situations, a counselor's values may conflict with an ethical principle, and a decision must be made.

Once you have determined which kind of ethical dilemma you are facing, there are steps to take in order to reach a conclusion and, ultimately, the resolution of the dilemma. The NASW lays out steps that should be taken when attempting to resolve an ethical dilemma.

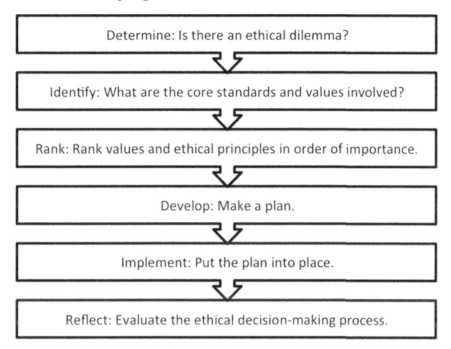

ACA Code of Ethics

The foundation of the ACA Code of Ethics is defined by the following six core values:

- **Autonomy**: freedom to govern one's own choices for the future
- **Nonmaleficence**: causing the least amount of harm as possible
- **Beneficence**: promoting health and wellbeing for the good of the individual and society
- **Justice**: treating each individual with fairness and equality
- **Fidelity**: displaying trust in professional relationships and maintaining promises
- **Veracity**: making sure to provide the truth in all situations and contacts

The **Code of Ethics** is comprised of nine sections that cover ethical guidelines to uphold these core values. These nine sections focus on the following:

The Counseling Relationship

The **counselor-client relationship** is one that is built primarily on trust. Counselors have the obligation to make sure the confidentiality and privacy rights of their clients are protected and, therefore, should protect and maintain any documentation recorded during services. Additionally, clients have rights regarding informed consent. Open communication between the client and counselor is essential; in the beginning of the relationship, the counselor must provide the client with information on all services provided, with sensitivity to cultural and developmental diversity. Counselors should also pay special attention to clients that are incapacitated in their abilities to give consent, and should seek a balance between the client's own capacities and their capacity to give consent to a more capable individual. Finally, with mandated clients, counselors should seek transparency in areas regarding information they share with other professionals.

Confidentiality and Privacy

With trust as the cornerstone of the counselor-client relationship, counselors must ensure the confidentiality and privacy of their clients in regards to respecting client rights through multicultural considerations, disclosure of documentation to appropriate professionals, and speaking to their clients about limitations of privacy. Some exceptions to confidentiality include the potential for serious harm to other individuals, end-of-life decisions, information regarding life-threatening diseases, and court-ordered disclosure. Counselors are encouraged to notify clients when disclosing information, when possible, with only the minimal amount of information shared.

Professional Responsibility

Counselors have the obligation to facilitate clear communication when dealing with the public or other professionals. They should practice only within their knowledge of expertise and be careful not to apply or participate in work they are not qualified for. Continuing education is part of the counselor's development as a professional, and the counselor should always be aware of evolving information. It's important for counselors to also monitor their own health and wellness, making sure to refer clients to other competent professionals if they find themselves unable to practice due to health or retirement.

Relationships with Other Professionals

Developing relationships with other professionals is important for counselors in order to provide their clients with the best possible resources. Being part of interdisciplinary teams is one way for counselors to provide the best, well-rounded services to clients. Counselors should always be respectful to other professionals with different approaches, as long as those approaches are grounded in scientific research. It is important for counselors to develop and maintain relationships with other professionals.

Evaluation, Assessment, and Interpretation

In order to effectively plan for a client's treatment, general assessments should be made at the beginning of the counselor-client relationship regarding education, mental health, psychology, and career. Clients have a right to know their results and should be informed of the testing and usage of results prior to assessment. Counselors must take into account the cultural background of clients when diagnosing mental disorders, as culture affects the way clients define their problems. Counselors should take care not to perform forensic evaluations on clients they are counseling and vice versa.

Supervision, Training and Teaching

It is important for counselors to foster appropriate relationships with their supervisees and students. A client's wellbeing is encouraged not only by counselors but everyone the counselor works with. For counselors who are involved in supervising others, continuing education is important in providing the students or trainees with correct information. Any sexual relationship with current supervisees or students is prohibited, as well as any personal relationship that affects the counselor's ability to be objective. Finally, counselors should be proactive in maintaining a diverse faculty and/or a diverse student body.

Research and Publication

When conducting research, counselors must take care to make sure they adhere to federal, state, agency, and institutional policies in dealing with confidentiality. Counselors should keep in mind the rights of their participants and facilitate safe practices during research that do not harm the client's wellbeing. As with any objective research, counselors should take care not to exaggerate or manipulate their findings in any way, even if the outcome is unfavorable. Counselors should take care where the identity of participants is concerned. All parties involved in the research of case examples must be notified prior to publication and give consent after reviewing the publication themselves. It's important for researchers to give credit to all contributors in publication.

Distance Counseling, Technology, and Social Media

The field of counseling is evolving to include electronic means of helping clients. Counselors should take into consideration the implications of privacy and confidentiality when treating clients online and take precautions in securing these, notifying the clients of any limitations to privacy. It's important to verify the client's identity when using electronic sources throughout the duration of treatment. In distance counseling, counselors must also be aware of the laws in their own state as well as the client's state.

Resolving Ethical Issues

This section ensures that all counselors act in an ethical and legal manner when dealing with clients and other professionals. It's important for counselors to make known their allegiance to the ACA Code of Ethics and try to resolve ethical issues following this manner. If the conflict cannot be resolved this way, counselors may be obligated to solve the conflict through the appropriate legal and/or government authority.

The ACA keeps an updated copy of their Code of Ethics, as well as other media and interactive resources relating to ethical practices, on their website at www.counseling.org.

Counselor–Client Roles

The relationship between the counselor and the client or client system is influenced by a number of components. These include the type of emotion that is shown by the parties during sessions, the general attitude toward the working relationship (e.g., positive, supportive), and the value each party places on the working relationship. The counselor should ensure that empathy, sympathy, and acceptance of the client and client system are shown during sessions to help foster a positive relationship. These aspects can be further supported by the counselor's initiative to build rapport with the client, such as through allowing the client to openly express feelings, work at a pace that feels comfortable, and encouraging them to shape and make decisions related to the intervention.

Additionally, a number of external tools may be a vital part of the counselor/client relationship. These include tools and documents that provide information related to the client's personality and behavior, and can help the counselor shape the intervention for the client. These might include items such as assessments, medical history, family history, current living situation, socioeconomic situation, and personal goals for the intervention.

Client's Rights and Responsibilities

When providing services, it is important to ensure that clients understand all aspects of the treatment they will receive. In addition to the plan of treatment, it is also necessary to ensure that clients understand the possible risks involved, the costs associated, the length of treatment, and any limitations to confidentiality that might exist due to both mandated reporting laws and third-party payers. Alternatives to the therapeutic plan may also be discussed with clients before beginning treatment. Clients need to be given the opportunity to ask questions and receive answers to ensure they completely comprehend what their therapies will entail. Informed consent should require that the client sign legal documentation stating that they fully understand what will be involved—including all the risks, limitations, and alternatives—prior to beginning treatment. This documentation should become a part of the client's chart.

25

There will be circumstances in which a person may be receiving treatment on an involuntary basis. In these situations, the counselor should fully explain the terms of the treatment as it pertains to the individual's situation, as well as any rights the person does have in regard to refusal. An example of this type of situation would be someone who is court mandated to receive treatment, such as drug and alcohol counseling, anger management, or other therapies.

Sometimes client information needs to be shared with other individuals such as the client's family or other professionals for referrals. In these situations, the client must agree to these disclosures, and consent for disclosure of information must be obtained.

Clients have a right to obtain their records. Counselors are permitted, however, by the Code of Ethics to withhold all or part of the client record from the client if the counselor determines there is a great risk of harm in releasing the information. In these cases, it is important to fully document the request, whether or not the records were released, and the rationale for either releasing or not releasing them.

Limits of Confidentiality

Counselors have a duty to protect confidential information of clients. Ethically, client information should not be discussed with anyone other than the client. Legally, a client has a right to keep their medical and therapeutic information confidential. The **Health Insurance Portability and Accountability Act of 1996 (HIPAA)** requires that medical information (including therapeutic and mental health information) be protected and kept confidential. However, there are certain limitations to confidentiality. These generally involve risk of harm to the individual being served as well as to others.

Counselors are not as protected as some other professionals when it comes to confidentiality and often find themselves being called to testify in court cases related to their clients. There are also certain situations in which counselors may have to release confidential information to protect the client or satisfy the duty to warn.

Providing services to minors can be challenging when it comes to confidentiality issues, especially since the legal rules and regulations vary from state to state. At times, there can be a conflict between the counselor's feeling of ethical responsibility to maintain the privacy of the minor and the legal right of parents to be informed of issues discussed. Adolescents in particular may discuss concerns with a counselor that they do not want their parents to be aware of, and it can be a violation of trust if these issues are subsequently revealed to parents. It is imperative that at the start of treatment, the expectations of the counselor's relationship with each person are discussed with the parents and minors, as well as the benefits and limits of confidentiality. Minors should never be promised confidentiality when the counselor cannot keep that promise, but the privacy and individuality of the minor should be maintained as much as possible. In cases where private information about the minor is going to be revealed, counselors should always inform the minor. This holds true whether it is with the client's consent, mandated reporting, or due to the parent utilizing their right to information.

Confidentiality also becomes more complicated when a counselor is working with two or more people, either in a family or group session. All participants must agree that any information shared within the context of treatment will be kept confidential and not shared with others. However, the counselor should stress with clients that they cannot force other members to abide by the confidentiality agreement and that breach of confidentiality is a risk.

It's important to note as well that counselors are considered mandated reporters in all states. This means there is a legal and ethical obligation to break confidentiality to report any signs and symptoms of child and elder abuse. In some cases, it will be impossible to know for sure if abuse or neglect is happening. Often the counselor will have only a small amount of information that may raise concerns but must make a report so that an investigation can occur. A counselor cannot be held liable for reports made in good faith to Child Protective Services or Adult Protective Services.

With technology being utilized extensively by counselors, confidentiality of electronic information is another important issue. Counseling sessions are now being provided by telephone, video chat, and online simulation, and these media open new possibilities for information abuse. If a counselor provides a video therapy session, they should be aware that it is possible for the client to have someone else in the room, off-camera, without informing the counselor or other participants. The same could be true with electronic communication such as texting or email. There is no way to know if a client is forwarding electronic information to third parties without the counselor's knowledge.

Counselor Agency Policies

The practice of professional counselors is guided by laws and policies. **Statutory law** is a body of mandates that is created and passed by U.S. Congress and state legislatures. Many of the laws are state-specific and may be more restrictive than federal legislation. Agencies such as schools or mental health facilities can also develop specific guidelines, procedures, and policies. In school systems, the local boards of education can rewrite policies and state regulations to meet the needs of their communities. For example, the ratio of students to counselors differs across the nation. In one state, the mandated ratio can be 1 counselor to 350 students, whereas in another state, the ratio may be 1 to 500. Other mandates may include the requirement of every school to provide comprehensive guidance and counseling programs, such as crisis assessment with referral, dropout prevention, and conflict resolution.

Similarly, a large number of state laws require healthcare service plans and insurers to provide some level of coverage for mental health services. Some outliers related to this mandate include copayments, deductibles, and limitations on the number of visits. It is important for a professional counselor to understand the difference between a mandate and a guideline. A **mandate** is a set of rules and regulations set forth by governing bodies that must be followed when practicing counseling. **Guidelines** are suggestions on how to meet mandates. Ethical standards should guide the professional counselor when conflicting mandates arise. Documentation of the logical course of action is key in legal defense. Mandates that result from federal legislation or court cases will usually cover all counselors. Some of these mandates include child abuse or neglect laws. Counselors who have multiple credentials should know the mandates and regulations that apply to their work setting. School counselors rarely require informed consent to meet with students. However, a mental health counselor who works in a school but is employed by an outside agency would have to obtain informed consent to see these same students.

Payment, Fees, and Insurance Benefits

A topic that must be discussed when obtaining informed consent from clients is payment and fees associated with the counseling services. Fees set by a counselor may be influenced by the standards of living in the local area of practice. A clear outline of the payment policy and fees associated with each counseling session should be provided and explained to the client. One form of payment is termed **sliding fee scale** wherein fees are adjusted depending on the client's income. Professional counselors

27

should consider that a sliding fee scale provides the same service to different clients for varying fees. Counselors who go through credentialing with insurance companies can become network providers.

A fee schedule will be discussed during the contracting phase with an insurance company. After providing counseling services to clients, counselors can bill the insurance. Claims will be reviewed and payment will be made to independent counselors directly. Government insurance options such as Medicare and Medicaid require the professional counselor to be within the network. Clients who do not have insurance or a health savings account can provide payment via private pay with cash or a credit card. The written agreement should include when payment is expected from the client or if the counselor plans to bill the client's insurance. The policy on missed appointments without notice should also be included in the disclosure along with a clear cancellation fee.

Counseling Processes, Procedures, Risks, and Benefits

Counseling Procedures, Risks, and Benefits

Counseling can provide individuals with the opportunity to learn about themselves with the guidance of a trained professional. It can be a time of self-discovery during which one's strengths and weakness are explored, inventoried, and modified. Counselors are bound by confidentiality, so the counseling environment is a safe one in which clients are free to open up and explore areas of themselves they might not feel comfortable doing otherwise. In addition to working with individuals, counselors are also able to help families and couples create healthier home environments by working on things like conflict resolution, communication skills, and parenting techniques. Individuals can also benefit from group counseling during which they can explore a variety of issues with others who are experiencing the same stressors or problems. **Counseling** also provides tools that can help to address various mental disorders such as depression, anxiety, bipolar disorder, etc. Counselors are trained to recognize when clients might need medication to help them successfully navigate their emotional issues. They can make referrals to appropriate medical professionals when necessary.

Although there are many benefits to counseling, there are also risks. Counseling can be unsettling for clients since the process explores potentially uncomfortable areas. Old images and memories may surface during and after counseling sessions that may leave clients feeling emotionally dysregulated. Some of the homework assignments may be difficult to complete and may even induce fear (for example, when clients are asked to face frightening situations or objects to overcome phobias). These assignments can be difficult because they challenge the way clients are accustomed to behaving and thinking. For these reasons, all potential clients should be apprised of the risks associated with counseling during the initial assessment and in the informed consent paperwork.

Counseling Process

Professional relationships with clients develop in six stages. In the first stage, counselors focus their efforts on building rapport and trust with clients. This involves the development of a comfortable and trusting working relationship using listening skills, empathic understanding, cultural sensitivity, and good social skills. In the second stage, the counselor identifies the problem(s) that led the client to seek the assistance of a counselor. Together, the counselor and client identify the initial problems that will be addressed, check the understanding of each issue through a conversation, and make appropriate changes as necessary. The third stage involves the counselor using skills that allow him or her to understand the client in deeper ways. The counselor begins to make inferences based on their theoretical orientation about the underlying themes in the client's history. Once these inferences are made, then goals can be established based on these overarching themes.

The fourth stage of professional relationship development involves working on the issues that were identified and agreed upon between the counselor and client. The client takes responsibility for and actively works on the identified issues and themes during and between sessions. As the client successfully works through issues, it becomes increasingly clear that there is little reason for the meetings to continue. Therefore, in stage five, the end of sessions is discussed, and both the client and the counselor work through feelings of loss. The sixth stage occurs after the relationship has ended if the client returns with new issues, if they want to revisit old ones, or if they want to delve deeper into their self-understanding. This stage is the post-interview stage and occurs with many—but not all—clients.

Relationship Phases

At the onset of the process, the counselor and client will progress through the relationship phase, which has four specific phases. These phases may be completed at a varying pace, depending on both parties. Some phases can be completed quickly, while others may take several sessions.

- Phase 1. **Initiation, or entry phase**: This is the introduction to the counseling process, which sets the stage for the development of the client/counselor relationship.

- Phase 2. **Clarification phase**: This phase defines the problem and need for the therapeutic relationship.

- Phase 3. **Structure phase**: The counselor defines the specifics of the relationship, its intended outcomes, and responsibilities of both parties.

- Phase 4. **Relationship phase**: The client and counselor have developed a relationship and will work toward mutually agreed-upon goals.

Advancement of Therapeutic Relationship and Reaching Goals

Once a working relationship is established, the client and counselor will need to develop and maintain positive interactions to ensure the effectiveness of counseling. Positive interactions ensure the therapeutic relationship advances and supports clients in meeting their goals. The counseling relationship has four stages.

- Stage 1. Exploration of feelings and definition of problem: Counselors will use rapport-building skills, define the structure of the counseling process and relationship, and work with their clients on goal setting.

- Stage 2. Consolidation: This is the process of the clients integrating the information and guidance from the counselor, allowing them to gain additional coping skills and identify alternate ways to solve problems.

- Stage 3. Planning: During this phase, clients can begin employing techniques learned in counseling and prepare to manage on their own.

- Stage 4. Termination: This is the ending of the therapeutic relationship, when clients feel equipped to manage problems independently and have fully integrated techniques learned in counseling.

Uses and Limits of Social Media

Social media has become a huge part of life for most people, so counselors must be aware of the appropriate uses of social media as well as its limitations. Some counselors may choose to promote their practices through social media. As long as their page is professional, this is a convenient and acceptable tool for marketing. For communication, it is best to provide a phone number and email address on the page rather than allowing messages through the social media page. This helps maintain confidentiality of current or future client information. Counselors may also use social media to connect with other counselors and discuss professional issues. In these instances, it is important that no personal information is shared that could reveal the identities of clients. Aliases should be used to keep specific information about cases that are being discussed from being connected to the counselor or clients. When sharing, commenting, or liking posts on social media, counselors should always be aware that clients might come across anything that is shared publicly. It is crucial to be conscious of whether these interactions and displays on social media could be harmful to clients.

Besides using social media professionally, it is likely that counselors have personal social media accounts. Some clients will want to connect with their counselors through social media, so it is best to address this during the first session. It should be explained that the policy is to never accept friend requests from clients. If this isn't explained up front, the rejection of a friend request could be detrimental to the therapeutic relationship and to clients who are emotionally fragile. By establishing and maintaining this policy, boundaries regarding dual relationships remain intact.

Informing Clients About Legal Aspects of Counseling

Some clients may disclose intent to harm themselves. It is necessary in these situations to fully assess suicidal intent and determine if the client is serious about carrying out a plan for self-harm. It might be sufficient, in cases where a client has considered self-harm but has no clear plan, to complete a safety plan with the client. The safety plan will outline what the client agrees to do should they begin to experience the desire to engage in self-harm. However, if the client has a clear plan of action and access to items necessary to carry out the plan, then confidentiality should be broken to protect the client. This would involve notifying police and having the client committed for observation for their own protection.

In addition to protecting clients from themselves, counselors also have a duty to warn third-party individuals if there is threat of harm. Duty to warn was established by the 1976 case **Tarasoff vs. Regents** of the University of California. In this case, a graduate student at the University of California-Berkley had become obsessed with Tatiana Tarasoff. After significant distress, he sought psychological treatment and disclosed to his therapist that he had a plan to kill Tarasoff. Although the psychologist did have the student temporarily committed, he was ultimately released. He eventually stopped seeking treatment and attacked and killed Tarasoff. Tarasoff's family sued the psychologist and various other individuals involved with the university. This case evolved into the duty to warn third parties of potential risk of harm. Satisfying the duty to warn can be done by notifying police or the individual who is the intended victim.

Because ethical dilemmas can involve legal situations, they may also have legal consequences for a counselor or necessitate involving the legal system. For example, a client may disclose that he frequently drinks large amounts of alcohol and then drives his children to school. Ethically, there is an obligation to keep what the client has said in confidence. However, the client's children are being placed in a situation in which they are in great danger of being injured or harmed. Due to laws protecting the welfare of children, the counselor would need to make a report to Child Protective Services. In some states, if someone has a good faith reason to believe that a child is being neglected or abused and does not report the situation, that person may face a civil lawsuit and even criminal charges.

When disclosing information due to legal requirements, it is always important to discuss the situation with the client. It should be noted that the counselor should evaluate their own safety when discussing disclosure of confidential information with the client. If the counselor believes the situation to be unsafe if/when the client learns of the disclosure, then it is not necessary to alert the client prior to disclosing the confidential information. This is something that should be discussed in detail with clients during the informed consent process and throughout the relationship.

One of the difficulties associated with breaking confidentiality to protect a third party is that the threat isn't always clearly established. If a client discloses during treatment that he is going to go home and stab his neighbor, this is clearly a plan of intended harm. However, what about an HIV-positive client who fails to warn sexual partners of her HIV status? What if the client fully understands the risk to her partners and has no intention of disclosing her status? This is a situation that would require thorough documentation, thoughtful debate, and possibly conferencing with colleagues to decide upon the best course of action.

Liability is another legal issue that counselors may sometimes face. Clients can sue a counselor for malpractice. When a counselor is sued, the liability does not stop with the counselor. In lawsuits, a counselor's supervisor can be named as a defendant, and liability can extend as far as the head of the agency that employs the counselor. Agencies that provide social services carry malpractice insurance for this very reason. It is good practice, however, for individual counselors to also carry malpractice insurance for extra protection.

Ethical and Legal Issues Regarding Mandatory Reporting of Abuse

Mandatory reporting laws require counselors, and other professionals, to report any suspected abuse or neglect. This means that any professional who has a suspicion of abuse or neglect of a child or a vulnerable adult must legally make a report to either child protective services or adult protective services. Note that some states, such as Tennessee, have laws that require all citizens to report suspected abuse or neglect, making everyone a mandated reporter.

Often when abuse or neglect is suspected, the concern about breaking confidentiality is at the forefront of the mind of the counselor. During informed consent, this requirement to report any signs of abuse or neglect should have been disclosed to the client. When such breaks in confidentiality occur, they can damage the relationship. In some cases, it may be necessary or appropriate to disclose to the client that a report is being made. For example, if a new mother has tested positive for cocaine and the infant has tested positive for cocaine while in the hospital, the infant will remain in the Neonatal Intensive Care Unit due to withdrawal. Disclosing to the mother that a report is being made, and why it's being made, could prepare her and create an opportunity to speak further with her about treatment options and other important considerations. It's important to note that counselors who fail to report suspected abuse or neglect can be subject to civil penalties and/or prosecution.

Obtaining Informed Consent

The majority of state counseling boards require professional counselors to obtain informed consent from clients prior to providing services. An **informed consent form** is a document signed by both parties agreeing to provide or receive a service. Some of the main topics included on an informed consent form are the qualifications and credentials of the counselor, risks and benefits of receiving the counseling service, goal expectations, and the provider's personal philosophy of counseling. The right to terminate counseling by either party and transfer service to another provider, if applicable, should also be discussed. Confidentiality is a prominent legal aspect of informed consent. The consent form should clearly outline situations in which confidentiality cannot be honored, such as in cases of neglect, intent to harm, and abuse of vulnerable populations. Additionally, informed consent documents should include clear expectations of fees, payment methods, and cancellation policies.

Confidentiality of Electronic Communication

Counseling is traditionally done in a face-to-face format. With the innovations in technology, virtual counseling is becoming more convenient. Some of the benefits of using technology include the ability to provide services to clients who may live in remote areas, those who do not have access to reliable transportation, and clients who are more comfortable receiving services online versus in person. One of the biggest challenges of using technology is maintaining client confidentiality. Professional counselors should be educated on the use of encryption standards that prevent unauthorized access to counseling sessions. **Encryption** is a safeguard to protect information that is being transferred online. Some common encryption methods include Transport Layer Security (TLS) and OpenPGP encryption.

OpenPGP encryption requires a password when accessing an e-mail or data that has been transferred to a recipient. If a data breach occurs, counselors should be prepared to show the efforts taken to safeguard **electronic protected health information (ePHI)**. Counselors may choose to use e-mail services that provide a **Business Associate Agreement (BAA)**, which places the responsibility on the service should a data breach occur. The informed consent should disclose the limitations of providing services via technology. Malfunctioning equipment or connectivity issues may arise and should be discussed with the client prior to providing services. Professional boundaries must also be established, and counselors should be cautious not to display any client information on social media. The **American Counseling Association (ACA) Code of Ethics** states that professional and personal presence in the virtual world should be kept separate.

Establishing Group Rules, Expectations, and Termination Criteria

Group counseling is a method of therapy in which clients with similar needs are grouped together to help share experiences and work toward an individual goal. The counselor's decision to place a client in group therapy is based on several factors, including the client's readiness to change, needs, preferences, and the services required. The decision to place a client in group therapy should be a joint decision between the client and the counselor. Clients should never be forced to participate in group counseling. Before the client can participate in group therapy, rules and expectations should be discussed with the counselor. Counselors will benefit from having a client sign an agreement delineating rules and expectations.

Some of the rules group members may be expected to adhere to are confidentiality, privacy, maintaining dignity, abstaining from violence, and regular attendance to the sessions. Clients should clearly understand that anything said in group counseling should not be shared and no group member is required to answer questions or engage in all activities. A clear expectation of attendance should be explained to the client. Clients are encouraged to remain in group counseling until the group members jointly decide it is time for a member to terminate their group therapy. Counselors acting as group leaders can guide members in determining when a group member is ready to leave. Some of the reasons clients may terminate group counseling include progress toward achieving their goals, a reduction or elimination of their primary symptoms, and the ability to independently cope with their issue. Alternatively, if a client no longer wants to participate in group therapy, their decision to leave should be respected.

Competency to Provide Informed Consent

In certain instances, a client may have difficulty in fully understanding the information being presented. This could be true especially if there is a language barrier or if the person receiving services either is not fully alert or is disoriented. Appropriate measures should be taken to ensure that the person receiving services fully understands the information provided to satisfy that informed consent has been achieved. This may require utilizing a translator or a third party, such as a durable power of attorney or family member, if the person is not able to make their own decisions. In the event that a client has a conservator or power of attorney acting on their behalf, it is also the role of the counselor to ensure that this person is making decisions that coincide with the wishes of the client.

Monitoring the Therapeutic Relationship and Building Trust as Needed

Rapport building begins during the initial contact the counselor has with the client, a crucial time for establishing trust and harmony. After building rapport, the client and the counselor can begin working on client issues and continue developing the relationship on deeper levels. The relationship that the client has with the counselor is representative of the relationships the client has in other areas of life; the counselor needs to engage with the client within this framework to effect the greatest change. As the principal conduit for client change and acceptance, the counselor/client relationship is primary to the problem solving and therapy process.

A common occurrence in counseling is **transference**. Without realizing it, the client misdirects feelings about another person onto the counselor. If transference isn't recognized or the counselor doesn't explain the transference to the client, the therapeutic relationship could be damaged if the emotions that the client is feeling are negative. Being mindful of transference and working on these feelings with the client can help to maintain the therapeutic relationship and assist the client in developing appropriate approaches for interactions outside of counseling.

If the counselor cannot develop a positive relationship with the client, the change process is hindered. The counselor/client relationship should be based on trust, empathy, and acceptance by both parties in order to facilitate growth. Some clients may have difficulty building trust with the counselor, and the counselor may need to be patient with the client in order to make treatment goal progress. If the counselor cannot develop an appropriate trusting, empathetic, and accepting relationship with the client, the counselor should seek supervision.

In some cases, the counselor will need to transfer the client because it will be very challenging for the client to make progress if trust does not exist. Counselors should also be alert for countertransference issues in the relationship with the client and address these issues promptly if they occur.

Reviewing Client Records

Counseling records serve as a reference for reviewing the client's plan of care and measuring goal achievement. Throughout the course of therapy, counselors may need to refer back to the treatment plan to facilitate interventions. Counselors should record and review any notes pertaining to client behaviors that indicate any chance of clients becoming suicidal or homicidal. These clients will require crisis intervention from other professionals, and their records will need to be reviewed. Counselors who decide to introduce new techniques, such as group or family counseling, will need to revisit the client's consent and revise the treatment modalities. Clients will need to consent to any amendments indicating a change in therapy techniques. Records also provide other counselors with information for continuity of care should the original counselor not be able to continue the sessions. In litigation, the client records will be reviewed by lawyers, and any applicable information will be admitted as evidence during court. Because client records are confidential, clients need to sign an informed consent form permitting the access of records by any third party.

Providing Adequate Accommodations for Clients with Disabilities

Enacted by Congress, the **Americans with Disabilities Act of 1990 (ADA)** is a comprehensive civil rights legislation designed to protect individuals with disabilities from discriminatory practices, such as refusal of employment or lack of access to buildings. Disabilities covered under the act include mental and physical impairments that may limit normal activities. An individual considered a viable candidate for employment is one who can perform the necessary activities with reasonable accommodation. Consequently, the ADA requires all workplace and public entities to provide the necessary accommodations and structures for access, unless doing so places an unreasonable burden on the entity. Counselors must abide by all ADA guidelines and provide appropriate accommodations for all clients with disabilities. Additionally, besides meeting the minimum requirements per the ADA, counselors should strive to make any and all additional accommodations for the comfort and ease of clients with disabilities.

Providing Information to Third Parties

Disclosure of client information will be necessary in certain instances. Some clients will require further medical treatment by a mental health provider. In order for a client to attain the best possible outcome, mental health providers will need to be informed of the assessments and interventions performed during the counseling sessions. Counseling services are often paid for by insurance companies. Basic information about the treatment, the client's diagnosis, and the frequency of counseling sessions will be necessary for billing purposes. In addition, clients may share with a counselor that they have a contagious communicable disease. If the disease is life-threatening, a counselor is justified in informing an identifiable third party of the situation. When court ordered, a counselor may reveal limited information about the client's counseling sessions that are relevant to the case. In the case of minors, each state has a minor-consent law that allows clients younger than 18 years of age to seek treatment without parental consent. Counselors should be knowledgeable about their state statutes related to counseling minors without parental knowledge. In any case where an outside agency or individual requests client records, the client must sign an informed consent agreeing to the release of their information.

Providing Referral Sources if Counseling Services are Inadequate/Inappropriate

In some cases, a client may require specialized service that is out of the scope of the counselor. At these times, a counselor may need to refer the client to another professional. It is important that the counselor is familiar with community resources and any specialized care a client may need. It is also essential to discuss with the client why a referral is recommended and ensure the client is comfortable with the decision and understands the next steps. The counselor must be familiar with ethical guidelines surrounding referrals and not refer out simply due to discomfort with or dislike for a client. A counselor who refers out for such personal reasons risks clients feeling abandoned, and the ACA Code of Ethics states that the needs of the clients must be put before those of the counselor. In these situations, the counselor should seek supervision and consultation regarding his or her personal issues. If the counselor is unable to provide appropriate care, then the client should be referred out.

Advocating for Professional and Client Issues

The **philosophy of counseling** includes the belief that counselors should encourage clients to advocate for their own needs. A counselor's duty is to intervene in the early stages of a client's problem to avoid a crisis situation in the future. Counselors may also assist clients with life's challenges, such as finances, job searches, and medical care, by facilitating phone calls or referrals to government assistance programs. Counselors are often faced with limitations of resources and insufficient representation of the profession. Advocating for their profession involves joining organizations that can make a difference. There are various state and national organizations, such as the **American Counseling Association (ACA)**, that encourage counselors to voice their concerns and advocate for change. Knowledge of public policy allows counselors to participate in committees that can produce changes in legislation.

Seeking Supervision or Consultation

Supervision takes place when a more experienced professional mentors or coaches an emerging professional counselor in fieldwork, practical application, or other service delivery settings. This requires strong interpersonal skills, a sense of respect, and open communication between both parties. The supervisor should be able to provide supportive instruction and guidance without arrogance and condescension; the supervisee should be receptive to instruction and have an honest desire for professional growth and learning. Some commonly used models of supervision in the counseling setting include individual-oriented types of supervision, in which the supervisor may ask the supervisee to reflect upon their interactions with different clients or their personal judgments and biases that may have arisen during a session. The supervisor may also present the supervisee with different forms of research and data and ask the supervisee to utilize the evidence to structure interventions. Finally, the supervisor may provide coaching related to the supervisee's development, by establishing small objectives that lead to larger professional goals.

In peer-oriented and group-oriented approaches, lateral-level colleagues (perhaps with the aid of one or two supervisors) learn from one another by sharing clinical experiences and lessons, new research and literature, or other professional development opportunities. This may take the form of team meetings at the beginning or end of the day, social events where work can be discussed, or conference settings. In some workplaces, individual, peer, and group models may be integrated to provide a more holistic sense of supervision.

Consultation can take place in any interaction that a counselor has with a client, regardless of setting or context. Consultation can primarily be divided into organizational, program, educational, mental health, and clinical cases. These can take place one-on-one with an individual or in group therapy settings.

Documentation for Each Aspect of the Counseling Process

Accurate case recording is an integral part of counseling practice. It is necessary to accurately document clients' information for effective treatment and protection of confidentiality. It is also required to protect the agency from possible legal ramifications and to ensure reimbursement from funders. Client records should be kept up-to-date, objective, and completed as soon as possible to ensure accuracy of information. Counselors should assume it is always possible that records may be requested as part of legal proceedings. Treatment notes should always be clearly written and only include information necessary to the client's treatment to protect confidentiality as much as possible. Counselors must also adhere to any state or federal legal requirements related to storage, disclosure of information, release of client records, and confidential information.

Both objective and subjective data are used during the assessment and treatment processes. The client provides their perspective on what happened and the correlated feelings and experiences felt, which is the **subjective data**. Subsequently, the counselor uses the information and may ask questions to better understand where the client is emotionally, while teasing out facts related to the client's situation. These facts are **objective data**.

The information from both the subjective and objective data is combined to formulate a concise, yet comprehensive, assessment for the client. In some note-taking practices, the identification of the subjective and objective data along with assessment formation is required. This style of documentation is known as the **SOAP method**, an acronym that stands for Subjective, Objective, Assessment, and Plan. Another note-taking style that focuses on the subjective and objective data is the BIRP documentation method. **BIRP** stands for Behavior, Intervention, Response, and Plan. It is not as commonly used as SOAP.

Awareness and Practice of Self-Care

Due to the highly emotional, interpersonal, and empathic demands of the counseling field, counselors must employ and sustain self-care practices to protect their personal health. Without self-care, counselors are highly susceptible to burnout and compassion fatigue—two risks that occur when working in a field that often provides exposure to disheartening humanitarian situations, abusive intrapersonal relationships, and cases that, for bureaucratic or personal reasons, take a long time to resolve. Unchecked, these experiences can lead the counselor to feel detached from work and hopeless toward cases or to consistently experience the ill effects of chronic stress.

Self-care practices may include establishing boundaries between one's work and personal life, having a regular meditation practice or other mental exercises that are shown to soothe the nervous system, eating a healthy diet and engaging in regular physical exercise (as these behaviors decrease inflammation in the body and reduce stress hormones), and having a trustworthy support system of friends and colleagues. Introspective exercises, such as daily journaling, can provide the counselor with a better understanding of which activities bring stress to their lives and which activities bring peace. By knowing these, the counselor can bridge the gap to reduce stress in areas they can control, such as setting a clear cut-off time for answering emails or scheduling personal activities that bring them joy. They can adopt healthy coping mechanisms for the areas in which they are unable to control factors that might contribute to their stress, such as an emotional case or external funding issues.

Practice Quiz

1. Nonparametric tests are more likely to result in which of the following?
   a. Type I error
   b. Type II error
   c. Confounding
   d. Independent variables

2. A school counselor is meeting with a 6-year-old student and notices the child has bruises in different stages of healing, is overly aggressive toward other children, and lacks basic social skills. The counselor should do which of the following?
   a. Dismiss the child from the session and document the behavior
   b. Recognize these as signs of abuse and contact Child Protective Services
   c. Ignore the symptoms since this is normal for a school child
   d. Consider these to be signs of neglect and make a note of it for the next session

3. Counselors may feel there are certain situations where it becomes necessary to make referrals for clients to seek other counselors, also known as "referring out." Which of the following is NOT a reason for counselors to refer out?
   a. Client issues outside of the counselor scope of practice
   b. Dislike for client
   c. Client need for specialized service
   d. Counselor retiring or taking leave from practice

4. "Do no harm" is deemed as a value in the ACA Code of Ethics by what principle?
   a. Nonhomogeneity
   b. Nonmalignant
   c. Nonmaleficence
   d. Nonchalance

5. Case studies, focus groups, and research observation are all examples of what kind of data collection methods?
   a. Qualitative data collection methods
   b. Quantitative data collection methods
   c. Purposive sampling
   d. Systematic random sampling

See answers on the next page.

Answer Explanations

1. B: Type II error is more likely to occur, provided a conventional α of 0.05, or a 95% likelihood that the result is not a false positive. The rate of a type II error, β, is inversely proportional to the test's power, is affected by the likelihood of a positive result, the size of the effect, and sample size. Conventionally kept at a minimum of 0.2, it is still greater than typical levels of significance. Therefore, Choice A is incorrect. Choice C, confounding, is an effect that occurs in an experiment or study due to the presence of an extra variable that can influence or correlate with the established independent or dependent variables, making this answer incorrect. Choice D is incorrect. Tests usually do not result in independent variables. Independent variables are variables that stand alone and are not changed by other variables attempting to be measured.

2. B: Unexplained injuries and erratic behaviors are signs of abuse and should be reported to CPS for investigation. Choice A is a dangerous intervention that won't protect the child if they are being abused at home. Choice C is incorrect because the physical and social signs point toward a problem. Choice D will delay investigation and put the child's safety at risk.

3. B: Counselors should refrain from referring out due to dislike for a client. This risks a client feeling abandoned and may be considered unethical. Needs of the client should be placed before those of the counselor. Counselors can refer out when retiring, taking a leave, when a client is out of the scope of their practice or expertise, or when a client needs specialized care, making Choices A, C, and D incorrect.

4. C: The term nonmaleficence means "do no harm" and is often used in ethical contexts. Choice A, nonhomogeneity, means composition from like parts, and does not make sense in this context. Choice B, nonmalignant, is a word used to describe something that is not threatening to health or life. Choice D, nonchalance, is the state of appearing relaxed and calm.

5. A: Case studies, focus groups, and research observation are all examples of qualitative data collection methods. These methods collect data related to descriptors and details, rather than data related to counts and numbers. Quantitative data collection focuses on the numerical mathematical, statistical, or otherwise quantifiable aspects of a phenomenon, making Choice B incorrect. Purposive sampling, Choice C, are non-probability sampling methods used when researchers have a precise purpose or target population in mind. In systematic random sampling, Choice D, researchers pick a random integer (n), and then select every nth person from the target population for the research sample.

Intake, Assessment, and Diagnosis

Biopsychosocial Interview

In order for an assessment to be comprehensive, the counselor must gather information and assess the individual holistically, which includes examining systems related to the biological, psychological, and social or sociocultural factors of functioning. In some cases, a spiritual component may be included. This process is based off of the **biopsychosocial framework**, which describes the interaction between biological, psychological, and social factors. The key components of the biopsychosocial assessment can be broken down into five parts: identification, chief complaint, social/environmental issues, history, and mental status exam.

Identification

Identification consists of the details or demographic information about the client that can be seen with the eye and documented accordingly. Some examples of identification information are age, gender, height, weight, and clothing.

Chief Complaint

This is the client's version of what the over-arching problem is, in their own words. The client's description of the **chief complaint** may include factors from the past that the client views as an obstacle to optimal functioning. It could also be an issue that was previously resolved but reoccurs, thus requiring the client to develop additional coping skills.

Social/Environmental Issues

This involves the evaluation of social development and physical settings. **Social development** is critical to understanding the types of support systems the client has and includes information about the client's primary family group, including parents, siblings, and extended family members.

The client's peers and social networks should also be examined. There should be a clear distinction between peers available online (such as through online social networks) and peers the client interacts with face-to-face, as online systems may provide different forms of support than in-person systems.

The client's work environment and school or vocational settings should also be noted in this portion of the assessment. The client's current housing situation and view of financial status is also included to determine the type of resources the client has. Legal issues may also be included.

History

This includes events in the client's past. Clients may need to be interviewed several times in order to get a thorough picture of their **history**. Some information in a client's history, such as events that occurred during the stages of infancy and early childhood, may need to be gathered from collateral sources. Obtaining the client's historical information is usually a multi-stage process and can involve the following methods of data collection:

Presenting Problem

Clients should be asked to describe what brings them in for treatment. Although a client may attempt to delve into information that is well in the past, the counselor should redirect the client to emphasize the past week or two. Emphasis is placed on the client's current situation when assessing the presenting problem.

Past Personal

When reviewing a client's history, noting biological development may determine whether or not the client hit milestones and the ensuing impact it had on their health. In reviewing biological development, other physical factors should also be assessed for impact on current emotional well-being, including those that may no longer persist, like a childhood illness. As much information regarding the client's entire lifespan (birth to present) should be gathered, with attention paid to sexual development.

Medical

During the medical component of the assessment process, information should be obtained on the client's previous or current physiological diagnoses. These diagnoses can contribute to the client's current situation.

For example, a client with frequent headaches and back pain may be unable to sleep well and therefore may be experiencing the physical and psychosocial effects of sleep deprivation. Additional information on other conditions, such as pregnancy, surgeries, or disabilities, should also be explored during this time.

Mental Health

Previous mental health diagnoses, symptoms, and/or evaluations should be discussed. If a client discloses prior diagnoses or evaluations, the counselor should determine the following:

- Whether or not the client has been hospitalized (inpatient)

- Whether the client has received supervised treatment in an outpatient setting (to include psychotherapeutic intervention)

- Whether the client has been prescribed medications

- Whether the client has undertaken other treatments related to mental health diagnoses

The client's psychological development should also be reviewed. It is important to gather details on how clients view their emotional development, including their general affect.

The client's cognitive development, in relation to information previously obtained regarding the biological development, should also be reviewed.

Substance Use

Without demonstrating judgment, counselors should encourage clients to disclose whether or not they have used controlled substances. It is important that thorough information is gathered and symptoms related to substance use are assessed BEFORE rendering a primary mental health disorder diagnosis.

Should a client disclose that they have engaged in the use of substances, information as to the type of substance, frequency of use, and duration of exposure to the lifestyle should be gathered. Additionally, information on what the client perceives as the positive and negative aspects of substance use should be gathered, noting whether or not the client perceives any consequences of substance use, such as job loss, decreased contact with family and friends, and physical appearance.

40

Mental Status Exam

A mental status exam is a concise, complete evaluation of the client's current mental functioning level in regard to **cognitive and behavioral aspects** (rapport-building, mood, thought content, hygiene). There are mini-mental status examinations available that allow counselors to provide a snapshot of the client's overall level of functioning with limited resources and time available. Mental status examinations are usually conducted regularly and discreetly through questioning and noting non-verbal indicators (such as appearance) in order for the counselor to best guide the session.

Diagnostic Interview

The **problem system** refers to factors that are relevant to the client's presenting problem, which may include other people or environmental elements the client deems relevant to the situation. It is important that questions be asked to determine what the client's perception of the presenting problem is. Additionally, the counselor should determine if there are other legal, medical, or physical issues related to the problem. For a **comprehensive assessment**, the client should also be asked how long the problem has been present and if there are any triggers they believe contribute to the problem. Identification of external supports and access to resources is also key when examining and discussing the problem system.

The presenting problem is generally revealed in the client's statement about why they have come in for treatment. If collateral sources are used, information can also be gathered from one or more of the collateral sources who have insight as to why the client is in need of assistance. Disclosure of the presenting problem allows the counselor to determine the prevailing concerns deemed important by the client. Counselors can gain a sense of how distressed the client is about the problem or situation and what client expectations are for treatment. The manner in which the client describes the presenting problem can also provide insight as to how emotionally tied the client is to the problem and whether or not the client came in under their own volition.

It is important to determine the true root causes of the presenting problem. Although a client may come in and voice a concern, it may not be the root cause of the issue. Rather, this concern may simply be an item the client feels comfortable discussing. For example, a client who is experiencing sexual issues may initially speak about anxiety before disclosing the actual problem. This may require an investment of time to allow the client to become comfortable trusting the counselor. The history of the problem is important to address because it clarifies any factors contributing to the presenting problem, as well as any deeper underlying issues. Gathering background information on the problem history is also helpful for developing interventions. There are three key areas to address when reviewing the problem history: onset, progression, and severity.

- **Onset**: Problem onset addresses when the problem started. It usually includes triggers or events that led up to the start of the problem; these events may also be contributing factors.

- **Progression**: Assessment of the progression of the problem requires determining the frequency of the problem. The counselor should ask questions to determine if the problem is intermittent (how often and for how long), if it is acute or chronic, and if there are multiple problems that may or may not appear in a pattern or recurring cluster.

- **Severity**: Counselors should determine how severe the client feels the problem is, what factors contribute to making the problem more severe, and how the situation impacts the client's adaptive functioning. This may be determined by addressing the following questions:

- o Does the problem affect the client at work?

- o Is there difficulty performing personal care because of the problem?

    - The counselor should ascertain whether or not the client has access to resources that can provide adequate care (running water, shelter, and clothing).

    - The client's living situation should be explored if there are difficulties with personal care activities.

    - The counselor should also ask if there are others for whom the client is responsible, like children or elderly parents/relatives.

- o Has the problem caused the client to withdraw from preferred activities?

- o Has the client used alcohol or other controlled substances to alleviate or escape the problem? If so, for how long and to what degree?

Cultural Formulation Interview

Culture

Cultural context is an essential factor when diagnosing, assessing, or treating individuals with mental illness. **Culture** is defined as the systems of knowledge, concepts, rules, and practices that are learned and passed on throughout generations. Culture is often used as an umbrella-term that encapsulates language, religion/spirituality, family structures, life-cycle stages, ceremonies, customs, and both moral and legal systems. Cultures are considered to be dynamic networks because they change so much over time. Individuals, more often than not, experience different cultures intersecting at once which allows them to gain a more specific understanding of their own identity. This conceptualization of identity then leads to the formation of other beliefs that extend to other areas of life such as relationships, career choices, and education. Due to the importance of culture and how it interacts with our experience as human beings, it is imperative for counselors to evaluate cultural factors when working with people in their practices and not fall into stereotypic or generalizable thinking.

Culture also includes the concepts of race and ethnicity, which are commonly mistaken to be the same thing. **Race** is a category of identity that differentiates individuals based on physical traits and biological characteristics. Racial categories vary across cultural societies. On a social basis, race is a construct that serves as a catalyst for racism, discrimination, and isolation. Existing empirical evidence demonstrates how racism can worsen the effects of mental disorders and racial biases impact diagnostic psychological assessment. Racial minorities are subject to these realities outside of clinical settings, so proper education and cultural competency is required in counselors in order to not emulate these concepts within the therapeutic relationship.

Ethnicity specifies an individual's community or group. They can exist across a common historical, geographical, linguistic, or religious domain. Ethnicity is able to be self-assigned or attributed by other people. In the essence of culture, ethnicities have evolved to intersect and introduce new variations of ethnic identities.

DSM-5-TR Cultural Formulation Interview

How individuals think about their symptoms or mental illness is greatly influenced by their cultural context. The **Cultural Formulation Interview (CFI)** is designed to evaluate these perspectives in order to gain a comprehensive understanding of the individual's specific experience. It consists of a set of sixteen questions that are typically asked when first meeting a new client during an initial interview. The CFI covers four domains of cultural assessment: cultural definition of the problem; cultural perceptions of cause, context, and support; cultural factors affecting self-coping; and past help seeking.

When obtaining cultural information about the client, counselors should do so in an inviting and welcoming manner. The CFI emulates a person-centered process, meaning that counselors encourage clients to explore their thought processes and experience. By using this approach, the diagnostic assessment becomes more valid and the individual becomes more engaged in the process. Stereotypic thinking is also controlled for as much as possible by this interview because counselors have the ability to understand how the client's particular culture affects their clinical presentation. Other variations of the CFI have been developed in order to assess certain populations such as children and adolescents, the elderly, immigrants, and refugees.

The CFI is such a vital part of diagnostic assessment as it provides extraordinary emphasis on the way mental illness is perceived through a cultural lens. Level of distress, one of the main indicators of psychological illness, can vary in the way it is expressed from culture to culture in how it is communicated (if at all), understood, or felt. A specific psychological experience that is shared among individuals in certain cultural groups, known as a cultural syndrome, may be presented through the CFI. Additionally, cultural idioms of distress and cultural explanations are able to be highlighted and understood through the process of the CFI. Culture will always affect the way in which mental illness presents. By extracting information about the client's experience in this context, counselors can avoid misdiagnosis, obtain useful clinical information, improve rapport and client engagement, guide clinical research, and possibly clarify cultural epidemiology.

Initial Interview

Communication Techniques

There are several communication techniques beneficial to counseling other than the basic interview process used to gather general demographic and presenting problem information. Here are several:

Furthering

A technique that reinforces the idea that the counselor is listening to the client and encourages further information to be gathered. This technique includes nodding of the head, facial expressions, or encouragement responses such as "yes" or "I understand." It also includes accent responses, whereby counselors repeat or parrot back a few words of a client's last response.

Close/Open-Ended Questions

Depending on the timing or information the counselor is seeking to elicit from the client, one of these types of questions may be used. **Close-ended questions**, such as "How old are you?" will typically elicit a short answer. Conversely, **open-ended questions**, such as "What are your feelings about school?", allow for longer, more-involved responses.

Clarifying and Paraphrasing

This is when counselors ask a client for clarification to ensure they understand the client's message. **Clarifying** also includes encouraging clients to speak more concretely and in less abstract terms to

43

provide clearer messages. When **paraphrasing**, counselors should convey a message back to the client to ensure an understanding of the client's meaning.

Summarizing
This is similar to paraphrasing, but **summarizing** includes more information. It's frequently used to help focus the session and allow the counselor to summarize the overall messages, problems, or goals of the client.

Active Listening
Active listening involves using facial expressions, body language, and postures to show that the counselor is engaged and listening to the client. Counselors should display eye contact and natural but engaged body movements and gestures. An example would be sitting slightly forward with a non-rigid posture. As with all communication techniques, counselors should be aware of cultural differences in what is appropriate, especially related to direct eye contact and posturing.

Methods of Summarizing Communication
Counselors may paraphrase and echo clients' verbal statements to acknowledge their feelings. **Summarizing** may involve reflecting back the statements made by the client to clarify what the client has said. Counselors also must summarize communication in order to provide sufficient records of the session. Further, during the end of the session, the counselor may wish to clarify goals and homework assigned for the next week so that the client is clear on the changes that need to take place.

Methods of Facilitating Communication
Counselors may facilitate communication with the client by verbally encouraging communication or by addressing the client with constructive information concerning the case. Counselors need to recall information concerning the client from session to session in order to facilitate communication and move forward with the client. Clarifying what the client has said and the client's feelings helps not only to ensure the counselor clearly understands what is being communicated, but also lets the client know that the counselor is engaged and actively listening. Development of trust with the client may facilitate additional communication, and counselors should be sensitive to the trust-building process because it is the cornerstone of the helping relationship. Counselors may provide clients with homework outside of a session that facilitates communication during the next session.

Mandated clients, including court-ordered clients or clients ordered to counseling from child protective services, may face challenges in communicating with the counselor because they do not choose to be in treatment. Developing trust with these clients to facilitate communication is especially important for progress to be made. It's helpful to acknowledge the client's feelings and possible frustration about the mandated treatment. Clients who require out-of-home placement need clear communication with the counselor to clarify what is happening and make appropriate psychological adjustments to their circumstances.

Eliciting Sensitive Information
Interviews are a critical component of counseling wherein clients provide verbal reports, accounts, or narratives that serve as the main source of information and data collected during the assessment process.

The basis of the interview is a verbal report that involves introductions between the counselor and client. In some practice settings, the verbal report may be supplemented by an **information sheet** that provides client demographics and a brief overview of the **presenting problem**. Presenting

44

problems are prevailing circumstances, symptoms, or difficulties that the client believes is a problem requiring psychotherapeutic assistance.

Principle: Counselors Need to Establish Rapport with the Client

Providing a description of the services provided and what the client can expect during sessions is the counselor's first opportunity to build rapport with the client. **Rapport development** impacts the thoroughness of the information provided from the client. If the level of rapport is limited, the client may not feel comfortable enough to provide sufficient information. The level of rapport also affects the type of impression the client wishes to make on the counselor. Consequently, it is linked to the client's perception of self-awareness. Some key points to remember are as follows:

- The counselor's own personal characteristics (gender, race, age, etc.) may affect the level of client interaction, based on the client's cultural background.

- Clients may adjust their responses to questions based on how they perceive the counselor's characteristics.

- The counselor's demographics may also have an impact on how the client feels about disclosing sensitive information, such as domestic violence, sexual conduct, or child abuse.

Principle: The Basics of Counseling Practice Should be Used When an Interview is Conducted

Once the introductions have been made and an overview of services and interview processes provided, the client should be asked to explain why they came in for treatment.

Empowering clients to share their concerns and emphasizing the point of hearing things from their perspective provides the counselor with an opportunity to gauge a client and start "where the client is" in the initial phases of the assessment process.

The use of encouraging, neutral phrases will help move the conversation forward and encourage the client to share, e.g., "What brings you in to see me today?"

While being encouraging to the client, it is important that counselors are genuine and not phony. Counselors should avoid overly complimentary statements, such as "I'm so glad you came in today!" If the client senses the interest is insincere, they may not wish to share.

Principle: The Counselor Should Start Where the Client Is

After engaging the client, they should be allowed to open up, "vent," or speak freely for approximately fifteen minutes.

While the client is delving into any emotions, the counselor should utilize active listening to keep the client engaged. Additionally, it is important to observe the client's **non-verbal cues** (posture, gestures, voice tone and pitch, and facial expressions) that lend to the emotional state. Once the client shares primary concerns, the counselor can focus on what is important to the client.

The counselor should observe the client's emotional state, allowing them to feel those emotions freely while providing the account of the problem. Demonstrating empathy is important when responding to the client's emotions. The emotion observed should be acknowledged. For example, if a client is crying, the counselor can state, "You seem saddened about this," to demonstrate empathy. This practice can also hone in on an important area of the client's life that may be addressed later.

Once the client has been allowed to speak freely, the counselor should utilize exploratory interviewing skills to delve into the specifics of topics that seemed particularly troubling for the client during the disclosure of the presenting problem.

After the client has revealed the presenting problem and the emotional state has been observed, the client should be asked to delve further into details about current life circumstances. This will provide an opportunity for the counselor to gain additional information related to the context of the client's problem. It also allows the counselor to uncover particularly troubling areas that can be explored later. Moreover, it may reveal certain boundaries for the client who is unwilling or unready to discuss certain details of their life.

Principle: It is Important to Engage the Client Verbally While Simultaneously Observing Non-Verbal Cues

The counselor should ask questions to provide clarification and deeper insight into the client's problems and level of functioning.

- Question Techniques

  - Open-ended questions may provide more detail and allow the client to expand into other areas that can be explored later.

  - Closed-ended questions are ideal for fact-finding from a client.

  - Clarification questions should be asked whenever necessary. This may be done through active listening and reflective sharing on the counselor's part, to foster comprehensive communication and further build rapport.

- Note Taking Techniques

  - If the client has questions as to why notes are taken, the reasoning behind it should be explained, and a copy should be offered to the client to make them feel more comfortable and involved in the interview process.

  - Observation of client behaviors during the interview may be indicative of how the client behaves or reacts in settings outside of the session. Conversely, clients may act outside of their norm, due to the perceived pressure from the interview process. The aforementioned questions and non-verbal observations are essential to determine factors of the client's personality and the context of presenting issues.

  - Counselors should also be aware that their interactions affect client behaviors and responses during the interview process. For example, the client may mimic rigid body language (folded arms, crossed legs, minimal eye contact) from the counselor and become defensive in speech pattern, pitch, or tone.

Interviewing Clients with Communication Barriers

Sometimes there will be communication difficulties between the counselor and client, most notably with language or cultural differences that hinder straightforward communication. It is ethically imperative that all clients have access to adequate language assistance, including the option of a translator, so that those with limited English proficiency are still receiving the same level of care. The optimal situation is for clients to have a counselor who can speak to them directly in their first language, and this should be arranged whenever possible. However, this is not always feasible and a translator must be used. In cases where interpreters are necessary or are requested by the client, they should be professional and trained interpreters, rather than family members or non-professionals. They must also understand and agree to the rules of privacy and confidentiality. Counselors should make sure their communication is simple and easy to understand and also make sure to clarify what the client is saying if there is any confusion. Counselors should also familiarize themselves with the cultural backgrounds of the clients they work with to better understand their unique perspectives and to minimize misunderstandings.

Using Bias-Free Language in Interviewing

When interviewing a client, a counselor must be careful to eliminate all personal bias from their language. This relates to all subtle negative phrasing related to race, ethnicity, socioeconomic status, gender, gender identity, life choices, disability, or psychological disorders. The job of the counselor is to support the client without bias, always promoting the client's self-identity. Phrases or expressions that demean or stereotype a particular group of people should never be used. Similarly, labeling someone can be hurtful, especially in cases where that label has a negative connotation or stigma attached to it. Sometimes it may even be appropriate for the counselor to ask the client how they wish to be identified or addressed. Inclusive and affirming language should be used when talking about all groups of people and especially when talking to or about the client. Terms that are known to be offensive or degrading should always be avoided.

Determining Diagnosis

The current American Psychiatric Association manual for the classification of mental disorders is the *Diagnostic and Statistical Manual of Mental Disorders, Fifth Edition, Text Revision*, or the **DSM-5-TR**. It is an updated and revised version of the APA's previous classification and diagnostic tool from 2013, the **DSM-5**. The **DSM-5-TR** serves as an authority for mental health diagnosis and functions as a tool for counselors to make treatment recommendations. The *DSM-5-TR* is organized in accordance with the developmental lifespan. In addition to guiding diagnosis, the updated framework of the *DSM-5-TR* is designed to help researchers and clinicians better understand how disorders relate to one another and ultimately improve treatment outcomes for patients.

There are several notable changes to the *DSM-5-TR* as of 2022:

- the addition of scientific knowledge accumulated since the 2013 update
- the recognition of the role of culture in psychiatric diagnosis
- the revision of language used regarding race, gender, and gender identity
- the description of a Cultural Formulation Interview for use in the counseling intake process
- the correction of ICD codes for mental health disorders
- the addition of more precise criteria for childhood conditions
- the addition of a new mental disorder, Prolonged Grief Disorder, to the category of Trauma- and Stressor-Related Disorders
- the addition of new conditions of clinical attention
- the updated names of two disorders, Functional Neurological Symptom Disorder and Intellectual Development Disorder
- the addition and removal of diagnosis specifiers, including those for Bipolar I, Bipolar II, Obsessive-Compulsive Related Disorder, Persistent Depressive Disorder, and Gender Dysphoria

Complete Listing of *DSM-5-TR* Diagnostic Criteria Chapters

- Neurodevelopmental Disorders
- Schizophrenia Spectrum and other Psychotic Disorders
- Bipolar and Related Disorders
- Depressive Disorders
- Anxiety Disorders
- Elimination Disorders
- Other Mental Disorders and Additional Codes
- Obsessive-Compulsive and Related Disorders
- Trauma- and Stressor-Related Disorders
- Dissociative Disorders
- Somatic Symptom and Related Disorders
- Feeding and Eating Disorders
- Sleep-Wake Disorders
- Sexual Dysfunctions
- Gender Dysphoria
- Disruptive, Impulse-Control and Conduct Disorders
- Substance-Related and Addictive Disorders
- Neurocognitive Disorders
- Personality Disorders
- Paraphilic Disorders
- Medication-Induced Movement Disorders and Other Adverse Effects of Medication
- Other Conditions That May Be a Focus of Clinical Attention

MSE

The **MSE (mental status exam)** is a tool used when evaluating a client and is part of the collection of information used to make a diagnosis. The purpose of the MSE is to determine how the client is functioning mentally and emotionally at that specific moment in time, whether it's during the initial interview or any session in the therapy process. The MSE is performed mainly by observation. Counselors can use a variety of checklists, but an MSE should always cover certain items such as the general impression of the client, their emotional state, their thoughts, and their cognitive functioning. The most obvious will be the overall impression of the client and includes their appearance, attitude, behavior, and motor functioning.

The client's current emotional state should also be noted, observing both their mood and affect. The counselor should observe and note the client's thought content, thought processes, and their self-perception as well as the how they perceive the environment around them. This could include observations of hallucinations or illusions. Additionally, the counselor should pay attention to the client's language and speech patterns. The cognitive portion of the MSE addresses elements such as orientation, memory, concentration, and intelligence. This is the portion of the MSE when observation alone will not be enough. The counselor can utilize various tests and questions to evaluate these areas. It's important that the counselor notes only current observations. Symptoms that the client has reported to be experiencing should not be part of the MSE if they are not observed by the counselor during that interview or session.

Co-occurring Diagnoses

Co-occurring disorders may also be known as **dual disorders** or **dual diagnoses**. Co-occurring disorders are more prevalent in clients who have substance use history or presently use substances. Substance use is diagnosed when the use of the substance interferes with normal functioning at work, school, home, in relationships, or exacerbates a medical condition. A substance use diagnosis is often made in conjunction with a mood or anxiety related disorder, resulting in a dual diagnosis.

Co-occurring disorders or dual diagnoses may be difficult to diagnose due to the nature of symptom presentation. Some symptoms of addiction or substance use may appear to be related to another mental health disorder; conversely, some symptoms of mental health disorders may appear to be related to substance use. On the contrary, there are some signs that a co-occurring disorder is present:

- *Mental health symptoms worsening while undergoing treatment*: For example, a client suffering from depression may be prescribed anti-depressants to address depressive symptoms. However, if the client is using substances, he or she may mix other medications with anti-depressants. This can be dangerous in itself, but it may also create a prolonged false sense of well-being while under the influence. Once this feeling fades, it can be confusing for the client to realize whether the prescribed medications are working. Even worse, the client may increase recreational substance use, leading to worse overall mental health symptoms over time.

- *Persistent substance use problems with treatment*: There are some substance use treatment centers that transition clients off of one medication and place them on another, for example, methadone. This may result in a transfer of dependence and ongoing substance use while the client is receiving treatment for mental health disorders.

Another scenario is that a client may seek treatment from a substance use treatment center with clinicians that are not equipped to provide adequate mental health treatment for the client. As the mental health problems persist or worsen while undergoing withdrawal, the client may continue to engage in substance use as a coping skill, therefore making the substance use problem appear resistant to treatment.

It is important for co-occurring disorders or dual diagnoses to be treated together because they occur simultaneously. This may be done utilizing a multidisciplinary team approach in an outpatient or inpatient setting. Treatment of dual diagnoses or co-occurring disorders at the same time in the same setting by the same treatment team is also known as an **integrated treatment approach**.

Determining Level of Care Needed

A client's need for care can fall on a wide spectrum. Some clients may comfortably live in their own residence but attend regularly scheduled meetings with a counselor to receive care. Other clients, after being appropriately assessed, may require institutional care where they can receive medical and therapeutic support as often as needed. Institutional care may be a long-term or short-term solution for a client. The level of care required for a client is assessed by examining a number of self-sufficiency factors, such as the presence of any formally diagnosed developmental disabilities, physical disabilities, or mental disorders.

Additionally, the client's ability to communicate needs, IQ level, ability to complete self-care tasks (such as dressing, toileting, grooming, etc.) alone or with assistance, and risk of voluntary or involuntary harm to self or others will also be taken into consideration. Based on the client's health and caretaking needs, they may receive outpatient services (such as regular therapeutic appointments), inpatient services (such as a behavioral program that lasts for a predetermined period of time), assisted living in a facility such as a nursing home, or in-home support (such as a home health nurse). Regardless of where a client falls on the care spectrum, services for mental wellness and adjusting to this new context of life will likely be beneficial to care.

Determining Appropriate Modality of Treatment

When utilizing a holistic approach for client assessment and treatment planning, counselors should utilize evidence-based research to support the selected interventions and treatment modalities. The interventions and treatment modalities selected will be based on a number of things, including the client's current level of functioning (based on the biopsychosocial assessment), level of care needed, presenting symptoms, and the counselor's background. Here are some things a counselor will want to consider when constructing interventions or treatment modalities:

- Are the selected interventions evidence-based?

- Do the selected interventions arise from a strengths-based perspective specifically tailored around the client's strengths, interests, and needs?

- Do the associated risks with the selected interventions outweigh the possible positive outcomes?

- Is the selected intervention culturally-sensitive and culturally-appropriate?

- Did the client participate in the construction of the intervention selection and/or consent to it?

- Does the counselor feel comfortable and well-versed in the selected intervention to increase the levels of intensity as needed and provide a continuity of care for the selected modalities?

- Does the selected intervention coincide with the client's financial ability to pay?

Assessing the Presenting Problem and Level of Distress

While formulating the treatment plan, the counselor should assess the level of care needed for a client with the whole person in mind and a desire for continuity of care. As the counselor starts where the client is, the treatment plan process should reflect levels of care that are in line with the client's needs, adjusting the intensity up or down based on the level of need as reflected in ongoing assessments and review processes.

For example, geriatric care is similar to behavioral health care as the client may present with a need for the most basic level of care, conducted through routine visits with a counselor, either at the counselor's office or at the client's residence. The intensity may move up to increased sessions with the counselor.

The highest level of intensity would be a multidisciplinary team approach in a residential or inpatient setting. For geriatric care, the highest level of need would be represented in a skilled nursing facility.

50

For child welfare or special needs, an inpatient medical facility would also represent the highest level of need.

Indicators of Client's Strengths and Challenges

Noticing a client's different characteristics can indicate particular strengths. Strengths are biological, physical, mental, social, spiritual, or emotional abilities that help them to solve problems and keep the mind, body, and spirit in a stable state. The counselor might also notice areas requiring intervention or treatment plans for the individual's overall growth. Focus is on the following indicators:

- Intelligence quotient (IQ) and cognitive ability
- Willingness to learn
- Willingness to understand oneself without judgment
- Ability to accept both positive feedback and constructive criticism
- Desire for personal growth
- Willingness to change
- Ability and desire to learn new concepts
- Temperament
- Optimistic or pessimistic thought patterns
- Reaction patterns to stressors (both initially and over time)
- Self-esteem
- Self-efficacy
- Self-worth
- Accountability for one's actions
- Emotional quotient (EQ), also called emotional intelligence (EI)
- Status and complexity of close relationships and friendships
- Ability to trust and depend on others
- Ability to be trustworthy and dependable
- Ability to empathize and sympathize
- Perspective on society at large
- Self-awareness
- Moods and what external events or internal thought processes affect them
- Involvement in social institutions (e.g., religious groups, social clubs)
- State of physical health
- State of finances
- Socioeconomic status

Evaluating an Individual's Level of Mental Health Functioning

Ideas about what is normal versus what is abnormal with regard to behavior are society-dependent. People tend to equate *normal* with "good" and *abnormal* with "bad," which means that any behavior labeled as abnormal can potentially be stigmatizing. Use of person-centered language is one way to reduce stigma attached to abnormal behavior or behavior health issues (e.g., saying "a person with schizophrenia," rather than "a schizophrenic.")

The **"Four Ds" of Abnormality** assist health counselors when trying to identify a psychiatric condition in their clients. Deviance marks a withdrawal from society's concept of appropriate behavior. **Deviant behavior** is a departure from the "norm." The *DSM-5-TR* contains some criteria for diagnosing deviance. The second "D" is dysfunction. **Dysfunction** is behavior that interferes with

51

daily living. Dysfunction is a type a problem that may be serious enough to be considered a disorder. The third "D" is distress. **Distress** is related to a client's dysfunction. That is, to what degree does the dysfunction cause the client distress? A client can experience minor dysfunction and major distress, or major dysfunction and minor distress. The fourth "D" is danger. **Danger** is characterized by danger to self or to others. There are different degrees of danger specific to various types of disorders. **Duration** is sometimes considered a fifth "D," as it may be important to note whether the symptoms of a disorder are fleeting or permanent.

Screening Clients for Appropriate Services

The **treatment plan** is dependent on the goals set by the client and counselor. Part of the intake process is obtaining a general overview of why the client is seeking counseling services. Data collection can be performed using various methods. The primary tool used to gather information about the client is an unstructured client interview. Counselors can also observe nonverbal behavior and build rapport during an unstructured interview. Structured interviews are used to ask clients questions that will improve reliability and ensure collection of specific information.

Some tools used to screen clients for appropriate services include questionnaires, checklists, rating scales, and standardized tests. **Standardized testing** is a formal process that produces a score and can be interpreted using a set of guidelines. Examples include personality and aptitude tests, such as the Minnesota Multiphasic Personality Inventory-2 or the SAT. Frequently used projective personality tests include the Thematic Apperception Test (TAT) and the Rorschach Inkblot Test (Rorschach). Objective personality tests rely on the client's personal responses and are considered a form of self-reporting. Examples include the Sixteen Personality Factors Questionnaire (16PF) and the Edwards Personal Preference Schedule (EPPS). Counselors should choose the screening tool that can best examine the client's presenting problem further.

Selection, Use, and Interpret of Appropriate Assessment Instruments

Psychological and educational tests play a critical role in understanding client backgrounds, belief systems, and perspectives as part of the overall assessment. They also indicate any current or potential psychological, social, or physical needs that the client may have. These pieces of information shape the way counselors develop and tailor interventions for a specific client; they also allow counselors to maintain the highest level of safety for the patient as well as themselves. Psychological testing usually includes an interview component in which the counselor may conduct the initial intake assessment, ask the client personal and family-related questions, and notice body language and other physical behaviors.

Answers to interview questions and body language observations are incorporated into assessments by indicating potential risk or protective factors, individual capacity to accept and receive services, and strengths and challenges that the counselor can incorporate into the client's treatment plan. Clients are also often tested for their communication, comprehension, reasoning, and logic skills in order to determine which methods of intervention will be best received. For example, a client who is unable to communicate verbally may not benefit from simply listening to the counselor providing counseling; a non-verbal, interactive approach will need to be developed for such a client. Clients may also take personality and behavior tests, which allow the counselor to incorporate aspects of the client's beliefs, attitudes, perspectives, and reactions into the assessment.

Many psychometric instruments exist to assess and diagnose psychological functioning. Some of the most common tests include:

Beck Depression Inventory–II (BDI–II)

BDI-II is a twenty-one-question inventory used to measure presence and severity of depression symptoms in individuals aged thirteen years and older.

Bricklin Perceptual Scales (BPS)

BPS is a thirty-two-question inventory designed for children who are at least six years old. It examines the perception the child has of each parent or caregiver and is often used in custody cases.

Millon Instruments

- **Millon Clinical Multiaxial Inventory III (MCMI-III):** This 175-question inventory is used to determine indicators of specific psychiatric disorders in adults aged eighteen years and older.

- **Millon Adolescent Clinical Inventory (MACI):** This 160-question inventory is used to determine indicators of specific psychiatric disorders in adolescents aged thirteen to nineteen years.

- **Millon Adolescent Personality Inventory (MAPI):** This 150-question inventory is used to determine specific personality indicators in adolescents aged thirteen to eighteen years.

- **Millon Behavioral Health Inventory (MBHI):** This 165-question inventory is used to determine psychosocial factors that may help or hinder medical intervention in adults aged eighteen years and older.

Minnesota Multiphasic Personality Inventory (MMPI–2)

MMPI-2 is a 567-item inventory. It is one of the most widely administered objective personality tests. It is used to determine indicators of psychopathology in adults aged eighteen years and older.

Myers–Briggs Type Indicator

Myers-Briggs is a 93-question inventory widely used to help people aged fourteen years or older determine what personality traits influence their perception of the world and decision-making processes. A preference is identified within each of four different dimensions: extraverted (E) or introverted (I); sensing (S) or intuitive (I); thinking (T) or feeling (F); and judging (J) or perceiving (P).

Quality of Life Inventory (QOLI)

QOLI is a 32-question inventory that determines the perception of personal happiness and satisfaction in individuals aged seventeen years and older.

Thematic Apperception Test (TAT)

TAT is a narrative and visual test that typically requires the individual to create a story and allows the counselor insight into the individual's underlying emotional state, desires, behavioral motives, and needs. It's used for individuals aged five years and older.

Rorschach Test

Rorschach test is a visual test that records an individual's perception and description of various inkblots. It's used to determine underlying personality or thought disorders in individuals aged five years and older.

<u>Wechsler Adult Intelligence Scale – Fourth Edition (WAIS–IV)</u>
WAIS-IV is a series of subtests that assesses cognitive ability in individuals aged sixteen years and older.

Formal and Informal Observations

Qualitative data can be collected through interviews, observations, anecdotes, and surveys, and by reviewing literature and other relevant documents. Qualitative data collection methods are often subjective and cannot be generalized to larger samples or populations. **Quantitative data** can be collected from experiments, recordings of certain events and timed intervals, surveys in which an answer choice must be selected for each question, data management systems, and numerical reports. Quantitative data methods are often objective and abstract, and they can be generalized to explain relationships between variables in large populations.

Assess for trauma

In normal circumstances, an individual is typically able to return to a calm state after a stressor passes. Traumatic stress and violence, however, cause long-term effects, and the patient may not be able to recover to a normal state. Indicators of traumatic stress and violence include:

- Unexplained anger or outbursts
- Substance use and abuse
- Uncontrolled behaviors such as binge eating, compulsive shopping, gambling, hoarding, or sex addiction
- Attachment issues
- Chronic and intense feelings of shame, regret, guilt, and/or fear
- Obsessive thoughts or behaviors related to the traumatic event
- Eating disorders
- Self-harm, self-injury, or other self-destructive behaviors
- Sleep problems such as insomnia or sleeping too much
- Intense anxiety, especially in social or crowded situations
- Fear, clinginess, aggression, withdrawal, or regression in developmental behavior in children

Trauma occurs when a client experiences a deeply disturbing experience that yields an intense emotional response. Traumatic events may interfere with a client's baseline level of functioning. It is important for the counselor to have an understanding of the detrimental effects, both visible and invisible, that traumatization can have on a client.

The counselor should have an understanding of the client's baseline level of functioning. This information may be gathered first-hand from the client or through collateral sources if the client is unable or unwilling to provide that information.

The counselor should have an understanding of how to guide the client gently through describing the traumatic experience and the emotions related to it. In doing so, the counselor should have an understanding of the widespread, lasting effects that trauma can have, as well as the multiple recovery and treatment options. This knowledge also helps prevent re-traumatizing the client.

54

An adult client may present with traumatic stressors due to one or more events that occurred during childhood. Symptoms of anxiety, depression, or other mood disorders that are actually related to the traumatic event(s) may present in session and daily functioning. A counselor should be aware that symptoms of trauma could manifest in places and interactions outside of the client, such as within the family system, with peers, and at work.

Assessing Substance Use

During the intake stage of the counseling process, a counselor may screen clients for substance use. The depth of screening will be determined by several factors. Many clients will confess to using substances recreationally or medicinally. The frequency of use, simultaneous use of other substances, and associated medical comorbidities should all be assessed. Counselors should also be aware of the differences between substance use and substance dependence. A client who is dependent on a substance is unable to function normally without it. The presence of polydrug use and dependency of substances for social survival should direct the counselor to do an in-depth assessment. Counselors should expect variations in the willingness of clients to respond to substance use questions.

Teenagers will be hesitant to respond honestly for fear of parental involvement. Examples of alcohol and drug screening tools include the Alcohol Use Disorder Identification Test (AUDIT) and the CAGE (cut-annoyed-guilty-eye) questionnaire. The **CAGE questionnaire** is a screening tool that determines the likelihood of alcohol problems. The risk is determined by the number of "yes" responses recorded. The **CAGE-Adapted to Include Drugs (AID)** questionnaire is similar to the CAGE tool but includes drug use in its questions. Substance use may cause clients to become suicidal or homicidal. Alternatively, chemical dependency may be the result of a suicidal state of mind. It is important to perform a suicide risk assessment concurrently when treating clients with substance use. The ultimate goal will be to assist clients in identifying and utilizing alternative coping mechanisms.

Obtaining Client Self-Reports

One of the ways to obtain data from clients is through self-reporting. **Self-reports** allow clients to disclose their own symptoms, beliefs, attitudes, and behaviors and can be done using a paper survey or electronic test. The **Minnesota Multiphasic Personality Inventory (MMPI)** is a common tool used to measure personality traits and can help diagnose mental health disorders. **Interest inventories** are a type of affective test that can help clients identify their areas of interest and match these preferences to work contexts. **Symptom checklists** can evaluate the presence and intensity of symptoms that appear with certain disorders and are useful in monitoring symptom reduction after treatment has been established. Examples of symptom checklists include the Beck Depression Inventory, the Connors 3 Rating Scales, and the Child Behavior Checklist. Counselors should be aware of client bias when they report their symptoms. Other factors to consider are the validity and reliability of the chosen test.

Evaluating Interactional Dynamics

Interpersonal relationships refer to interactions (often of a close, friendly, romantic, or intimate nature) between people. They can form due to shared personal, professional, social, charitable, or political interests. Strong interpersonal relationships are built over time as participants are willing to honestly communicate on a regular basis, support one another's well-being, and develop a shared history. Psychological, evolutionary, and anthropological contexts suggest that humans are an inherently altruistic, community-oriented species that relies on interpersonal relationships to survive and thrive. These types of relationships (when healthy) provide security, a sense of belonging, an exchange of benefits and rewards, and a sense of self-esteem. **Healthy interpersonal relationships** are characterized by mutual respect, care, and consideration between members. Almost all groups assemble into a power structure of some kind, with natural leaders taking over decision-making, resource sharing, and other tasks that affect the group as a whole. **Dysfunctional interpersonal relationships** may be characterized by an extreme power imbalance and dominance by one or more involved members, often leading to submissiveness, learned helplessness, and feelings of low self-esteem in the relationship's less powerful members. Submissive members of a group may find themselves without material resources or respect from the rest of the group.

In some cases, information about interactional relationships, as well as the client's current functioning and past history, can be obtained from collateral sources. **Collateral sources** are persons other than the client, such as family members, police officers, friends, or other medical providers, who can provide information related to the client's levels of functioning, life events, and other potential areas of significance in the client's treatment.

Prior to obtaining collateral information from any source, a signed **release of information (ROI)** form should be obtained from the client (or from a parent/ guardian if the client is a minor). The necessity for an ROI may be waived if there is explicit legal consent granting access to collateral sources. This is most commonly seen during forensic interviews. It is important to explain the purpose behind collecting an ROI to the client. Relatedly, it is also important to make the collateral source aware of the reason behind the request for information on the client.

Information from collateral sources is useful in cases when the client is unable to provide reliable information. The inability to provide reliable information could be due to a number of factors, such as substance use issues, severe cognitive impairment, or severe mental illness/disorder. Based on the client's background, there could be a number of collateral sources from which to solicit information. Thus, it is important to filter these sources based on those who have had regular or recent contact with the client.

It is important to select collateral sources that can provide information about significant experiences and events relating to the client's presenting problem. Collateral sources can provide a level of objectivity when discussing the client's situation. Additional examples of collateral sources include physician's reports, police reports, reports from other medical professionals or mental health agencies, school reports, and employment records.

Ongoing Assessment for At-Risk Behaviors

The counselor conducts **risk assessments** to determine any influence that could result in harm or increased risk of harm to the individual. Assessing risk can be an ongoing process, as it's important to always have updated, accurate information. Risk-assessment methods will also vary depending on the circumstance (e.g., criminal justice, child abuse or neglect, community care). Some common methodology themes in risk assessment include the following:

Universal Risk Screening

This is a general screening for certain risky behaviors (e.g., violent behavior, substance use problems, self-harm) that may result in additional screenings, referral for treatment, or stronger outcomes such as institutionalization (in the instance of high suicide risk, for example). This screening often takes place in initial consultations or as part of the individual's intake forms and may be administered on an ongoing basis (e.g., at every session) to remain current.

Unstructured Methods

These typically include clinical assessments without any specific, prepared structure. While high-level professionals often make judgments during this process, outcomes can sometimes be considered biased and unreliable.

Actuarial Methods

These include highly logical, regimented tests and scales used to predict the likelihood of certain behavior patterns in a specified time frame. While scientific and evaluative in nature, some argue that these methods may place undue blame on individuals or be too inflexible to allow for the likely interplay of many influencing factors in an individual's presenting issue.

Structured Professional Judgment

This combination of the previous two methods is generally the most accepted. It uses structured tools appropriate for the scope of the case but allows for the judgment and flexibility of the counselor to decide what information is useful and to note any external information that may not be caught by standardized assessments.

Client's Danger to Self and Others

Counselors should always be alert to indicators that individuals may pose a threat to themselves or others. These indicators may be obvious or discreet and may include:

- Substance use and abuse

- Sudden apathy towards others or society

- Sudden lack of personal care or grooming

- Isolation

- Apparent personality change

- Drastic mood shifts

- Marked change in mood. Both depressed mood and a positive change in mood can be associated with suicidal thoughts or plans. A sudden positive change may indicate that the individual has made a decision and is no longer experiencing personal turmoil.

- Verbalization of feelings such as extreme self-loathing, desire to be dead, being a burden to others, or volatility toward others.

Risk Factors for Danger to Self and Others

A client who presents as a danger to self or others should be assessed through a biopsychosocial lens. In addition, tailoring crisis management techniques to the immediate problem can help de-escalate the situation. Open-ended questions should be used to gather as much information from the client as possible. It is also important to consult collateral information from any nearby family members to document other pertinent information about the client.

- The client should be asked if there are plans to harm anyone. If the client states yes, the counselor should determine what the plan entails.

57

- Any and all threats made should be taken seriously and reported to the proper authorities. Colleagues may be consulted to determine the validity of a threat, if the counselor is unclear on the client's intent.

- Identifying the critical event and antecedent that preceded it is important. The client should be asked to provide as much information on this as they are willing, in order for the counselor to gain a better perspective of the client's point of view.

- Determining whether or not the client has engaged in self-injurious behaviors (SIB) is also important. Here are a few examples of SIB:

  o Excessive use of alcohol or other substances

  o Cutting

  o Banging one's head against a hard object

  o Ignoring necessary medical advice (not taking prescribed pills, leaving a hospital against medical advice)

- The counselor should also evaluate the social and cultural factors that contribute to how the client reacts to stressful situations, including the following:

  o History of violence

  o Stability of relationships (school, work, and home)

  o Social isolation or withdrawal from others

  o Limited access to social resources

- Any recent life stressors that would lead to the client carrying through with a plan to harm self or others

- Assessing the client's current thought process is important. Do they present with confusion, clarity of the situation, or irrational thinking?

- If the client has a clear, concrete plan of action, then the risk for harm to self or others should be considered high.

Risk Factors Related to Suicide

The following are risk factors related to suicide:

- Previous attempts at committing suicide
- History of cutting
- Multiple hospitalizations related to self-injurious or reckless behavior, such as those noted below:
  - o Drug overdose
  - o Alcohol poisoning
  - o Inhalation of carbon monoxide
  - o Statement of a plan to commit suicide/suicidal ideations and access to the means to complete it

58

- Ownership or access to a lethal firearm
- Stated plan to cut one's wrists "the right way"
- Warnings or statements that suicide is planned
- Other factors related to suicide risk
- Age—middle-aged adults present highest suicide risk over other age groups
- Gender—males more likely to commit suicide than females
- Adolescents—high suicide risk, especially those heavily-entrenched in social media groups as a means of support and socialization
- Presence of a mental health disorder
- Life stressors from work or school
- Family history of suicide
- Family discord or other relationship trauma (divorce, break-up, widowed)
- Excessive drug or alcohol use
- Chronic illness
- Job loss

Pre-Test and Post-Test Measures for Assessing Outcomes

Counselors can employ **pre-tests** before an intervention to serve as a baseline data set, and they can employ a **post-test** to measure changes from the baseline. Counselors can also administer surveys, Likert scale questionnaires, or specific intervention evaluation assessments to the client or client system. These tools can measure quantitative results as well as provide an option for anecdotal or testimonial information. Entrance and exit interviews with the client or the client system can also provide a wealth of evaluation information. When evaluating clients face-to-face or through a survey, it's important to create an environment that fosters comfort, open dialogue, and honesty. Clients may feel pressured to provide positive evaluations if they are answering directly to the counselor or if they feel as though a satisfaction survey that they are completing can be traced back to them. This can bias the evaluation process and produce skewed results.

Evaluating Counseling Effectiveness

Evaluation is an important component of any field of study, as it allows counselors to understand which processes are working well and providing results. Evaluation also allows one to identify areas of opportunity and areas for improvement. The process often utilizes data and consumer feedback, and it focuses on processes that are in place and specific desired outcomes of the practice.

Counselors should continuously evaluate their practice. This evaluation begins with what exactly they would like to evaluate. An evaluation typically focuses on processes (such as clinical intake, client satisfaction, time spent with clients, frequency of sessions, type of intervention) and outcomes (such as were specific goals met for a client, how many clients return after being discharged). Many healthcare organizations provide evaluation tools for counselors, such as benchmark reports that provide client satisfaction responses or practice outcomes.

Practice Quiz

1. Which of the following is NOT a personality test?
   a. Minnesota Multiphasic Personality Inventory (MMPI-2)
   b. Beck Depression Inventory
   c. Stanford-Binet Intelligence Scale
   d. Myers-Briggs Type Inventory (MBTI)

2. What concurrent assessment is important to perform with substance use clients?
   a. A cognitive assessment
   b. A suicide risk assessment
   c. A fall risk assessment
   d. An environmental assessment

3. Which of the following clients would benefit from substance use treatment?
   a. A 21-year-old male who drinks three days a week and is an A student at school
   b. A 50-year-old accountant who drinks a glass of wine daily after work
   c. A 35-year-old female artist with a history of back pain who takes narcotics for pain relief
   d. A 46-year-old male who reports marijuana use and works two jobs to manage increasing debt

4. Which of the following is an index that measures someone's cognitive, critical, and abstract thinking abilities?
   a. Intelligence
   b. Intellectual Achievement
   c. Intelligence Quotient
   d. Emotional Quotient

5. What kind of test is used to explore the client's unconscious attitudes or motivations?
   a. Objective test
   b. Projective test
   c. Free choice test
   d. Vertical test

See answers on the next page.

Answer Explanations

1. C: The Stanford-Binet Intelligence Scale is an intelligence test. The other three answers, Minnesota Multiphasic Personality Inventory (MMPI-2), Beck Depression Inventory, and Myers-Briggs Inventory (MBTI), are types of personality tests.

2. B: Clients with substance use problems may be prone to suicide or homicide and should be screened appropriately. Choice A is appropriate for clients who display memory impairment. Choice C is not an appropriate assessment for a client with a primary problem of substance use. Choice D is a holistic evaluation of how the environment affects the client, family, or group.

3. D: One of the signs of substance use is financial struggles; clients will prioritize purchasing substances over essentials. Choice A is still able to perform well academically. Choice B does not depict binge behavior. Choice C is socially functional, and the substance is used for medical purposes.

4. C: Intelligence Quotient. More commonly known as IQ, this index measures someone's intellectual ability. The average person's IQ falls between 90 and 110. Over 125 is considered exceptional and under 70 is considered intellectually deficient. Choices A and B are too broad to be considered actual terms in psychology. Choice D is an index used to measure someone's ability to show empathy and connect with others, so this is incorrect.

5. B: A projective test would be given to explore the client's unconscious attitudes or motivations. An objective test, Choice A, gives questions with clear correct or incorrect answers and is not open to interpretation. A free choice test, Choice C, allows for an open-ended response, but this is a much more general answer choice than Choice B, making it incorrect. A vertical test, Choice D, is a same-subject test given to different levels or ages, which is incorrect.

Areas of Clinical Focus

Adjustment Related to Physical Loss/Injury/Medical Condition

The client's medical history is important information that should be gathered during the intake stage of the counseling process. Medical comorbidities can have an interrelationship with psychiatric illness. Clients who suffer through physical trauma and end up with a disability may have questions related to functionality as members of society, being able to work, and body image changes related to loss of limbs or disfigurement. **Pain** is a major concern for clients who have chronic injuries and may exacerbate psychological conditions. Clients who receive a diagnosis of terminal diseases such as cancer may go through episodes of hopelessness and despair.

Counselors should be prepared to perform crisis interventions and collaborate with other professionals if needed. Other concerns counselors should be prepared to assess are coping strategies, quality-of-life perception, and the effects of the illness on the client's independence. Clients should be assessed for spiritual or religious beliefs, as they may find comfort in these practices. The client's social support systems, including family and friends, should be established. The degree of social support systems will determine how well a client can handle the treatment and recovery of the illness. Psychological responses to physical illness may lead to anxiety, substance use, or depression. Counselors should be prepared to establish a treatment plan that addresses the client's emotional support, coping strategies, and social ties.

Aging/Geriatric Concerns

Aging is an inevitable phase of human development, and the impact is physical, psychological, social, and economic. **Self-image** is the perception of oneself, but the perception is influenced by societal values. Some cultures revere the elderly and look to them for wisdom and strength. These cultures include the Native Americans, Chinese, Koreans, and Indians. In the United States, there is a different perception of aging. Many elderly Americans feel less valuable or important once they enter retirement. At the same time, they are coping with undesirable body changes and learning to accept that, physically, they can no longer do what they once did. In the U.S., youth and physical attractiveness are highly valued. The elderly are seldom seen as important social figures. They are also less connected with families today, with only 3.7% of homes reporting multigenerational households, per Census Bureau reports. Currently, family support and family contact are less available. However, for some segments of the population, technology has allowed relatives to visit regularly with grandchildren and even participate in family meals or get-togethers.

In gerontology, **aging** is viewed as occurring in four separate processes:

- **Chronological aging**: based on actual years lived.

- **Biological aging**: based on physical changes that have an impact on the performance of the body's organs and systems

- **Psychological aging**: based on changes in personality, cognitive ability, adaptive ability, and perception

  o Basic personality traits appear to be relatively stable through the lifespan, as does an individual's self-image.

  o One aspect that does tend to change, however, is the tendency to become more inwardly focused, which may also result in reduced impulsivity and increased caution.

  o Studies have shown that a pattern of age-related changes in intelligence can typically be observed after age sixty, although changes vary widely across individuals. Furthermore, the somewhat poorer testing results are reflected in **fluid intelligence** (i.e., reasoning, problem-solving, and abstract thinking unrelated to experience or learned information), but not in **crystallized intelligence** (i.e., knowledge based on skills, learning, and experience).

  o Normal age-related changes in memory typically involve acquisition of new information and retrieval of information from memory storage.

  o **Sensory decline** is also a common experience for aging individuals.

- Social aging: based on changes in one's relationships with family, friends, acquaintances, systems, and organizations

  o Most older persons experience a narrowing of their social networks. However, they are more likely to have more positive interactions within those networks, and they are more likely to experience more positive feelings about family members than younger persons do.

  o **Disengagement theory** states that it is natural and inevitable for older adults to withdraw from their social systems and to reduce interactions with others. This theory has been highly criticized and is incompatible with other well-known psychosocial aging theories.

  o **Activity theory** proposes that social activity serves as a buffer to aging; successful aging occurs among those who maintain their social connections and activity levels.

  o **Continuity theory** proposes that with age, individuals attempt to maintain activities and relationships that were typical for them as younger adults.

Social Clock Theory (Bernice Neugarten)

Neugarten proposed that every society has a **social clock**—an understood expectation for when certain life events should happen (e.g., getting married, buying a home, having children). When individuals do not adhere to this timeframe, they often experience stress, the sense of disappointing others, or the experience of an internal "clock ticking" and reminding them that time is running out.

Gerontology

Gerontology is the study of biological, cognitive, and psychological features of the aging process. It includes the study of the impact of an aging population on social and economic trends. Gerontologists practice in the fields of medicine, psychology, physical and occupational therapy, as well as

63

counseling. **Geriatric counseling** practice refers to a range of services provided to the population of those over age 60. Geriatric counselors are found in nursing homes, counseling programs, advocacy centers, and other programs serving seniors. Aging adults must deal with the very real issues of palliative care, hospice, and other end of life issues. The job of counselors is to support them through difficult decision-making processes and to counsel them as they deal with the complicated emotional and spiritual concerns of aging.

Behavioral Problems

Children who struggle with behavioral problems may require counseling services. Professional school counselors often treat students who may require complex counseling services, increased consultations, and collaboration with teachers and administrators. Childhood behavior problems are often the result of anxiety or stress in the home or school setting. In the home setting, one parent may be absent or have extreme or no disciplinary behavior. Children may also be the victims of bullying at school. Behavioral problems are often a way to communicate a lack of social or language skills. Understanding how negative behavior is manifested in children can help create positive change. Counselors should collaborate with teachers and parents to establish a behavior management system. The goal is for children to understand what constitutes acceptable behavior and the consequences of negative behavior. Children with behavioral problems should also feel supported and have a safe place to talk about their feelings. Therapeutic activities, such as sculpting, art, music, and crafts, may help the child project their behavior toward a positive concept. Some of the most common behavioral problems counselors will encounter are abusive language, lying, manipulation, and disrespect.

Bullying

Bullying is widespread among school-aged children and teenagers and may require intervention by a professional school counselor. **Bullying** is defined as intentional, unwanted, and aggressive behavior that is repetitive in relationships in which there is a perceived power differential. There are various types of bullying. **Physical bullying** can be a physical assault or damage to someone's property or belongings. **Verbal bullying** is any type of verbal statements that tease or threaten a person. **Name-calling** is a type of verbal bullying. **Relational bullying** is an attempt to discredit or tarnish another person's reputation by spreading rumors or ignoring the target of bullying. **Cyberbullying**, a growing concern with the influence of social media, is destructive behaviors through e-mail, texting, or social media sites.

Those who bully others are more likely to have substance use issues later in life and can potentially practice criminal behavior. Those who are bullied can suffer from emotional distress, suicidal ideation, and a decrease in academic performance. Counselors should be aware of the intervention programs funded by the ACA Foundation. Counselors should also identify advocates who can act as defenders when a bullying incident is occurring. The goal is to empower the person being bullied to speak up and communicate that bullying behavior is not acceptable. Defenders work to involve adults when necessary, support the person being bullied, and encourage empathy in the person doing the bullying. **Workplace bullying**, which can happen to clients of any age, are patterns of behavior that are intended to intimidate, humiliate, offend, or degrade a coworker. Clients affected by workplace bullying can experience a loss of confidence, anxiety, helplessness, and physical symptoms, such as loss of appetite and/or sleep. Clients should be encouraged to review employer violence prevention programs and report the harassment according to the policy.

Caregiving Concerns

Impact of Caregiving on Families

There are about 10 million Americans over the age of fifty who are caring for aging parents. In the last fifteen years, thanks to modern medicine, the adult population has begun living longer. As a result, the number of adult children between the ages of fifty and seventy who provide care to aging parents has tripled. This amounts to about 25% of adult children who provide either personal or economic assistance.

Research indicates that becoming a personal caregiver to a parent increases the rates of depression, substance use, and heart disease. These adult children sometimes take significant financial blows in the form of lost income, earlier than planned retirement, and reduced pension plans, due to leaving the workforce earlier. At the same time, these adult children are assisting their own children as they move towards independence. Those in the youngest generation may still be in college or in the early stages of starting a career and still look to parents for some financial assistance. From a different perspective, the positives of this situation are that children are able to form deeper bonds with grandparents, and the longevity of life in loved ones can have a very positive impact on all involved.

Cultural Adjustments

Impact of Cultural Heritage on Self-Image

Although personal factors play a large role, self-esteem is also based on how closely a person matches the dominant values of his or her culture. For example, Western society tends to value assertiveness, independence, and individuality. Living up to these values is seen as an important accomplishment, and thus, children receive messages about their personal competence and success based on whether or not they are living up to these ideals.

Children are more likely to develop a positive self-concept when they are able to exhibit behaviors that are valued in their family, home, and culture.

One study suggests that across cultures, self-esteem is based on one's control of life and choices, living up to one's "duties," benefiting others or society, and one's achievement. However, the degree to which one's culture values each of those factors has an impact on how the individual derives his or her self-esteem.

A widely cited example of the way that a culture can affect a person's self-image is in the portrayal of women's bodies in the media. In the United States, young women are exposed to underweight models and unrealistically drawn cartoon "heroines," which can lead to the development of unachievable expectations and significant negative perceptions about their bodies.

Impact of Race and Ethnicity on Self-Image

Culture, race, and ethnicity can greatly impact one's self-image, whether one is part of a majority population or a minority population. One's ethnic and racial background provides a sense of belonging and identity. Depending on a country's treatment of a particular group, self-image can be negatively impacted through racism and discrimination. Racial jokes and racial slurs are common. Stereotypes abound, and some people judge entire racial groups based on the behavior of a few. Such treatment consistently impacts the self-esteem of minority groups. Non-white Americans who grew up in the fifties or earlier were denied access to restaurants, theaters, high schools, professions, universities, and recreational activities. Even within the last fifty to sixty years, African Americans who had achieved great status in the fields of music, sports, and entertainment were still denied access to certain clubs, hotels, or restaurants.

Every person must explore and come to terms with his or her own culture, ethnicity, and race. Sometimes, this even means rejecting cultural aspects with which he or she disagrees and embracing new and evolving cultural norms. This is a significant part of self-identity development among teenagers and young adults as they are part of a new generation that may be culturally different from their parents. Those who have more exposure to other cultures and backgrounds will have a more open perspective and are better able to evaluate their own culture and ethnicity objectively.

End-of-Life Issues

Death is an inevitable concept. Clients who are nearing end of life may experience emotional distress and functional roadblocks. Poor health, mental health issues, neglect, and depression are common problems experienced by those nearing end of life. **Aging** is a natural process that can have an effect on purposeful activities of daily living. Clients who lack caregiver involvement and suffer from neglect may require counseling services to address feelings of despair and helplessness. Counselors should be familiar with the various service providers in their communities. These clients may require a referral to a long-term care facility or caregiver services or be enrolled in wellness programs. The overall goal of counseling is to help clients envision a healthy perception of life. Similarly, clients who receive a life-threatening diagnosis may experience anticipatory grief. The client and their family members may require counseling for the expected loss and course of illness. Helping clients acknowledge and express their grief via listening, understanding, and accepting can encourage them to develop coping mechanisms. Counseling for anticipatory grieving can assist with resolving unfinished business before end of life occurs.

Fear and Panic

Fear is a natural reaction to a specific danger. Fear triggers the flight-or-fight response, which results in physical symptoms such as increased heart rate and respirations. Fear can be a result of phobias, perceived failure, or past experiences, such as violence, war, and aggression. On the other hand, **anxiety** results from the fear of an unspecified danger. The most extreme level of anxiety is known as **panic**. Clients who exhibit panic behavior may experience hallucinations, delusions, the inability to focus, and disorganized thought processes. Some of the screening tools used to detect panic disorders are the five-question Mental Health Inventory (MHI-5) and the Panic Disorder Self-Report Scale (PDSR) questionnaire.

The PDSR contains twenty-four items that are answered in a yes/no format or a five-point Likert scale. Clients experiencing extreme fear and panic have poor situational awareness. Other symptoms include extreme regression and aimless movements. Counselors should speak to clients in firm, simple statements and reinforce reality if a client is experiencing delusions. Clients will benefit from being in quiet settings and minimal environmental stimuli. One of the most effective treatments for clients experiencing panic disorders is cognitive behavioral therapy (CBT). CBT focuses on identifying and modifying thought patterns, which, in turn, can impact emotions and behaviors. Other interventions include exposure therapy and establishing coping mechanisms, such as mindfulness.

Financial Issues

A significant source of stress for many clients is money and financial issues. Financial distress can interfere with personal relationships and family life. The inability to provide for the family, pay debts, or keep up with finances may affect a person's mental and physical health. Clients who experience an unexpected loss of income, bankruptcy, or poverty may seek counseling services to deal with the mental and emotional toll. Mismanagement of money due to lack of financial planning, impulsive purchases, or gambling can also lead to financial issues. Studies have shown that people with financial debt are three times more likely to experience issues with mental health. Other associated risks of financial distress are drug dependency, depression, and contemplation of suicide. Counseling and therapy can help clients identify the emotional need that is met by overspending or impulsive behaviors. The goal is to develop coping tools to suppress the habit. Certified financial therapists focus on the psychological and emotional complications of financial issues and help clients identify the cause of poor financial decisions. Financial therapists can help clients develop money management strategies and productive behaviors.

Poverty is often the foundation of a number of other socioeconomic and health problems faced by individuals, families, and communities. Without resources such as money, transportation, or housing, it becomes difficult to buy healthy food, access medical care, drive to work, have quality childcare, or live in a safe area. For adults in poverty, the extreme level of stress that arises from trying to pay bills, provide basic necessities for themselves and their families, and manage multiple jobs often leads to a number of mental, physical, and emotional problems.

These can include substance use, domestic violence, inability to maintain family units and romantic relationships, hopelessness, depression, and desperation. Children who live and grow up in poverty are prone to traumatic and catastrophic health risk factors, such as experiencing or witnessing violence, chronic malnutrition, higher rates of illness, and mood disorders. Experiencing such adverse events in childhood is associated with high levels of stress, impaired functioning, and impaired cognitive ability that can be irreparable. Individuals experiencing poverty are more likely to visit the emergency room for health problems (and often be unable to pay), require government assistance, and commit crimes (often in order to obtain necessary resources). These outcomes create a financial burden on the community and local economy.

Gender Identity Development

Gender identity is the subjective term that describes how people identify their internal sense of self. Regardless of assigned sex at birth, a person may identify as a different gender. Gender identity is usually established by the age of 4 but may happen later or earlier in life. Children can be influenced by social factors, such as gender roles, authority figures, and influential people in their lives. Additionally, children learn language that characterizes males and females and may subconsciously adjust their behavior to match gender roles. Societal norms have established ideals of male and female expression, outward appearance, and expected behaviors. Clients who do not conform to a specific gender may often identify themselves as **gender fluid**. Nonexclusive identification of gender is defined as **gender nonbinary**. Clients who identify as neither male nor female, both, or a combination of genders is said to be **gender queer**.

While developing their gender identity, one of the biggest issues clients experience is social isolation. These clients may be discriminated against, stereotyped, or bullied and therefore may experience depression, suicidal ideations, and anxiety. Crisis resources, such as The Trevor Project and the National Suicide Prevention Lifeline, should be provided to clients who express intent to harm themselves. The ACA has endorsed guidelines for counseling clients who are developing their gender identity. Some of the guidelines include using nonsexist language, facilitating client knowledge on the physical and psychological effects of sexism, and increasing their own knowledge on the connection between sexism and other forms of oppression. Joining support groups and community organizations that encourage acceptance of gender identity development can help reduce social isolation.

Grief/Loss

The concept of loss is at the root of many depressive episodes. **Losses** can include anything one holds dearly. Losing a loved one, a pet, a job, housing, or financial or social status can all bring emotional pain. Other losses include the loss of physical or mental health. **Separation** is a form of loss that can occur in many forms, including divorce, military deployment, a job that requires one to move far away, or the loss of custody of a child. **Grief** is the emotional response to loss. Grief includes the main emotion of sadness, but other strong emotions may be present as well. Other feelings include confusion, anger, frustration, anxiety, or guilt.

The **five stages of grief** is a concept developed by **Elisabeth Kubler-Ross** in her book *On Death and Dying* in 1969. The five stages model originally pertained to those experiencing the dying process as the result of a terminal illness, but the model has been widely used to understand the grief reactions that people have in response to a number of situations, including loss of a loved one. The stages were first posited to be linear, but Kubler-Ross later stated that they are five common experiences that may or may not be experienced during grieving.

Denial
This is the first stage. It occurs when a person becomes aware that they have lost someone or something dear but refuses to accept the truth. This stage is generally brief as the person begins to process irrefutable evidence.

Anger
This is a period of venting anger at anyone who the person feels contributed to the loss occurring. It may be towards God, the drunk driver who caused an accident, or the CPS worker who takes a child from the home. In the case of a suicide, there could be anger at the deceased for choosing to leave.

Bargaining
This stage is almost a form of magical thinking. A person may think that if they promise to do better, work harder, or pray harder, the loss process can be reversed. This is generally a short-lived phase as one realizes that promises made will still not bring back that which has been lost.

Depression
During the fourth stage, a person allows themself to feel the sadness, and they may experience an even deeper emotional pain while learning to accept the loss and move forward. It may be a time of crying, despondency, and anguish. It must be experienced in order to move to the next stage.

Acceptance
The last stage is the point at which the grieving person recognizes that, while the pain is tremendous, they will be able to handle it. Those at this stage understand that time will ease some of the suffering. They are learning to make peace with the experience and move forward with their lives.

Hopelessness/Depression

Hopelessness is a key characteristic in clients who suffer from depression and suicidal ideations. Clients who experience **hopelessness** believe their current situation will never change. **Depression** is a leading cause of disability and is prevalent in adolescents and more commonly observed in females. In the elderly, symptoms of depression differ from other age groups and often go unnoticed because they commonly occur in combination with other medical illnesses and disabilities. Symptoms of depression in the older adult include confusion, changes in weight or appetite, physical aches and pains, irritability, trouble sleeping, and suicidal thoughts. A caregiver may attribute confusion to a cognitive disorder such as dementia and not address it as possible depression. Hopelessness is considered a cognitive and emotional state and has attributes such as loss of control, negative expectations for the future, and negativism expressed as despair or depression. Counselors can use various screening tools to assess for depression and symptoms of hopelessness.

The **Beck Depression Inventory (BDI)** is used to measure the behavioral manifestations of depression and assess its severity. The BDI is a twenty-one-item self-report inventory that can be used in clients between the ages of 13 and 80. Similarly, the **Beck Hopelessness Scale (BHS)** assesses an individual's negative expectations about their future. The **Hamilton Depression Rating Scale (HAM-D)** is a useful tool that measures depression before, during, and after treatments. This twenty-one-item test is measured on a three-point or five-point scale. **The Children's Depression Inventory (CDI)** is a modified BDI used in children. The CDI can be used in adolescents up until the age of 17 and assesses the severity of depression. Counselors should work with clients to establish a list of worries with possible resolutions. Brainstorming problem-solving solutions and building resilience can assist clients with improving their perception of the future. Other interventions include CBT and interpersonal therapy (IPT) to assist clients with managing negative thoughts and improving their relationships with others.

Loneliness/Attachment

The **attachment theory** is based on the belief that people have the desire to form interpersonal relationships, feel safe, and engage with others. When an interpersonal relationship is disrupted, clients with an **anxious attachment style** can experience distress, grief, and loss. Clients with an **avoidant attachment style** avoid depending on someone else or create distance from others to avoid having anyone depend on them. In times of stress, clients with an avoidant attachment style will withdraw from support systems and experience isolation. The goal of counseling is to make the client understand their attachment needs, communicate them with others, and identify functional coping patterns. Counselors may also use **complimentary** interventions that encourage clients to break old patterns and establish new coping mechanisms. In clients with avoidant attachment styles, practicing empathy and increasing their closeness with others can help decrease loneliness and depression. Counselors can also provide clients with opportunities for social interaction by placing them in group therapy.

Hypomental and Hypermental Focus

When an individual spends an excessive amount of time thinking about a certain topic or idea or doing a certain activity, it is referred to as **hyperfocus**. Hyperfocus is commonly seen in clients with ADHD or ASD. They have a hard time turning their focus from interesting activities to responsibilities that they don't have much interest in. Often, individuals with ADHD are thought of as having no ability to focus. However, they are capable of focusing their attention continuously for hours on things they enjoy. When the focus can't be switched to important tasks, such as homework or cleaning, it appears that they aren't able to focus. Hyperfocus can become a problem when hours are spent on one thing and duties, or even family and friends, are neglected.

Excessive focus can cause individuals to lose awareness of what is going on around them. They may fail to recognize that they missed a meal or that it is hours past bedtime. Although the intense focus is on something that the individual finds enjoyable, the amount of time spent on the activity and the resulting neglect of other areas of the individual's life can lead to feelings of guilt or anxiety. Since those who tend to hyperfocus do it for the immediate gratification they receive during the activity, one solution for getting them to shift their focus is to create pleasurable feedback in the otherwise boring tasks. Some clients will simply need help diverting their attention to a different task. Creating a schedule with set time-limits for activities (managed with the use of an alarm clock) is a great way to help clients handle issues with hyperfocusing.

On the flip side of hyperfocusing is **hypofocusing**. This is demonstrated by the inability to concentrate. Clients who suffer from PTSD, anxiety, or depressive disorders are often troubled by lack of concentration. There tends to be an emphasis on dismal thoughts that suppresses the ability to focus. Decreased sleep and appetite can also affect the ability to focus; these problems are common with PTSD, anxiety, and depression. Additionally, issues with concentration in clients with depression may be caused by decreased volume of gray-matter in the brain. If a counselor is working with a client who has trouble focusing, the counselor can help the client make a list of necessary but attainable tasks. Being able to reference the list can prevent clients from losing track of what needs to be done. The list should be easily manageable, not daunting. Having a list that can be checked off as tasks are completed can provide the client with a sense of accomplishment that can break the pattern of feeling additional anxiety or depression over being too unfocused to get anything done.

Intellectual Functioning Issues

Clients with decreased intellectual functioning have diminished learning, problem-solving, and reasoning abilities. Intellectual disabilities usually develop before the age of 18, and these clients exhibit signs of cognitive limitations and lack of adaptive behaviors. Children with decreased intellectual functioning will have issues with abstract thinking, academic learning, and planning. In adults, decreased intellectual functioning results in the inability to follow rules, socially engage with others, or understand important concepts, such as time and financial means. A counselor can use various interventions to treat clients with decreased intellectual functioning, including behavioral therapy, **Individualized Education Programs (IEPs)**, and talk therapy. IEPs are common in schools and require collaboration of school staff to meet the educational needs of the student. Clients with intellectual disabilities require trust, repetition, concrete communication, and simplified language. Counselors should be aware that up to 40% of clients with an intellectual disability will have mental health challenges, such as anxiety and depression, and should be addressed accordingly.

Insomnia/Sleep Issues

Sleep deprivation occurs when a person does not get the optimal amount of sleep on a daily basis. Lack of sleep or trouble sleeping can lead to issues such as unstable mood, chronic fatigue, and medical comorbidities. Chronic sleep deprivation may result in delusions and hallucinations. **Insomnia** is the most common sleep disorder reported and can be associated with anxiety, depression, and posttraumatic stress disorder (PTSD). Counselors should explore the root cause of sleep disorders and develop interventions related to the source of the problem.

Counseling should primarily focus on having the client change behaviors, develop relaxation skills, and establish sleep goals. There are various methods a counselor can use to address sleep disorders, such as keeping a sleep diary, improving sleep hygiene, and discussing dark therapy. **Sleep diaries** can help determine any causative triggers that disturb sleep patterns. **Sleep hygiene** is a personalized plan in which the client develops a list of activities to perform and/or avoid before bedtime. **Dark therapy** involves restricting light sources, which can delay the circadian clock. Clients should be encouraged to limit exposure to blue light that is found in screens, such as cellphones and televisions, before bedtime. CBT is commonly used in clients with insomnia and aims to change sleep schedules and habits that can contribute to sleep disturbances.

Maladaptive Eating Behaviors

An **eating disorder** is a persistent disturbance in eating behaviors that leads to poor health. Maladaptive eating patterns can lead to psychological, physical, and emotional disturbances. Some of the most common eating disorders are anorexia nervosa, bulimia nervosa, and binge-eating disorder. Clients who practice extreme forms of dieting can also be classified as having an eating disorder. Extreme dieting can lead to sleep disturbances, decreased energy, mood swings, irritability, and social isolation. Additionally, clients who experience high levels of emotional or mental stress can use food to suppress their negative thoughts. This type of maladaptive eating behavior can be attributed to atypical depression. **Atypical depression** results from chronic stress and a sustained level of increased cortisol in the body. **Cortisol** is a stress hormone that increases appetite.

Stress eating satisfies the client's emotional needs as opposed to their physical hunger. Clients who experience these maladaptive eating behaviors may also experience low self-esteem and anxiety. Adolescents are the population most commonly affected by eating disorders and may develop maladaptive behaviors because of bullying, body shaming, or peer pressure. Screening tools, such as the SCOFF questionnaire (Sick, Control, One, Fat, Food), the Body Attitudes Questionnaire, and the Eating Disorder Inventory, are useful in assessing the presence of an eating disorder. Behavioral therapy is an important part of recovery and aims to help clients build good eating habits, stop harmful behaviors, and develop healthy coping skills. Clients may be placed in group therapy to obtain support from others who experience the same condition. Counselors should encourage clients to develop healthy coping skills to deal with emotional distress and ultimately be comfortable in their own body.

Remarriage/Recommitment

After separating from a partner or divorcing a spouse, people experience a sense of loss and may go through stages of grief. There are multiple stages of grief, including denial, anger, bargaining, depression, and acceptance. The final stage is **rebuilding**. During this stage, acceptance of the situation increases and a plan for the future emerges. Clients may seek counseling to process their emotions, learn to establish healthy boundaries with their former partners, and attempt to rebuild their lives. Counseling can help clients identify unhealthy behaviors that ended the relationship. It is important to include the client's new partner in the counseling so they can establish a sense of vulnerability and increase effective communication. Some of the problems to address include jealousy, lack of closure in previous relationships, resentment, and lack of trust. Counselors who specialize in couples counseling should focus on helping partners communicate their needs and develop healthy solutions to their conflicts.

Developmental Processes/Tasks/Issues

Client needs in counseling vary depending on their developmental stage. Counselors should be aware of the challenges their clients face as they progress through their lifespan. In every psychosocial stage, there are two concepts all clients will face. For example, children from the age of 3 to 6 years will experience **initiative versus guilt**; through imaginative play, children begin to experiment with who they are. If they do not feel supported by their parental figures, they may feel guilty about not following a set of rules. In middle adulthood (approximately ages 40 to 65), **generativity versus stagnation** challenges a person to contribute something meaningful to new generations.

Failure to do so will lead to stagnation without a meaningful sense of accomplishment. Knowledge of the different developmental stages can help the counselor guide the client through anticipated challenges and put their problems into perspective. A client's culture and diversity factors may also influence how they meet their developmental tasks. Clients who have low socioeconomic status or are victims of racism, prejudice, or oppression may have limited opportunities to reach their developmental goals. Interventions include individual, family, and group counseling. Classroom guidance can facilitate younger clients' understanding of the emotional, cognitive, physical, and social aspects of self-development.

Obsessive Thoughts/Behaviors

Obsessions are impulsive thoughts that are persistent and recurring in the mind. Obsessions and compulsions often exist together. **Compulsive behaviors** are ritualistic and aim to decrease the severe anxiety that is caused by not performing them. Clients with an **obsessive-compulsive personality** have an overwhelming need to follow a strict set of rules, moral codes, and fixed routines. On the other hand, clients diagnosed with **obsessive-compulsive disorder (OCD)** have a pattern of unwanted thoughts followed by a repetitive compulsion, and an intense need to carry out compulsive behaviors. Examples of obsessive themes include violence, sexual ideation, contamination, and doubt. For example, a client who believes that every surface is contaminated may avoid touching all objects and will repeatedly wash their hands if forced to touch a surface.

Other clients may return to their home to check the door lock many times a day to satisfy the intrusive thought of doubt. There are a couple of interventions counselors can use during therapy to decrease the compulsion that follows the obsessive thought. **Exposure and response prevention (ERP)** aims to control the anxiety of not reacting to a particular obsession. The goal is to have the client confront the obsession and refrain from performing the usual compulsive action. CBT can help clients place their obsessions into perspective. The goal is to recognize unrealistic thoughts and become desensitized to the obsession. Clients should also be encouraged to develop coping skills to deal with the anxiety caused by not reacting to an obsessive thought. When counseling children with OCD, parents should be educated on supportive strategies. Praising the child when they resist compulsions, allowing uncertainty, and avoiding criticism can reassure control of the issue.

Occupation and Career Development

One of the most important aspects of an adult's life is their career choice. **Career counseling** can help clients choose, change, or leave a particular occupation by providing resources, interpreting aptitude assessments, or discussing the development of career choices. Counselors should assist clients in identifying their strengths, personality type, and skills set. The **Myers-Briggs Type Indicator (MBTI)** is a tool used to determine personality type based on self-reporting. Choosing a career based on personality type can decrease the probability that an individual will experience burnout in their occupation. Some of the topics to discuss with clients during career counseling are financial goals, educational capacity, advancement opportunities, and work environments. Demanding occupations may lead to job stress, and clients may present with psychological issues, such as depression, anxiety, and substance use, or physical symptoms, such as decreased appetite, difficulty sleeping, and headaches. Counselors can help clients identify patterns that contribute to stress and develop relaxation techniques, such as meditation, yoga, and deep breathing, to decrease the effects of burnout.

Physical Issues Related to Anxiety

Anxiety is defined as having a sense of dread, uncertainty, or uneasiness. Although anxiety usually disturbs thought processes, it can also manifest through physical symptoms. Some of the most common physical signs of anxiety are elevated heart rate, sweating, dizziness, tense muscles, and headaches. Physical symptoms that are more severe, such as difficulty breathing, can signal a panic attack. Counselors should be able to recognize that anxiety will affect each client differently. Based on the level of anxiety, counselors can develop interventions to help the client develop healthy coping skills. The most common type of therapy to treat the symptoms of anxiety is CBT. CBT works by retraining how clients think via exposure. For example, if a client struggles with being out in public for long periods of time, progressive exposure to social situations in time increments may ease the anxiety. **Biofeedback** is another form of therapy that helps clients understand the physical reaction to anxiety and become aware of how their bodies respond to triggers. Introducing self-care habits, such as exercise, meditation, yoga, and journaling, can help clients reduce their anxiety and, consequently, their physical symptoms.

Physical Issues Related to Depression

Depression is usually characterized by feelings of hopelessness, anger, sadness, and suicidal ideation. However, depression can also cause physical manifestations. Eating disorders are common, and clients may experience decreased appetite and weight loss or increased cravings that lead to binge behaviors. Depression can lead to slow body movements, slouched posture, back pain, and headaches. In children and teenagers, oversleeping and overeating are common manifestations. In the older adult, fatigue and non-medical impotence are physical signs that are often overlooked and may delay a depression diagnosis. **Goal setting** during an initial counseling session can help clients determine what priorities to address. Counselors can help clients recognize their strengths and use them to change behaviors and develop healthy coping mechanisms. Common goals of overcoming depression include improving physical well-being, building meaningful relationships, and performing productive activities of daily living. Counselors should also encourage clients to develop healthy lifestyle habits, such as exercise, which releases endorphins; eating foods that are rich in omega-3 fatty acids, which increases serotonin; and meditation, which can increase dopamine levels.

Physical/Emotional Issues Related to Trauma

Trauma affects everyone differently. The reaction depends on the person's emotional resiliency, history of past trauma, and other factors. Some trauma survivors exhibit symptoms that clearly meet the criteria for PTSD, while others exhibit smaller clusters of symptoms, such as anxiety or depression. Others show little or no symptoms. Below is an overview of common responses:

- Foreshortened future: This refers to the sense that one's life is shortened or forever altered and that a normal life may never be experienced again.

- Emotional responses: These may be fear, sadness, shame, anger, guilt, and/or anxiety.

- Physical reactions: Survivors of trauma often have multiple somatic issues, including gastrointestinal complaints, neurological problems, poor sleep, and muscle pain.

- Hyperarousal: Trauma survivors often become hypervigilant. They are frightened by neutral stimuli, such as a dog barking or a child screaming. They may experience a continual feeling that something terrible is going to happen.

- Intrusive thoughts: Survivors can become flooded with unwanted thoughts and memories about the trauma.

- Trigger/flashbacks: Triggers are stimuli that set off memories and provide a sensory reminder of the traumatic event.

- Dissociation: This coping mechanism allows the person to "check out" temporarily. This process severs connections to the painful memories.

- Self-harm: Some survivors use self-harm as a means of distraction from emotional pain. This could transition into more serious self-harm and can result in suicidal behaviors if not treated.

- Substance use: Many survivors use substances to medicate unpleasant emotions, such as fear or shame.

Common Effects of Stress, Trauma, and Violence

Many people equate stress with an emotional experience, but stress can actually have a profound effect on the body, cognition, and behavior as well.

Common Effects of Stress		
Body	**Mood**	**Behavior**
• Headache • Muscle tension or pain • Chest pain • Fatigue • Change in sex drive • Stomach upset • Sleep problems	• Anxiety • Restlessness • Lack of motivation or focus • Irritability or anger • Sadness or depression	• Overeating or under eating • Angry outbursts • Drug or alcohol abuse • Tobacco use • Social withdrawal

Although everyone experiences some degree of stress, stress becomes trauma when the intensity of the stress causes a person to feel helpless and seriously threatened, either physically or psychologically. Unfortunately, trauma and violence are common experiences for both adults and children, and the risk for traumatic and/or violent events is particularly high for individuals suffering from mental illness. Some people will experience a trauma with little to no lasting impact, while others may struggle with the aftermath of the trauma for the rest of their lives.

Many variables can either exacerbate or ameliorate the impact of trauma:

- Whether the event occurred once or was ongoing
- Whether the event occurred during childhood or adulthood
- Intensity of the traumatic event
- Personal experience vs. observation

74

- Ability to access supportive resources
- The way in which people and systems respond to the individual who has been traumatized

Potential effects of trauma and violence:

- Substance use and abuse
- Mental health problems
- Risk-taking behavior
- Self-injurious behavior
- Increased likelihood or exacerbation of chronic illnesses, including cardiovascular disease
- Difficulties with daily functioning, including navigating careers and relationships

Post-Traumatic Stress Disorder (PTSD)

Some people who have experienced trauma or violence will experience an impact significant enough to be diagnosed with **PTSD**. Symptoms must last for more than one month before the diagnosis of PTSD is considered and must include the following:

- One or more *re-experiencing symptoms* (flashbacks, disturbing dreams, frightening thoughts)

- One or more avoidance symptoms (avoiding reminders of the trauma, experiencing emotional "numbing," losing interest in activities that one previously enjoyed)

- Two or more arousal and reactivity symptoms (startling easily, experiencing tension, hypervigilance, difficulty falling or staying asleep, eruptions of anger)

- Two or more cognition and mood symptoms (difficulty remembering the traumatic event, persistent negative thoughts, excessive feelings of blame or guilt)

Process Addictions

Behavioral process addictions are compulsive activities performed to satisfy an impulse. Clients with process addictions perform activities despite the possible consequences. Addictions are particularly problematic when they interfere with the ability to function academically, socially, and professionally. Clients who develop habitual behaviors that result in guilt, distress, or shame can benefit from counseling to decrease the anxiety caused by abstaining from the addiction. Common process addictions include chronic gambling, sex urges, hoarding, excessive exercising, and unrestrained shopping. Clients with a **gambling addiction** may lie about the extent of their gambling, ignore family and work responsibilities, progressively increase the amount that is gambled, and use gambling as a means to escape life problems. **Compulsive spending** is classified by investing an excessive amount of time and resources to shop.

The **Bergen Shopping Addiction Scale** is a screening tool that measures the severity of a shopping addiction. The scale consists of twenty-eight statements that rate each item in a five-point continuum of agreement. Behaviors that increase the likelihood of a shopping addiction include consistent and obsessive thoughts about shopping, using shopping as a mood stabilizer, inability to decrease the amount of shopping, and guilt if the activity is not performed. Process addictions require discovering the underlying emotional need that necessitates the compulsive behaviors. Counselors should work with clients to establish adaptive skills and impulse control. CBT, support groups, and twelve-step programs can help clients overcome process addictions. The development of new hobbies, avoiding

75

places that encourage the behavioral addiction, and strengthening supportive relationships can facilitate recovery.

Racism/Discrimination/Oppression

Making unjust distinctions between people or groups based on characteristics such as race, sex, age, religion, disability, or sexual orientation is **discrimination**. Discriminatory treatment and practices must be consciously combatted in the counseling profession to ensure that all clients receive appropriate care. Counselors should be aware of the various forms of discrimination and their effects, including those defined below.

Direct discrimination refers to unfair treatment based on someone's characteristics. An example would be refusing to hire someone because of their ethnicity.

Indirect discrimination refers to situations in which a policy applies the same to everyone, but a person or group of people are negatively impacted due to certain characteristics. For example, a company might require that everyone help unload shipments that come to the office. The policy is the same for everyone, but it's discriminatory towards any disabled employees. In a workplace environment, indirect discrimination can sometimes be allowed if there's a compelling reason for the requirement. For example, firefighters have to meet certain physical criteria due to the nature of their work.

Another form of discrimination is **harassment**. This involves unwanted bullying or humiliation intentionally directed to a person. **Secondary victimization** refers to the unfair treatment received when a person reports discrimination and is not supported by authorities.

Effects of discrimination on the individual may include depression, anxiety, other mental health issues, and medical/health-related problems caused by lack of access to health resources. Effects of discrimination on society include diminished resources (e.g., employment, educational opportunities, healthcare) and a culture characterized by fear, anger, or apathy.

Religious Values Conflict

Religion and spirituality are two distinguishable terms that can cause distress in an individual if not followed according to their ideals. **Spirituality** is a sense of connection to the universe, nature, or a higher power that may not be directly identified. Individuals who share a common faith and practice a particular set of beliefs may identify themselves with a formalized **religion**. Religion can influence a person's life and may be helpful in coping with hardship. When religions operate under principles that deviate from their doctrine, an individual may question their faith, which can lead to unstable emotional and mental well-being. Clients who are questioning their faith may experience anxiety and can potentially self-harm, experience suicidal ideation, and have substance use issues. Clients who experience religious discrimination and are potential victims of physical violence may have PTSD, depression, and mental distress. Counseling should focus on guidance as opposed to supporting or rejecting a person's beliefs. Clients should be encouraged to reconcile the areas of conflict between their life and religion and uncover areas of concern. Helping the client align their emotional needs with their fundamental beliefs can help them develop a greater understanding of mental and spiritual well-being.

Retirement Concerns

Planning for retirement usually includes financial stability and affordability of living. However, retirement can also lead to emotional and mental instability. Work provides a social structure and sense of community. Careers often fulfill a sense of purpose and passion. Retirement can cause emotional distress and lead to feelings of uselessness, loneliness, boredom, and disillusionment. Retirement can cause an identity crisis, and clients will be seeking counseling to establish a new sense of productivity. There are several interventions counselors can implement to help clients adjust to retirement. Setting small goals and establishing milestones can give clients a sense of purpose. Clients should be encouraged to become involved within the community and build friendships to avoid the isolation that follows retirement. Setting up a schedule for the day's activities allows for structure and can help clients feel a sense of normalcy to their routine. Volunteering, developing new hobbies, and expanding social ties can decrease the mental and emotional effects of retirement.

Ruminating and/or Intrusive Thoughts

Persistently focusing on a situation or thought process is known as **rumination**. Ruminating thoughts are concerns with possible loss, failure, or hopelessness. People who experience rumination focus on negative thoughts, feelings, and past experiences. As intrusive thoughts persist, the result can be in anger, sadness, and agitation. Rumination is a maladaptive form of self-reflection and focuses on psychological distress. Clients who have ruminating thoughts are more likely to become depressed and develop unhealthy coping mechanisms, such as alcohol abuse and binge-eating habits. The Ruminative Response Scale (RRS) is a twenty-two-item questionnaire that measures the intensity of ruminating thoughts when feeling sad. CBT for ruminating thoughts focuses on developing new ways of thinking and targets the issues that are causing the intrusive thoughts. **Functional analysis** is a component of CBT that aims to identify problematic thinking and change behaviors that exacerbate habitual thought processes. During behavioral activation and cognitive restructuring, clients take action, reward healthy behaviors, and learn reality-based thinking. The goal of counseling for rumination is to encourage mindfulness and defuse negative thoughts.

Separation from Primary Caregivers

Throughout their development, children form attachments to their primary caregivers. **Secure attachment** is a healthy bond between a child and a caregiver. Some of the behaviors that define secure attachment include eye contact, verbal and nonverbal display of emotions, and recognition of familiar caregivers. Other forms of attachment include the anxious-resistant insecure, anxious-avoidant insecure, and the disorganized/disoriented style. These attachment styles typically indicate that the child's needs are not consistently met by the caregiver. A weak attachment bond can result from early separation from caregivers and lead to social and emotional developmental issues. Signs that children have insecure attachments include rejection of emotional connections, frequent crying, avoidance of eye contact, and lack of interest in interactive play.

To determine the effect of detachment from a child and their caregiver, the **Strange Situation** test can be performed prior to initiating counseling. The test consists of eight episodes lasting a couple of minutes in which the caregiver, child, and a stranger are introduced, separated, and later reunited. In a secure attachment style, separation anxiety is marked when the caregiver leaves the child. In the resistant attachment style, the child will display intense distress when the caregiver leaves. In the avoidant attachment style, children show no sign of distress when left alone. Counseling can help children understand healthy relationships, develop coping skills for separation anxiety, and form constructive bonds with caregivers. Interventions include behavioral therapy, such as systematic desensitization and flooding. Gradual exposure to anxiety-producing situations can diminish the fear that is initially experienced.

Sexual Functioning Concerns

Sexual dysfunction is characterized as any problem that prevents an individual from obtaining satisfaction from sexual activity. More than 40% of women and 30% of men report issues with sexual functioning. There are four categories of sexual dysfunction: a lack of sexual desire, inability to become sexually aroused during intercourse, delayed or absent climax, and pain during intercourse. Sexual dysfunction has both physical and psychological causes. Physical causes include heart disease, diabetes, high blood pressure, hormonal imbalances, among many others. Psychological causes include stress, anxiety, depression, body image issues, and past sexual trauma. Counseling should focus on the underlying cause of sexual dysfunction. For example, clients who have a history of sexual assault may benefit from **depth therapy**, which focuses on unconscious feelings and aims to change unhealthy coping behaviors. After recovering from sexual trauma, sex therapy can address intimacy concerns. Sex counseling can help individual clients and couples reflect on their internal conflicts and concerns. The goal of counseling is to remove mental and emotional barriers that prevent clients from achieving sexual satisfaction.

Sleeping Habits

A disturbance in sleep patterns is known as a **sleep-wake disorder.** Sleep-wake disorders can affect mental, emotional, and physical health. Several psychological factors that affect the sleep cycle include depression, anxiety, trauma, and stress. Sleeping less than the recommended hours can lead to sleep deprivation. Sleep deprivation can cause fatigue, impaired judgment, and trouble focusing. Alternatively, consistently sleeping more than the recommended hours can lead to headaches, back pain, lack of productivity, and depression. Poor sleep habits, such as late or early bedtimes, remaining in bed for prolonged periods of time, and excessive daytime napping, can cause sleep-wake disorders. It is important to recognize if poor mental health is affecting sleep or if sleep disorders are causing disruptions in mental health. Counselors should focus on the behaviors or emotional disturbances causing the disruption in sleeping habits. Interventions include helping clients set a consistent sleep schedule, create bedtime rituals, and eliminate stimuli before bedtime.

Spiritual/Existential Concerns

Spirituality is a sense of connection to the universe, nature, or a higher power that may not be directly identified. An individual may continuously be searching for an ultimate meaning of life or personal growth. Spirituality can also connect people to one another and is expressed via various rituals, such as meditation, yoga, and dance. Spiritual beliefs may also provide social and emotional support, offer comfort in times of grief, and provide ethical guidelines for a way of life. When an individual questions their spirituality and is faced with a life challenge, such as the loss of a loved one or diagnosis of a chronic health condition, they may struggle to find meaning in life. Similarly, clients who experience doubts about their place in life and develop an internal conflict may experience an **existential crisis**.

Some of the reasons an individual may experience an existential crisis include unresolved emotional challenges, unfulfilled social lives, inability to overcome guilt, and overall dissatisfaction with their path in life. The sense of hopelessness can lead to depression and anxiety. Clients seeking counseling for spiritual or existential concerns may struggle with self-compassion or a lack of belonging or may be unconcerned with life. **Pastoral counseling** is a realm of practice with education on theology and can help clients discover their own spirituality. Being empathetic and incorporating a twelve-step program can guide clients toward resolving their spiritual concerns. Encouraging clients to replace pessimism with positive thoughts, reflect on reasons for being grateful, and identify positive qualities in oneself can help to resolve an existential crisis.

Stress Management

Counselors will often encounter clients with stress related problems and should be well versed in stress management techniques to offer clients suggestions for this issue. Counselors may engage clients to practice relaxation techniques in order to manage stressors. Clients may engage in physical exercise at their physician's discretion to relieve stress. Deep breathing exercises are also beneficial for relieving stress. To reduce stress, clients may use treatments such as cognitive behavior therapy or rational emotive therapy to change fallacious thinking patterns and distorted perceptions. Clients may be stressed concerning basic living needs and counselors can link clients to services in the community to assist them with these issues. If clients are at the safety and physical stages of the hierarchy of needs, these stressors should be addressed before other issues are included in the therapeutic process.

Substance Use/Addiction Issues

Addiction is a complex process involving biological, social, cultural, and genetic factors. There is some disagreement in the addiction treatment community about the causes and best treatments for substance use disorders. There are several models of addiction.

The earliest theory of addiction is called the **Moral Model**. This model implies that the person abuses substances because they are morally weak. The addict is viewed as a sinner or criminal and one who does not have the intestinal fortitude to change negative behaviors, therefore choosing to wallow in the misery of their sins.

The **disease model** or **medical model of addiction**, upon which the twelve-step program of Alcoholics Anonymous (AA) is based, specifies that the addict suffers from an illness that will never be cured and is progressive in its development. Even if the individual ceases alcohol intake, the disease remains. AA literature indicates that when one relapses, even after years of sobriety, the addict picks up, not where he left off, but where the disease would have taken him if the drinking had continued. It is seen as a medical disorder and, at times, referred to in the Big Book of AA as having an allergy, with alcohol as the identified allergen. This theory is accepted and understood by many successful AA participants who have maintained sobriety throughout this program for years and who have shared their experience of strength and hope to help others struggling with addiction.

The **bio-psychosocial model of addiction** focuses on the role of the environment. Cultural and social factors influence one's beliefs and attitudes about substance use. In certain religions, it is unacceptable to use alcohol. In others, it may be encouraged—such as the huge sale and consumption of beer at Catholic picnics and fish fries. An addict's observation of others and their patterns of alcohol ingestion influences their attraction to drug or alcohol use as a means for tension relief or a form of celebration. Exposure to family or community members who use large quantities of intoxicants may serve to normalize dysfunctional patterns of use. Some youth observe their parents drink a quart of vodka each night and believe that their family members are just normal drinkers whereas other youth are raised in environments where alcohol is unacceptable or served only on rare occasions.

The **learning theory of addiction** is based on concepts related to positive reinforcement. The assumption underpinning this model is that addiction is a behavior learned through operant conditioning, classical conditioning, and social learning. Social learning takes place through observation. Learning theory posits that the interplay between these three factors contribute to the initiation, maintenance, and relapse of addictive behaviors. The intoxicant serves as an immediate reinforcement in the form of increased euphoria or relaxation. In some cases, it also deters withdrawal symptoms. Both of these forms of reinforcement increase the likelihood that the behavior will be repeated in an effort to recreate the sensation of feeling better.

Genetic theory is based on research indicating that biological children of parents who struggle with addiction are more prone to addiction than children of non-addicts. According to genetic therapy, this genetic predisposition towards addiction accounts for about half of one's susceptibility to becoming an addict. Theorists of this model agree that other factors, such as social experiences, have an impact upon the formation of an addiction.

The repercussions of the addict's behavior can affect many significant aspects of life. The impact of addictions is felt not only by the addict, but also by everyone in that person's family and circle of social support. Those most powerfully affected are the immediate family members—particularly those who live under the same roof as the addict. Friends, extended family, co-workers, and employers also experience fallout from the addict's behaviors.

The spouses or partners of people who struggle with addiction often feel depressed, anxious, and angry. Persons in the throes of addiction often lie and steal to maintain their habit. It is not uncommon for people who struggle with addiction to steal from friends, family, or employers. Families must deal with the anxiety of not knowing when their loved one will come home or what mood or condition the person may demonstrate upon arriving home. Some families must deal with the shame of seeing their loved one arrested or knowing that this person harmed others while under the influence. Others simply become embarrassed by behaviors that loved ones exhibit in public or their failure to show up for an important event, such as a graduation.

Children of parents who struggle with addiction experience embarrassment, fear, anxiety, and sadness. They are more likely to be abused or neglected, especially in single parent homes. Children may suffer when money intended for basic needs is spent on drugs or alcohol instead. When abuse and/or neglect are reported to CPS, these children may be taken from parents and placed in a series of group or foster homes. In some cases, custody is completely severed. Such experiences may lead to deep psychological scars for those closest to the addict.

Suicidal Thoughts/Behaviors

Suicidal ideation is an emergent thought process that should be addressed promptly. Suicidal thoughts or behaviors can occur as a result of experiencing severe anxiety, depression, hopelessness, or panic attacks. When clients express suicidal ideation, counselors should promptly perform a suicide risk assessment. There are various tools used to assess for suicide risk, such as the Columbia-Suicide Severity Rating Scale (C-SSRS), the Beck Scale for Suicide Ideation, and the Suicide Assessment Checklist. In general, these tools assess the suicidal intent of the client. Counselors should also observe for warning signs, such as direct or indirect suicidal statements, depressive symptoms, emotional disturbances, negative behavioral thoughts, and situational challenges. Some of these signs include long-term depression, preoccupation with death, suicide notes, and lack of interest in life. Specific information should be obtained if the client verbalizes that they have a suicide plan. Clients should be questioned on the frequency of suicidal thoughts and if the means to carry out the specific plan are available. Crisis interventions, such as emergency hotlines, hospitalization, and notification of social support systems, may be warranted.

Terminal Illness Issues

A medical diagnosis of a terminal illness is impactful. Examples of terminal diagnoses include cancer, acquired immunodeficiency syndrome (AIDS), and Lou Gehrig's disease (ALS). End of life is expected within a short time frame, and a person may feel intense grief, sadness, and despair. Support systems may also be emotionally affected by the individual's diagnosis. Clients and their loved ones often seek counseling to come to terms with the diagnosis and find resolution of their feelings. Clients trying to cope with their diagnosis may experience guilt, regret, fear, frustration, and uncertainty about their life. Loved ones who take on the role of a caregiver can develop anxiety, depression, resentment, and burnout. Counseling interventions will commonly address feelings during the stages of grief (denial, anger, bargaining, depression, acceptance, and rebuilding). Clients may be encouraged to join support groups for the terminally ill and seek companionship from those going through the same situation. The goal of counseling is to have the client and their loved ones process their feelings, communicate their needs, and find emotional relief.

Visual/Auditory Hallucinations

Hallucinations are false perceptions of reality. The most common types of hallucinations are visual and auditory. A person may see and/or hear someone or something that does not exist. Hallucinations occur as a result of multiple conditions, including schizophrenia, psychosis, extreme emotional or mental stress, and as a side effect of medications. Substance use can also cause hallucinations, which are more prominent during withdrawals. Auditory hallucinations can sometimes direct a person to perform a harmful action. Clients experiencing auditory hallucinations should be questioned regarding suicidal or homicidal intent. Counseling interventions for clients experiencing hallucinations include assessing and acknowledging the client's feelings about the hallucinations, being objective about reality, and developing coping strategies to manage the hallucinations. CBT can help clients restructure delusional beliefs and distinguish what is real and what is not. Counselors should explore when hallucinations are more likely to occur and encourage clients to perform distracting activities, such as singing, reading, or talking to a friend, when experiencing the issue.

Worry and Anxiety

Worrying, defined as dwelling over actual or possible problems, is a symptom of many mental health diagnoses, such as generalized anxiety, psychosis, OCD, and PTSD. It is important for counselors to assess other underlying factors, such as toxic relationships, financial concerns, and workplace issues, and develop interventions that address those circumstances. Excessive worry can prevent clients from finding enjoyment in everyday activities. Individuals who obsess over potential scenarios can experience distress, insomnia, and panic attacks. CBT can help clients identify when the worry happens and break the cycle of negative thinking by identifying fears and putting them into perspective. Clients can also be encouraged to make a list of specific stressors, identify behavior patterns, and develop strategies that will minimize the time spent worrying. Activities such as exercising, socializing with friends, and listening to music can minimize the negative thoughts that occur with worry and anxiety.

Adoption Issues

Many children who go through the adoption process do not have a positive outcome. Issues with the foster care system, neglectful adoptive parents, or issues with placement can lead to emotional stress and trauma. Children may also experience anxiety and anger from not knowing their background. The rate of teens who develop behavior disorders is almost double for those who are adopted. While in foster homes, up to 45% of children leave the system and can experience homelessness, unemployment, and imprisonment. Other problems adopted children face include attachment issues, developmental delays, and decreased trust. Counseling interventions to help clients cope with adoption issues include family therapy, play therapy, and support groups. **Family therapy** can help caregivers and children learn to relate to one another and establish empathy. **Play therapy** allows children to verbalize their thoughts and emotions through self-expression and can help counselors develop strategies to support the child. **Support groups** may help clients find people who share similar thoughts, encourage each other, and discuss problem-solving techniques for emotional challenges.

Blended Family Issues

A high percentage of children live in a **blended family** with a biological parent, a stepparent, and possible stepsiblings. Children who are part of a blended family may experience stress from conflict between separated parents or siblings, differing parenting styles, and opposite family routines. Children who become part of a blended family may resent the new parent, be bullied by stepsiblings, or express their frustration through behavioral outbursts. Alternatively, adults who become stepparents can experience tension in the family due to ongoing communication with their partner's ex or trying to gain acceptance from the child. Counseling can provide blended families with an opportunity to establish roles, boundaries, and parenting goals. Family therapy can help children express their concerns and allow the caregivers to show their affection. Couples counseling can help partners adjust to their new blended family life and provide open communication about challenges and compromises.

Child Abuse–Related Concerns

Children develop attachment early in life. The bond that is created between a child and their parental figure is determined by the amount of nurturing and how well the child's emotional and physiological needs are meet. Children who develop a sense of trust that is later broken will develop emotional disorders. Child abuse is reported frequently and can be in the form of neglect, exploitation, abandonment, physical, or sexual. Teachers are often the first to notice signs of child abuse. A child may present with physical signs, such as unexplained cuts or bruises. The child's behavior may also be erratic, and interacting with others may be troubling. Children who are abused by their parents or an older authority figure will struggle with anxiety, fear, and severe emotional distress.

The mental and emotional effects of abuse can also linger into adulthood and interfere with academic performance, social interactions, and independence. Counselors who treat young clients who experience abuse can intervene with psychodynamic techniques such as play therapy. Play therapy allows the child to imitate or re-create the experience, enabling the counselor to discuss right from wrong with the child and help them develop healthy coping skills to begin the healing process. **Talk therapy** is a goal-oriented technique that aims to remedy unhealthy behaviors that result from trauma. Talk therapy is geared toward clients who understand the concept of abuse. The overall goal

82

of counseling is to provide the child with a safe environment to express their emotions and begin the healing process.

Child Development Issues

Social skills and emotional intelligence are developed as children age. To understand the needs and behavior changes throughout life, **Erikson's Stages of Psychosocial Development** serves as a reference for the different stages of growth. There are eight stages in life, and four of them happen throughout childhood. It is important to meet the needs in every stage because lack of fulfillment can lead to issues such as abandonment, academic challenges, neglect, and intellectual disabilities. During **infancy**, the need for a safe environment is established when parental figures meet their infants' needs and provide trusting behavior. If the emotional and physiological needs are not met, infants are faced with mistrust. During the **toddler stage**, children begin to develop their own independence and autonomy. Defiance and stubbornness are common during this stage.

If autonomy is not established, they are left with a sense of shame and doubt. Initiative versus guilt occurs during the **preschool years** and focuses on developing social roles and emotions through imaginative play. During **school age**, relationships and academic performance are important. Children who struggle with bullying or inferiority may experience mental health problems such as depression and anxiety. Other events that may interfere with positive development include child abuse, domestic violence between parents, parental divorce, homelessness, and death of a loved one. Counseling can help young clients process emotions and experiences through play therapy, art therapy, or family therapy. For instance, family therapy can strengthen relationships and help family members understand and meet each other's developmental needs.

Dating/Relationship Problems

Relationships typically go through three phases. During the **romance or rejection phase**, a couple begins to learn about each another and build intimacy. Idealization occurs during this phase, and partners may ignore each other's flaws for fear of conflict or rejection. During the **trust or disillusionment phase**, partners will encounter more disagreements regarding activities of daily life. Couples who have positive conflict resolution strategies will establish trust and learn to rely on one another during challenging times. Couples who are unable to overcome their differences may constantly argue and grow apart. The final phase is **adjustment or separation**. Couples who are able to respect differences in opinion and trust each other will adjust and stay together. Those who are unable to compromise will separate emotionally and end the relationship. Unhealthy relationships have similar characteristics and include jealousy, insecurity, unsuccessful resolution of disagreements, lack of romance, and imbalanced responsibilities. The **Gottman Method** is an intervention that helps partners identify each other's aspirations and worries and teaches conflict management. Couples counseling can help partners address concerns, identify areas of differences, develop conflict resolution techniques, and improve communication.

Divorce

Separation of marriage can occur for several reasons, including lack of commitment, disproportionate responsibilities, poor communication skills, an affair, and abuse. After divorce, partners may experience anger, guilt, grief, and anxiety. Additionally, divorced couples with children may experience intense stress. Individuals who experience a divorce may be unable to cope with adjustments, such as finances, social relationships, and single lifestyles. The goal of counseling is to help clients navigate through the divorce or recover emotionally and mentally after a divorce. Couples therapy can facilitate a healthy divorce and establish guidelines regarding financial obligations, living arrangements, and parenting. Individual therapy helps clients gain a new perspective on life and develop coping skills to deal with depression, anxiety, or stress caused by the divorce. Clients should be encouraged to perform stress-reducing activities, such as self-care, meditation, exercise, and contacting friends for support.

Family Abuse/Violence

People may experience abuse at the hands of strangers, caretakers, or close friends and family. The effects of abuse are traumatic, pervasive, and long lasting. Beyond affecting the abused parties, abuse often impacts those who are close to the victims. Physical, sexual, and psychological child abuse can lead to impaired intellect, learning disabilities, deficits in trust and language skills, long-term inappropriate behaviors, or lack of coping mechanisms. As abused children grow, they may be unable to make healthy friendships or lack the ability to desire or maintain intimate relationships. They may have failed marriages, or they may perpetuate the cycle of abuse when they become parents. They may often feel unworthy or that they did something to cause the abuse. This often has an impact on their attachment styles and how they relate to others.

In adults, abuse may cause permanent or temporary physical damage, low self-esteem, shame, despair, or feelings of helplessness. Victims of abuse as an adult may experience mental health disorders such anxiety and depression. If children witness their loved ones experiencing abuse, it may be traumatic for them, or they may normalize the behavior and perpetuate abuse themselves. Elder abuse, especially in nursing homes, often goes undetected as victims may be weak or losing mental faculties. Elders are especially vulnerable to physical and financial abuse. Effects may include rapid physical or mental deterioration, submissiveness, bedsores, increased rate of illness, or premature death.

In traumatic cases, both children and adults may become severely depressed or anxious. They may abuse substances or commit suicide.

Interpersonal Partner Violence Concerns

Domestic violence commonly occurs when one partner attempts to gain control over the other. There are various types of domestic violence, including physical, sexual, emotional, and psychological abuse. **Physical abuse** includes hitting, choking, or biting that may result in bodily injury. **Sexual abuse** is any sex act that is forced, coerced, or demeaning to an individual. **Emotional abuse** and **psychological abuse** can include threats, verbal statements that diminish self-worth, and actions that prevent socialization. Individuals who stay in an abusive relationship for a long period of time can develop physical and psychological problems. Some psychological effects of domestic violence include anxiety, depression, trust issues, fear of intimacy, suicidal thoughts, and emotional distancing. Counseling can help treat the lasting effects of domestic violence. Domestic violence survivors require counseling that helps build upon their individual strengths and improve their self-esteem. Individual therapy can help identify the pattern of violence and establish a plan to keep the client safe. Group therapy allows clients to normalize their feelings by sharing experiences with others who have gone through the same situation. Providing a creative outlet, such as music or art, can also help clients express their emotions.

Marital/Partner Communication Problems

Troubled relationships can often be attributed to poor communication. Many individuals find it hard to talk about their troubles as a result of negative childhood experiences or past failed relationships that affected them emotionally and psychologically. There are four different styles of communication. The **assertive communication style** is characterized by clear, honest, and direct statements that positively express feelings and thoughts. An **aggressive style of communication** focuses on expressing feelings with a clear disregard of the other's feelings. Partners with an aggressive communication style may make the other person feel like their opinions are not valued. **Passive communicators** rarely voice their feelings or opinions and may become overwhelmed by their partner's decisions. **Passive-aggressive communication** is characterized by unclear or confusing statements and may lead to internal frustration and resentment. Counselors should take communication styles into consideration when developing interventions between partners that help improve the quality and frequency of communication. The goal is to encourage partners to have open lines of communication, voice their emotions, practice active listening, and respect each other's opinions.

Parenting/Co-Parenting Conflicts

Good parenting practices are essential for raising emotionally healthy children. When parents, either married or divorced, have conflicting parenting styles, both the children and the marriage can be negatively affected. Through counseling, parents can discover their parenting styles and work together to provide their children with consistent parenting. Child psychologists vary on what types of parenting styles are most effective, but there are four generally recognized styles of parenting:

- *Authoritarian parenting style*: This style of parenting reinforces the role of parent as controller and decision maker. Children are rarely given input into decisions impacting their lives, and the parent takes on a dictatorial role. Children raised by this kind of parent are often obedient and tend to be proficient. The drawback is that they do not rank high on the happiness scale.

- *Authoritative parenting style*: This style of parenting allows for a greater sense of democracy in which children are given some degree of input into issues that impact their lives. There is a healthy balance between firmness and affection. Children raised in this environment tend to be capable, successful, and happy individuals.

- *Permissive parenting style*: This type of parenting allows children to be more expressive and freer with both feelings and actions; they are allowed to behave in whatever manner they please. There are very few rules, and no consequences will be given, even if a rule is violated. These children are more likely to experience problems in school and relationships with others. In the long run, they are often unhappy with their lives.

- *Uninvolved parenting style*: This form of parenting often occurs in dysfunctional families in which parents are emotionally or physically unavailable. They may be remiss in setting clear expectations, yet they may overreact when the child misbehaves or fails to understand what is expected. This is often seen in families where poverty is extreme or addictions or mental illnesses are present.

The authoritative style of parenting is considered to be the most effective form of parenting, yet much depends on the individual child or parent and the economic situation or cultural setting. One rule of

85

thumb is that whatever style one chooses, it is helpful to remain consistent. A parent who is permissive one day and authoritarian the next sends mixed and confusing messages to the child. It is also important that the child is completely aware of rules, expectations, and consequences that may follow if the rules are broken. Communicating a sense that children are loved, wanted, and accepted is one of the most important parts of parenting.

Emotional Dysregulation

Emotional dysregulation is a mood disorder that makes it difficult to regulate emotional responses and behaviors. Individuals with emotional dysregulation may be seen as aggressive, controlling, entitled, or problematic. Emotional dysregulation may be caused by an abusive childhood, brain injuries, or a disruptive home environment. Those who experience emotional dysregulation have a difficult time maintaining personal and professional relationships due to their conflicting and misunderstood behavior. One of the most common interventions to treat emotional dysregulation is **dialectical behavior therapy (DBT)**, which incorporates CBT and methods that help create mindfulness, such as meditation, music, and yoga. The goal of DBT is to help clients establish skills for confronting their emotions and regulating the behavioral response. Other interventions include anger management to identify stressors and Schema Therapy, which helps to identify and change unhealthy ways of thinking.

Practice Quiz

1. During a counseling session, a client voices they feel a sense of despair and believe their future will not change or become better. Which of the following emotional states is the client experiencing?
    a. Anxiety
    b. Panic disorder
    c. Hopelessness
    d. Delirium

2. A counselor is providing therapy to a 48-year-old client who is experiencing burnout in his career. This client falls into which psychosocial stage?
    a. Ego integrity versus despair
    b. Generativity versus stagnation
    c. Identity versus role confusion
    d. Intimacy versus isolation

3. Which of the following type of therapy helps clients confront their emotions and regulate the behavioral response?
    a. Accelerated resolution therapy (ART)
    b. Exposure therapy
    c. Gottman Method
    d. Dialectical behavior therapy (DBT)

4. Which of the following clients might a counselor suspect has an eating disorder?
    a. A 16-year-old female who uses several fitness apps and takes a daily laxative
    b. A 15-year-old male athlete who exercises vigorously and eats 2,500 calories a day
    c. A 28-year-old female on a 1,400-calorie per day diet who is preparing for her wedding
    d. A 68-year-old male who eats very small meals three times a day

5. What is the difference between habitual behaviors and addiction?
    a. Habits are compulsive needs, whereas addictions are repetitive acts.
    b. Addictions continue despite negative consequences, whereas habits require less effort to change.
    c. Habits are accompanied by obsessive thinking, and addictions are not.
    d. Habits affect personal relationships, and addictions strengthen social ties.

See answers on the next page.

Answer Explanations

1. C: Hopelessness is the belief that the current situation will not improve in the future and is accompanied by feelings of despair and depression. Choices *A* and *B* are incorrect; anxiety and panic are characterized by fear of an unspecific danger. Choice *D* is characterized by confusion and decreased awareness.

2. B: This client falls under the generativity versus stagnation phase. During this phase, middle adults (age 45-60) are concerned with working conditions and policies. Choice *A* is the stage for older adults (over the age of 60). Choice *C* is the adolescent stage, and Choice *D* is young adulthood.

3. D: Dialectical behavior therapy (DBT) is a comprehensive cognitive behavioral therapy (CBT) used in emotional dysregulation that focuses on change and acceptance; DBT involves a consultation team to assist with phone coaching, assigned tasks, and conditioning of severe mental health issues. Choice *A* reduces the effects of trauma and reconditions stressful memories by using rapid eye movement and image rescripting; clients are asked to visualize a traumatic event and incorporate stress-relieving techniques as needed. Choice *B* is a type of behavioral therapy that manages problematic fears by progressively exposing clients to items or situations that cause them fear and anxiety. Choice *C* is a couples counseling approach; the Gottman Method works to decrease conflicting verbal communication, remove barriers, and increase respect and affection between couples.

4. A: Obsessing over fitness trackers and dieting apps can signal an unhealthy habit, and the use of unnecessary laxatives are a sign of an eating disorder. Choice *B* requires a higher intake of calories for his lifestyle. Choice *C* is a short-term plan to achieve a situational goal. Choice *D* is not restricting food and may require lower calories due to aging.

5. B: The main difference between a habit and an addiction is that addictions cause distress and will continue despite negative consequences. Choice *A* is an opposite definition of terms; habits form from repetitive behaviors, and addictions are compulsive needs that cannot be controlled. Choice *C* has opposing definitions for habit and addiction; addictions have an intense focus on a behavior or substance. Choice *D* is incorrect because addictions cause problems with interpersonal relationships.

Treatment Planning

Collaborating with Client to Establish Treatment Goals and Objectives

Goal setting should occur in collaboration with a client's treatment plan. Intervention strategies, tasks, and timeframes should correspond with the desired goal and objectives. The primary goal should be to assist clients in returning to pre-crisis functioning. However, there will likely be additional and related goals and tasks as the plan of action is implemented.

Whenever possible, counselors should invite their clients to take a collaborative perspective in designing interventions, establishing objectives, and developing program goals. This allows the client to feel empowered and engaged as an active member of the problem-solving process. These factors are associated with higher incidences of positive outcomes, as they encourage clients to feel accountable for their behaviors, actions, and personal changes.

Collaboration should begin at the intake process. This is a period in which the counselor can make assessments, but they can also get information directly from clients about why they are in the session and what they hope to achieve. The counselor can also ask clients the steps they believe they need to take to reach their desired outcomes. While clients may or may not provide useful or feasible answers, this process still sets the tone that allows clients to feel acknowledged and involved in their own care.

In the intake session or in the sessions that immediately follow, the counselor can invite the client to develop SMART objectives to reach their goals. This may also include establishing accountability tools, documenting plans of action to address potential barriers and how to overcome them, and identifying any other support protocols that clients may need for their individual situations. Depending on the client's specific case, this process may take one session or may take much longer. Counselors should continuously show patience, compassion, and a welcoming desire to engage the client in the process.

Establishing Short- and Long-Term Counseling Goals Consistent with Diagnoses

Setting goals is an important aspect of the therapeutic process. Talk therapy may seem unstructured or capable of lasting for long periods of time; however, both the client and the counselor are responsible for setting and working toward measurable change. Goals of counseling can include the desire for physical change, such as getting into shape or losing weight, and career aspirations and/or social goals, such as gaining increased support or modifying relationships. Other types of goals can be emotional, spiritual, and intellectual. Goals can be immediate, short term, or long term, and clients may want to achieve several goals at different paces.

Identifying Barriers to Client Goal Attainment

Goal setting must be specific to each client and should be mutually agreed upon. Setting clear time frames that are supported by the counselor is essential to success. Goal setting may cause issues if goals are too ambitious or vague or have no identifiable benefit. It is also important to explore what motivation exists for a client to work toward a goal. If adequate motivation is present, the counselor also needs to consider what will happen if the goal is not met. In some cases, failure to meet goals can cause a client to become highly discouraged and unwilling to stick with the process of reformulating goals. During the process of working toward goals, a client may realize another goal is better suited. It's important to reevaluate goals during the process to help the client grow and embrace personal change.

Identifying Strengths That Improve Likelihood of Goal Attainment

Goals can take the form of **SMART goals**, which are specific, measurable, achievable, relevant, and time-bound. **Specific** means detailing why you want to accomplish the goal, what specifically there is to accomplish, who is involved, the setting for the goal, and what kind of resources are involved. **Measurable** means designating a system of tracking your goals in order to stay motivated. **Achievable** is making sure that the goal is realistic, such as looking at financial factors or other limitations. **Relevant** means making sure it's the right time for the goal, if it matches your needs, or if the goal seems worthwhile to pursue. Finally, **time-bound** is developing a target date so that there is a clear deadline to focus on. A client's strengths should also be identified and recognized when the goal is set, as this will help the client feel empowered in the attainment of the goal.

Referring Clients to Different Levels of Treatment

When planning a client's treatment, the counselor will need to decide which type of therapeutic environment will coincide best with the client's needs. The most extreme level of treatment is inpatient. **Inpatient treatment** provides professional supervision and monitoring along with daily counseling sessions. Clients who require inpatient treatment will be diagnosed with more problematic and complicated mental health issues or issues that are chronic or unusual. Inpatient treatment will provide an orderly routine, allowing focus to be on therapy, and it will eliminate environmental factors that aggravate the client's issue. This level of treatment is best for clients who can commit to weeks or months in a treatment facility. Inpatient treatment should be chosen for clients who are in danger of harming themselves or others and/or if their condition is interfering with day-to-day functioning. In cases of substance use, if the client has attempted treatment in the past and relapsed, inpatient treatment is a viable option.

The next level under inpatient treatment is residential. This type of treatment environment is more like a home. Clients are monitored but not to the same degree as they would be in inpatient treatment. Inpatient treatment is preferable for problems such as eating disorders or substance use. The daily focus will be on treatment. Counselors should refer clients to **residential treatment** if they don't need constant supervision but still need to get out of an environment that encourages or provokes the problem. In residential treatment, clients benefit from the group environment where others who are going through the same problems support and push each other to reach their goals.

The most flexible option for treatment is outpatient as it allows clients to continue working or going to school while going through therapy. Clients who only need to meet for sessions once a week or once a month should receive **outpatient treatment**. Outpatient treatment allows clients to retain privacy regarding treatment while learning how to cope in their usual environment. The options for outpatient treatment include short- and long-term counseling and individual, group, or family therapy. Typically, clients who are referred to outpatient treatment show more motivation to change and will show signs of being able to commit to this level of treatment. Outpatient treatment is acceptable for clients who suffer from disorders such as depression or anxiety. Occasionally, after inpatient treatment, patients will need to maintain treatment in an outpatient setting.

Referring Clients to Others for Concurrent Treatment

Counselors sometimes work concurrently with other providers of mental health services. One of the most common examples is when counselors work with psychiatrists. If a counselor believes that their client is not making sufficient improvement or their symptoms are worsening, they can refer the client to a psychiatrist for medication evaluation while continuing to counsel the client.

Counselors can also refer their clients to another counselor if the client desires another type of therapy (e.g., marriage counseling). In such cases, individual counselors may maintain communication with the other counselor, but they are not required to do so. The level of collaboration with other mental health providers should always be done with the client's best interests in mind.

Guiding Treatment Planning

Creating SMART objectives allows for data-driven and measurable intervention plans. When creating objectives, counselors should be able to measure the desired behavior that is exhibited, the number of times the desired behavior is exhibited over a period of time, the conditions in which the desired behavior must be exhibited, and progress from the undesired behavior to the desired behavior through baseline evaluation and evaluation at pre-determined intervals.

Termination Process and Issues

An important part of treatment planning is discharge planning. There are numerous reasons that services for a client may end. Clients may feel that they no longer need the services, that they are not compatible with the counselor providing the services, that an increased level of care is needed that is beyond the scope of the counselor, or they may have successfully met goals for treatment.

Discharge planning should begin with the onset of the initial assessment for the client. The counselor should not delay discharge planning, as discharge may occur at any time. Making the client aware of the choices for discharge and the discharge planning process empowers the client during treatment. It also provides continuity of care for the client.

The main purpose of **discharge planning** is to develop a plan of care that goes beyond the current treatment sessions to promote success once services have concluded. In the event that the client is going to a higher level of care or to a different professional, effective discharge planning is useful in disseminating pertinent information about the client to assist in continuity of care and effective treatment. In this sense, the current counselor should prepare to become a collateral source linked to the client's level of care for the next professional.

In addition to benefitting the other counselors the client may meet with, effective discharge planning is a benefit to the client as well. If services have been completed successfully and the client has met the stated goals, then discharge planning ensures that the client has a plan to sustain a stable level of function and maintain the successes achieved. This is particularly useful with clients who suffer from substance use or other addictive behaviors, as effective discharge planning can prevent relapse.

Upon the conclusion of the client discharging from services, a discharge summary should be created and placed in the client's file. The ***discharge summary*** should include the following information:

- Reason for discharge
- Description of treatment goals and the degree to which they were met

91

- Client's response to the interventions
- Description of the client's levels of functioning
- Baseline
- Progress during treatment
- Functioning at discharge
- Recommendations for follow-up care
- Links to community resources
- Appointment dates for other providers (if available)
- Provision of additional contacts, client supports
- Description of potential risks post-discharge
- Contact information for post-discharge support and crisis intervention

Transitions in Group Membership

There are two kinds of groups in counseling: open and closed. A **closed group** has a specific starting date, and only the clients who begin on that date are admitted to the group. Once the group starts, no other clients are permitted to join. In an **open group**, clients can begin and end treatment at any time during the life of the group. Prior to the beginning of either type of group, counselors should interview all potential members individually to determine their suitability for the group. Once new members are admitted, the counselor should go over the group's rules and describe the limits of confidentiality. When a group is coming to an end, counselors should prepare their clients in advance.

This can be done by addressing issues such as the sadness some members may experience because they have come to rely upon the group for support or they have formed bonds within the group. Counselors can facilitate this process by having open conversations and encouraging clients to express their feelings. In preparation for termination, counselors should also talk about the progress made by the group members. Additionally, counselors can provide referrals to individual counselors if clients need or desire further treatment. Helping clients transition out of group therapy is an important stage of the process.

Follow-up After Discharge

At the final session, the counselor and client can schedule a follow-up session at a predetermined time to evaluate the client's continued progress after termination. Another option is to propose a time to meet and alert the client that the counselor will contact the client to schedule a follow up. The **follow-up session** enables the counselor the opportunity to determine how well the client has progressed and to determine the effectiveness of the intervention(s) used during sessions.

Using Assessment Instrument Results to Facilitate Client Decision-Making

Psychometric assessment tools can provide valuable pieces of information. Many assessment tools are available for free, while others must be purchased. **Assessment tools** often come with rating scales that indicate the level of training needed to interpret the results. Assessment instruments can be used at the beginning of treatment to help counselors make diagnostic decisions. Counselors can also have clients take personality assessments, which can provide them with information about the best ways to work with their clients. Some counselors use a battery of tests that provide them with multifaceted views of their clients' disorders and personality structures. Assessment tools can also be used throughout counseling to give counselors feedback on the effectiveness of their treatment methods. If the testing devices indicate that a client's symptoms are remaining the same or worsening, then counselors might consider changing their treatment plans.

Reviewing and Revising the Treatment Plan

Treatment evaluation is a necessary part of direct practice. Counselors should strive to exercise best practice techniques by using evidence-based practice evaluation. It is beneficial for clients to see the progress they have made, while simultaneously providing information to funders and insurance companies that typically require documentation and outcome measures for reimbursement of services. Other benefits include providing indicators that interventions should be modified or that treatment is complete and termination is warranted. Several factors are important in the evaluation of a client's progress, including identifying specific issues to be addressed; creating appropriate goals, objectives, and tasks; using effective and relevant techniques and tools to measure success; and routinely documenting progress.

Client progress may be measured using a quantitative or qualitative approach used in research. Quantitative measures relate to the rate of occurrence or severity of a behavior or problem. When performing quantitative evaluation, first establish a baseline, which is a measurement of the target problem, prior to intervention. Qualitative measures are more subjective and reflective of the client's experience (information is gathered largely from observation and different forms of interviewing) and provide a view of whether progress is being made.

Engaging Clients in Review of Progress Toward Treatment Goals

Clarifying the roles and responsibilities of the counselor, the client, and the client system in the intervention process can reduce the chance of miscommunication, misunderstanding, and interventions not working as intended. This clarification process can be developed during the intake process and initial sessions by actively listening to what the client hopes to achieve, and working together to develop a step-by-step intervention methodology. When possible, the stages, objectives, and milestones of the intervention should be documented in order to have an available reference point, drive accountability, and reduce any confusion around the expectations of all involved parties.

The **problem-solving approach** to interventions is a commonly used framework to cover these points. This is a seven-stage model that encourages active listening and engagement techniques (such as eye contact and other receptive body language); fostering trust and collaboration with the client (such as by showing genuine interest in the client as a person, rather than just in the context of the issues at hand); working together to identify the problem to be addressed and possible solutions; introducing allies in the resolution processes (such as clinical providers, a yoga or meditation teacher, or other experts that could help the client); developing a documented resolution plan and actively engaging all parties to follow it (such as through accountability cues, positive reinforcement, and celebrating small victories); and support for sustaining the desired behaviors until the client is capable of terminating the intervention.

While one can be hopeful that the client and client systems will be cooperative and willing in this framework, that is not always the case. Clients may show distrust, anxiety, fear, or apathy, especially in the beginning. Often, the most important role of the counselor is building trust with the client and the client system. The counselor should continue to encourage a trusting, collaborative relationship until the time of service termination.

93

Documentation When Collaborating with Other Providers and Client Support Systems

Counselors can provide a holistic level of care for their clients by collaborating with providers of other health-related services. For example, if a client suffers from depression, a counselor could contact the client's primary care provider (after receiving permission from the client by means of a signed HIPAA form) to discuss medical tests that might rule out organic causes of depression. Likewise, if the depressed client is obese, the counselor could work with the client's dietician to discuss dietary and exercise changes that might aid the client's recovery. In all cases, it is important for counselors to keep comprehensive records of their interactions with other providers. Any test results and other communications obtained from these providers should be kept in the client's secure treatment file. If the counselor writes a report for another provider, it should provide only the minimally required information.

Discussing Integration and Maintenance of Therapeutic Progress with Clients

The **problem-solving therapeutic model** serves to teach clients how to manage stressors that come in life. Often, clients do not possess skills that allow them to effectively navigate negative events or emotions without increasing personal harm. The goal of the problem-solving model is to teach clients the skills necessary to deal with negative life events, negative emotions, and stressful situations. In particular, goals of this model should be to assist clients in identifying which particular situations may trigger unpleasant emotions, understanding the range of emotions one might feel, planning how to effectively deal with situations when they arise, and even recognizing and accepting that some situations are not able to be solved.

The counselor, however, may be an instructional guide to facilitate problem solving for the client. Because problem-solving skills are one of the primary methods of resolving issues and often are skills that clients lack, the counselor may need to model them for the client so that the client can then develop their own skills. Counselors need to maintain empathy and congruence with the client during the problem-solving process, and even though they may have verbally instructed or modeled problem-solving methods, they need to maintain rapport in the relationship.

Educating Clients to the Value of Treatment Plan Compliance

When determining a client's motivation, the engagement and assessment stage is crucial. When clients voluntarily seek services and/or are facing a crisis, the commitment and motivation will likely be high. **Non-voluntary clients** are identified as those who are seeking assistance based on pressure outside of the legal system (e.g., a woman gives her spouse an ultimatum to get help or she will leave). When working with non-voluntary or involuntary clients who are mandated legally to seek treatment, the counselor must help determine client-identified problems. This should be in addition or complementary to the presenting problem. The counselor and client collaboratively should create a treatment plan that addresses both types of issues.

Additionally, the counselor must help the client overcome any negative feelings of anger or mistrust about treatment. With all clients, appropriate relationship building between the counselor and client is a necessary part of engagement and motivation. Clients must feel they are in a safe, empathetic environment. They also should experience a sufficient level of trust for the counselor in order for treatment to be effective. To create an effective treatment relationship, the counselor must project an attitude free of judgment; recognize the client's individual attributes, strengths, and abilities; and encourage the client's right to be an active participant in his or her own treatment.

Practice Quiz

1. What are SMART goals?
   a. Specific, meaningful, achievable, realistic, and time-sensitive
   b. Special, manageable, action-oriented, realistic, and timely
   c. Specific, measurable, action-oriented, relevant, and time-bound
   d. Specific, measurable, achievable, relevant, and time-bound

2. Which of the following is important for a counselor to consider when treating clients with addiction issues?
   a. Legal consequences will deter clients from continuing addictive patterns.
   b. Relapsing is common, and a prevention plan is essential.
   c. Clients with addictions do not benefit from support groups.
   d. Clients with addictions should isolate themselves to prevent hurting their family.

3. To encourage clients to take responsibility for their treatment progress, counselors can do all of the following EXCEPT:
   a. Ask clients how many counseling homework assignments they have completed.
   b. Ask clients if they are medication compliant.
   c. Ask clients to evaluate how much effort they are putting toward their stated goals between sessions.
   d. Ask clients to provide feedback on the counseling services.

4. When counselors work collaboratively with physicians, what should guide their level of disclosure about clients' personal issues after receiving a signed HIPAA?
   a. Counselors should provide specific details about clients' lives because a signed HIPAA allows for full disclosure.
   b. Counselors should only provide general information that will be helpful to the physicians when determining which medications and dosages should be prescribed.
   c. Counselors should not speak with physicians about their shared clients because their roles are vastly different.
   d. Counselors should only share information with physicians if a court order requires it.

5. When counselors evaluate their clients' ability to achieve treatment goals, all of the following would be important considerations EXCEPT:
   a. Past successes
   b. Socioeconomic status
   c. Siblings' history of mental illness
   d. Personal strengths

See answers on the next page.

96

Answer Explanations

1. D: SMART goals are a way of planning an effective goal-setting and goal-accomplishing process. The SMART goals are specific, measurable, achievable, relevant, and time-bound. Specific is being detailed about what the goal is and how it can be accomplished. Measurable is tracking the goal or improvements to keep up motivation, achievable is making sure the goal is realistic, relevant is asking yourself if it's the right time for the goal, or if you're the right person for it, and time-bound is setting a clear date to achieve the goal by so as not to lose focus. Choices *A*, *B*, and *C* are incorrect.

2. B: A large percentage of clients with addictions will relapse during the course of treatment; a prevention plan can equip clients with necessary resources. Choice *A* is incorrect; clients with addictions participate in the behavior despite legal and social ramifications. Choice *C* is incorrect; support groups can help the client feel a sense of belonging. Choice *D* is not beneficial to the client; educating family and encouraging support of the client is essential to the client's recovery.

3. D: Asking clients to provide feedback would not encourage the client to take responsibility for their own treatment progress. The remaining choices are appropriate questions for the counselor to ask.

4. B: Counselors should only provide general information that will be helpful to the physicians when determining which medications and dosages should be prescribed. Even though a signed HIPAA *allows* for full disclosure, specific details should generally remain confidential. Therefore, Choice *A* is incorrect. Choice *C* is incorrect because the mind and the body are connected. Choice *D* is incorrect because a signed HIPAA allows counselors to disclose clients' personal information.

5. C: Siblings' history of mental illness may or may not impact clients' ability to achieve their treatment goals. Choice *A*, past successes, helps counselors know where clients have achieved goals previously. Choice *B*, socioeconomic status, is an important consideration because clients may or may not have the means to achieve certain goals. Choice *D*, personal strengths, helps counselors draw upon their clients' natural abilities while working toward goals.

Counseling Skills and Interventions

Aligning Intervention with Client's Developmental Level

A client's development level will vary from client to client, and it may even vary for the same client over the full course of an intervention. Therefore, the counselor should make no assumptions about the client's ability to cope, the way the intervention will be accepted and utilized, or any other aspect of the working relationship. These factors should be assessed upon intake and at regular intervals thereafter, the frequency of which may vary on a case-by-case basis.

Assessments should holistically take into account the client's development, including age, psychological factors, emotional factors, social factors, acute personal conditions (such as an impending divorce or recent refugee status) that may temporarily impact the client's functioning, and any other scope of development that may be appropriate for the client's need. For example, a client who has a history of violent behavior and a history of playing physical sports with extreme contact may find it beneficial to undergo neurological development assessments. By viewing the client through a holistic perspective, counselors can ensure interventions are appropriate across all domains of development; if so, the interventions are more likely to be effective and received positively by the client.

Aligning Intervention with Counseling Modality

Individual

Individual therapy can be an appropriate option for many reasons. A few considerations for choosing this modality would be if the client needs individualized treatment, requires scheduling flexibility, or prefers the privacy of individual counseling. Issues addressed in individual counseling are numerous and can include the same issues that would be focused on in family or group counseling, but in individual counseling the client is the priority. The counselor can decide with the client whether the client's goals and needs would best be met through individual therapy. Interventions such as exposure therapy and psychodynamic therapy work well in individual therapy as these interventions are unique to the client and allow them to progress and open up emotionally at their own pace in an intimate and safe setting.

Couples

Many couples enter treatment after experiencing long-standing problems and may seek help because all other options have failed. One of the goals of **couples' therapy** is to help clients develop effective communication and problem-solving skills so they can solve problems throughout and after treatment. Other goals include helping the couple form a more objective view of their relationship, modifying dysfunctional behavior/patterns, increasing emotional expression, and recognizing strengths. Counselors should create an environment to help the couple understand treatment goals, feel safe in expressing their feelings, and reconnect by developing trust in each other. Interventions for couples are often centered on goals geared toward preventing conflicting verbal communication and improving empathy, respect, and intimacy in a relationship. Therapeutic interventions, along with exercises, are designed to help couples learn to treat each other as partners and not rivals. Cognitive Behavioral Therapy is also used when working with couples. It uses cognitive techniques to help change distorted thinking and modify behavior.

Family Therapy Models, Interventions, and Approaches

One of the main goals of family therapy is to allow each family member to function at his or her best while maintaining the functionality of the family unit. When working with families, the counselor must do the following:

- Examine and consider all systems affecting a family and each individual member to determine problems, solutions, and strengths and also consider the functionality of the family subsystems.

- Respect cultural, socio-economic, and non-traditional family systems and not automatically define those systems as dysfunctional if they are not the norm. The overall and individual family functioning should be accounted for.

- Work to engage the family in the treatment while considering the specific traits of the family (i.e., culture, history, family structure, race, dynamics, etc.).

- Assist in identifying and changing dysfunctional patterns, boundaries, and family problems.

Important Concepts

Boundaries: Healthy boundaries around and within the family must exist for families to function effectively. The boundaries must be clear and appropriate.

Emotional Proximity and Distance: the type of boundaries that exist within a family system

Enmeshed: Boundaries are unclear and pliable. Families that have very open boundaries within the family unit may have very fixed boundaries between outside forces and the family.

Disengaged: Boundaries are rigid with little interaction and emotional engagement. Families that are disengaged within the family system tend to have very open boundaries around the family unit.

Family Hierarchy: The power structure within the family. For families to function effectively, there must be a clear delineation of authority. There must be an individual or individuals who hold the power and authority in a family system. In a traditional family, this should ideally be located within the parental system.

Homeostasis: Family systems should maintain homeostasis or remain regular and stable. When life events become too stressful and the family can no longer function as it normally would, the state of homeostasis is threatened. This is usually when many families seek help.

Alliances: Partnerships or collaborations between certain members of a family. When alliances exist between some members of a family, it can lead to dysfunction (e.g., parent and child have an alliance that undermines the parental subsystem).

Group Work Techniques and Approaches

Group work can be defined as a goal-directed intervention with small groups of people. The intention of this work is to improve the socioemotional and psychoeducation needs of the individual members of the group through the group process. There are two types of groups in counseling: therapeutic and task groups. **Task groups** are created to perform a specific task or purpose. These groups differ in the amount and type of self-disclosure, confidentiality, and communication patterns. There are several types of treatment groups, including support, educational, and therapy groups. Groups can also be long-term or short-term, depending on the type and purpose.

Groups can be open or closed. **Open groups** are ongoing and allow for new members to enter at any time. Open groups are typically used for support and life transitions. There are challenges to this type of group, since the members are at different stages in the group process. The frequently changing membership can be disruptive to the group process because members may not feel as emotionally safe to share with others. **Closed groups** are time-limited, and new members can only join during the beginning stage. The advantages to this type of group are more engagement and better trust by the members, since the group process is more stable. A disadvantage is that if several members leave the group, the group process may not be as effective.

Aligning Intervention with Client Population

An intervention's success depends in part on whether the intervention plan is aligned with the individual's cultural experience and life experience. All individuals are part of cultures with specific traditions, habits, and norms. These can vary by race, ethnicity, immigration status, income level, geographical location, or social status. It's important to take culture into context in order to show respect for the individual's way of life, tailor interventions to be easily understood, create trust and cooperation, and avoid wasting time or resources. Cultural contexts can be understood through researching the community, reading literature or periodicals from the area, and networking with people in the setting.

The intervention should also be appropriate for the client's life. For example, counselors may specifically tailor the intervention for a veteran or a client with a physical or intellectual disability.

Implementing Individual Counseling in Relation to a Plan of Treatment

Licensed professional counselors are obligated to provide their clients with time-limited and effective treatment methods. Time-limited treatments can actualize clients' treatment objectives in the fewest number of sessions possible. Effective methods have been established empirically through scientific research. Once a counselor determines a diagnosis and understands the clients' treatment goals, they develop a treatment plan. The treatment plan is based on the diagnosis and a particular treatment method. For example, a counselor may choose to use Cognitive Behavior Therapy for a client diagnosed with depression because CBT has demonstrated efficacy in the treatment of depression. The treatment plan would follow CBT protocol, adjusted as necessary to fit the client's needs. The counselor would plan for a limited number of sessions to complete the treatment and would evaluate along the way whether the treatment is effective. If the treatment is not effective, it would be extended and/or altered.

Establishing Therapeutic Alliance

An important element of the counseling relationship is the establishment of a **therapeutic alliance**, or collaborative effort between the counselor and the client, that will predict the success of the counseling experience. Generally, counselors who are inviting and interpersonally sensitive will be able to form a positive therapeutic alliance with the client. The working alliance can be assessed using a couple of tools. The **Working Alliance Inventory** is a self-reporting Likert questionnaire that explores how well the client's and counselor's thoughts about therapy are aligned. Both the counselor and the client answer more than thirty questions pertaining to counseling goals, first impressions, and the effectiveness of counseling sessions. The Barrett-Lennard Relationship Inventory is another tool used to measure congruence, regard, and empathy of a relationship. It is important for the therapeutic alliance to be established in the early counseling sessions to ensure the development of a positive working relationship.

Applying Theory-Based Counseling Interventions

Modeling

Modeling is a technique used in therapy to allow clients to learn healthy and appropriate behaviors. Counselors "model" certain actions and attitudes, which can teach a client to behave in a similar fashion in their own life. Modeling is somewhat indirect. It is not suggested to the client to act in specific ways; rather, the counselor demonstrates desired behaviors, and the client begins imitating them.

Reinforcement

Reinforcement is a tool of behavior modification, used to either encourage or discourage specific thoughts or behaviors. **Positive reinforcement** rewards desired behaviors, thus encouraging the client to continue them. Counselors can provide positive verbal reinforcements, for example, to a client sharing difficult feelings, which in turn will encourage the client to continue sharing. The term **positive** in this case does not refer to a "good" outcome but to the act of applying a reward, such as a positive reaction from the counselor. **Negative reinforcement** works to discourage unwanted thoughts or behaviors by removing a stimulus after a specific action. The negative does not make it "bad"—rather, it is the act of removing a negative stimulus to eliminate a specific thought or behavior.

Extinguishing

Extinguishing is the process of ending, or making extinct, a specific maladaptive thought pattern or behavior. Previously occurring behaviors were reinforced, and when reinforcement (either positive or negative) ceases, the behavior will eventually be extinguished. It may be a goal in counseling to extinguish unwanted thoughts or behaviors that are harmful or a hindrance to the client.

Cognitive Behavioral Techniques

Cognitive Behavioral Therapy (CBT) is typically a short-term treatment that focuses on transforming behavior by modifying thoughts, perceptions, and beliefs. Conscious thoughts affect behavior. Consequently, to promote consciousness of behavioral patterns in the client, the counselor (in the therapist role) will often assign homework in the form of exercises or journaling. The premise is that by identifying and reframing negative or distorted thoughts, the desired behavioral change can occur. CBT combines techniques and traits of both behavioral (positive and negative reinforcement) and cognitive therapies (cognitive distortion and schemas).

Cognitive restructuring is a concept used in CBT. The goal of cognitive restructuring is to help clients change irrational or unrealistic thoughts so that, ideally, change will lead to development of desired behaviors.

The steps for cognitive restructuring are as follows:

- Accept that negative thoughts, inner dialogue, and beliefs affect one's feelings and emotional reactions.

- Identify which thoughts and belief patterns or self-statements lead to the target problems. Clients use self-monitoring techniques, including a log to track situations as they occur and the accompanying thoughts or feelings.

- Identify situations that evoke reoccurring themes in dysfunctional thoughts and beliefs.

- Replace distorted thoughts with functional, rational, and realistic statements.

- Reward oneself for using functional coping skills.

In-Life Desensitization

Desensitization is a behavior modification technique designed to replace an anxiety-producing stimulus with a relaxation response. Also known as **systematic desensitization**, it is a process to help the client manage fear or phobias. The client is taught relaxation techniques, which can include breathing, mindfulness, and muscle relaxation. Next, a "**fear hierarchy**" is created to rank stimulus from least to most fearful. The client is gradually exposed to the object or action that causes anxiety and then moves up the fear hierarchy and practices relaxation techniques. The goal is for the client to reach the most feared object or action and be able to react with calmness and control.

Addressing Addiction Issues

Addictions can be in the form of drugs, alcohol, or behaviors that cause financial instability and social impairment. It is important for counselors to distinguish when a behavior or addiction has become problematic for the client. Clients who continue to use substances or participate in behaviors despite legal or social consequences may require a counseling intervention. When assessing for substance use addiction, tolerance is an important aspect to consider. **Tolerance** is having to use more of the substance to obtain the same desired effects as before. Additionally, clients who continue taking substances to avoid withdrawal symptoms demonstrate dependence. After establishing a trusting relationship, counselors can encourage addiction recovery by helping their clients locate support groups, engage in twelve-step programs, secure social connections, and develop a relapse prevention plan. CBT helps clients focus on reducing problematic behavior that is associated with the addiction. The development of coping strategies, such as avoidance and self-control, helps to prevent a relapse. Counselors can assist clients with identifying and modifying cravings, triggers, and risky behaviors that can enable the addictions. Incorporating **motivational enhancement therapy** can encourage clients to address self-destructive behaviors and improve motivation to change.

Motivational Interviewing

Motivational interviewing (MI) is a communication technique that focuses on altering the patient's behavior. It is often used as a counseling tool for patients with substance use disorders, behavioral alterations, smoking, and obesity. There is a subset of skills used in MI that facilitate the progress in each of the MI phases. The **OARS** skills are a set of verbal and non-verbal interview techniques, which can be tailored to the specific needs of the MI process. The acronym OARS stands for **open-ended questions**, **affirmations**, **reflections**, and **summaries**.

Open-ended questions encourage two-way conversation because they are not generally answerable with a simple "yes" or "no." Questions beginning with the word "why" can potentially elicit a defensive patient response and should be avoided. **Affirmations** acknowledge the patient and convey a message of empathetic understanding. These statements can also build a patient's self-efficacy which positively affects motivation. **Reflections**, or reflective listening, improve the interviewer's understanding of the patient's narrative. Periods of reflection after the patient speaks slow the pace of the conversation so that it is not simply a series of questions and answers. **Summaries** provide a review of the substance of the conversation and an opportunity for closure by the interviewer and the patient.

The OARS skills are used with each process of MI to maximize the outcomes. If the work of the MI process is slowed down or is unsuccessful at any point, the provider returns to the initial process and reestablishes it. MI is not a linear process; it is responsive to the flow of the conversation, which depends on the skill of the interviewer and the use of the OARS techniques. The four processes of MI include engaging, focusing, evoking, and planning. **Engaging** is the process of establishing a rapport, assessing and reducing any defensive behavior, and creating a collaborative environment for the discussion of change. The interviewer is able to assess the focus of the patient's conversation, in other words, is the patient actually engaged in the work of MI. If the patient is resistant to participating in the process of MI, the interviewer often finds that empathy is effective in re-establishing the interviewer-patient relationship.

The second process of MI is **focusing**. Communication experts advise that it may take several sessions before the interviewer can direct the conversation to the issue at hand. The potential for success at this stage is enhanced when the patient has already reached a state of contemplation for the desired change. The process of **evoking** focuses on the discussion or "**change talk**" for two behaviors: identification of the specific steps necessary for the desired change and the steps required for an ongoing commitment to the changed behavior. There are two forms of change talk: **preparatory** refers to the desire to change, and **mobilizing** addresses commitment and action. The **planning** process may be optional, but when it is included in MI, it identifies the "how" for the planned change.

Addressing Cultural Considerations

Culture refers to the way a group of people lives, behaves, thinks, and believes. This can include behaviors, traditions, beliefs, opinions, values, religion, spirituality, communication, language, holidays, food, valued possessions, and family dynamics, among other factors. Geography, social status, economic standing, race, ethnicity, and religion can determine culture. Culture can be found within any organized community, such as in a place of worship or workplace. The following are examples of specific types of culture:

- **Universal**: the broadest category, also known as the human culture, and includes all people
- **Ecological**: groups created by physical location, climate, and geography
- **National**: patterns of culture for a specific country
- **Regional**: patterns for specific areas of a country that can include dialect, manners, customs and food/eating habits
- **Racio-ethnic**: group that shares a common racial and ethnic background
- **Ethnic**: group that shares a common background, including religion and language

Counselors must be culturally competent to meet the needs of all clients. One way to do this is to have the staff demographics reflective of the community served. Counselors must also recognize the differences in individuals of the same culture and not use a cookie-cutter approach to deal with people

103

of the same demographic group. Counselors must also work to create agency policies that encourage culturally sensitive treatment and do not allow discriminatory practices. When choosing interventions, treatment methods, and evaluation techniques, counselors must also consider the appropriateness of the selection for the client's cultural background.

Attitudes and Beliefs

Counselors should be culturally aware in their attitudes and beliefs. This requires a keen awareness of their own cultural background and gaining awareness of any personal biases, stereotypes, and values that they hold. Counselors should also accept different worldviews, be sensitive to differences, and refer minority clients to a counselor from the client's culture when it would benefit the client.

Knowledge

Counselors should have the appropriate knowledge of different cultures. Specifically, counselors must understand the client's culture and should not jump to conclusions about the client's way of being. Throughout their careers, counselors should be willing to gain a greater depth of knowledge of various cultural groups and update this knowledge as necessary. This includes understanding how issues like racism, sexism, and homophobia can negatively affect minority clients. Counselors should understand how different therapeutic theories carry values that may be detrimental for some clients. Counselors should also be aware of how conventional barriers affect minority clients' eagerness to use mental health services.

Cultural Skills

Counselors should be well-versed in cultural skills. They must be able to apply interviewing and counseling techniques with clients and should be able to employ specialized skills and interventions that might be effective with specific minority populations. Counselors should be able to communicate effectively and understand the verbal and nonverbal language of a client. They also should take a systematic perspective in their practice, work collaboratively with community leaders, and advocate for clients when it's in their best interests.

When working with clients from diverse backgrounds, counselors should be able to shift their professional strategies. Below are techniques and strategies counselors should keep in mind when working with clients of different cultures.

Various Cultural and Racial Backgrounds

- Have appropriate attitudes and beliefs, gain knowledge about the client's background, and learn new skills as needed.

- Encourage the client to speak in his or her native language and arrange for an interpreter when necessary.

- Assess the client's cultural identity and how important it is to the client.

- Check accuracy of any interpretations of the client's nonverbal cues.

- Make use of alternate modes of communication, such as writing, typing, translation services, and the use of art.

- Assess the impact of sociopolitical issues on the client.

- Encourage the client to bring culturally significant and personally relevant items.

104

- Vary the helping environment to make it conducive to effective work with the client.

Various Religious Backgrounds

- Determine the client's religious background in the beginning sessions.
- Check personal biases and gain information about the client's religion.
- Ask the client how important religion is in his or her life.
- Assess the client's level of faith development.
- Avoid making assumptions about the religion.
- Become familiar with the client's religious beliefs, important holidays, and faith traditions.
- Understand that religion can deeply affect the client unconsciously.

Address Family Composition and Cultural Considerations

In the United States, a long-standing definition of the family unit has been the **nuclear family**, which consists of a single man and a single woman (typically married to one another) and their immediate children. However, there are other concepts of family reflected in other cultures that can encompass alternate dynamics.

Families can consist of any small group of individuals that are related by blood or choose to share their lives together. These can consist of heterosexual or homosexual couples with or without children, single parent households, childfree households, homes with extended family all living under one roof, blended families involving step-children and step-parents, or lifelong partners that choose not to marry legally.

Culture and ethnicity play a large role in defining a family unit. For example, many Eastern cultures value living with extended family and consider everyone in the physical household to be a member of the immediate family unit.

American psychiatrist **Murray Bowen (1913–1990)** first established the family systems theory, which later served as the basis for family, or systems-focused, counseling. The family systems theory seeks to explain the high level of emotional interdependence that family members have with one another and how this interdependence individually affects each member of the family system. This theory states that the unique and complex cohesiveness that is found in family systems promotes positive behaviors like teamwork and taking care of one another; however, it can also cause negative behaviors, like anxiety or addictions, to diffuse from one person into the entire system.

The family systems theory is made up of eight distinct concepts:

- **Triangles**: refers to three-person systems, considered to be the smallest system that can still be stable. A third person adds extra support to manage intense emotions, tension, or conflict. The theory states that a two-person system cannot usually weather high levels of emotion, tension, or conflict over time.

- **Differentiation of Self**: how much an individual's personal beliefs differ from that of his or her group's beliefs. It is an important function of developing one's self. A strong self usually correlates with confidence and pragmatism, while a weak self usually correlates with an unhealthy need for approval from others.

- **Nuclear Family Emotional System**: referring to four different relationship patterns in this system. The patterns are marital conflict, dysfunction in one spouse, impairment in

105

one or more children, and emotional distance, which refers to the fact that it occurs and how it affects the way problems are handled within the family.

- **Family Projection Process**: how parents project emotional conflict onto their children. The process can lead to pathologies in the child's psyche.

- **Multigenerational Transmission Process**: regarding the variance in differentiation of self between generations. The differentiation of self between parents and children over time leads to a widespread difference in beliefs between the oldest generation and the youngest generation of the family.

- **Emotional Cutoff**: regarding issue resolution. The act of failing to resolve issues between family members by reducing or eliminating contact with one another is emotional cut-off.

- **Sibling Position**: the importance of birth order and its influence on someone's functioning. It incorporates not only the birth order as it relates to how that person will function in workplaces and relationships, but also focuses on the birth order of each of the individual's parents and the influences those have on parenting styles.

- **Societal Emotional Process**: how the previous seven concepts hold true for any society. All families and societies will have progressive and regressive periods of development over time.

Important Terms

Affectional Orientation: a term used to describe one's romantic orientation toward a specific sex; an alternative term to *sexual orientation*

Alternative Family: any group of people that considers themselves a family unit but does not fall into the definition of a nuclear family

Emic: being aware of a client's culture and using counseling approaches accordingly

Empty Nest Syndrome: feelings of isolation, depression, or purposelessness that some parents may feel when their children move out of the family home

Ethnocentrism: a belief that one's culture is superior to another's

Ethnocide: purposely destroying another's ethnicity or culture

Ethnology: a branch of anthropology that systematically studies and compares the similarities and differences between cultures

Etic: an objective, universal viewpoint of clients

Gender Schema Theory: a theory by **Sandra Bem** in 1981 that describes how people in a society become gendered, especially through categories of information such as schemata

Heterogeneous Society: a society that is diverse in characteristics, cultural values, and language

High Context Culture: information is implicit and communicated through unspoken messages, with a focus on personal relationships and with fewer rules

Homogenous Society: a society that primarily consists of people with the same characteristics, cultural values, and language

Low Context Culture: information exchanged with little hidden meaning, with clear, explicit rules and standards, and relationships deemed less important than tasks

Modal Behavior: statistically, the most common and normative behaviors of a society

Nuclear Family: a family unit that consists of a married man and woman and their immediate children

Nuclear Family of Orientation: the family one is born into

Nuclear Family of Procreation: a family created by marriage and childbearing

Reciprocity: a social norm that says people should pay back what has been provided to them. This type of exchange relationship is used to build continuing relationships with others.

Sexual Orientation: an individual's sexual preference toward a specific gender

Stereotype: a preconceived notion about a group of people, not necessarily based in fact

Tripartite: awareness, knowledge, and skills of multicultural counseling

Evaluating and Explaining Systemic Patterns of Interaction

Systemic patterns of interaction are based on the belief that multiple factors impact the relationship between individuals. A client's social, familial, political, and cultural beliefs are all environmental factors that influence a current state of mind. This belief is part of **systems theory**, which aims to conceptualize a client's issue based on their surroundings. The theory focuses on viewing individuals as their own system whose behaviors, thoughts, and emotions affect everyone in connection with them. In order to create a system that works for all members involved, counselors must help clients identify each person's expectations, behaviors, and desires. Using a systemic approach, insight into each member's role can help determine how that role affects the functionality of an entire group.

For example, a woman can be a nurturing mother at home, a disciplinary leader at work, and an encouraging friend within her social circle. All of these roles help to fulfill the overall system of interaction. Alternatively, there are negative interaction patterns that can strain communication and cause conflict among individuals. An example is individuals who rapidly escalate an argument with minimal provocation and have low frustration tolerance. This pattern is usually directed at another person who does not engage in shouting and will remain silent. Other individuals will attempt to control a situation by verbalizing threats of exposure, abandonment, or harm. Effective communication and constructive dialogue can help attain positive relationships and encourage clients to become an active participant within a system.

107

Exploring Family Member Interaction

Components of a Family History

Family history can provide insight into an individual's influences. The **family unit** is the most immediate system to which an individual belongs, so understanding it can provide invaluable perspective.

Counselors often use a genogram to understand the individual's family dynamic. A **genogram** is a visual chart that depicts an individual's familial relationships over a specified period of time by collecting relationship dynamics, attachments, interactions, and behavioral patterns. It can also aid clients with self-understanding and help the counselor choose appropriate assessments.

Inquiries about family history may explore:

- ethnic and cultural background.
- immigration status and experiences.
- family composition (i.e., nuclear, blended, fostered or adopted children, divorced parents, co-parenting status).
- socioeconomic status.
- educational levels of family members.
- employment status of family members.
- personal and occupational goals and ambitions of family members.
- achievements of family members.
- traumas or loss experienced by any family members.
- medical, financial, or domestic problems.
- values held by each family member and the priority of each value.
- any perceived favoritism experienced to certain children or adults.
- roles held within the family.

Some of these topics may be sensitive to discuss and should be approached empathetically.

Family Theories and Dynamics

Family systems theory is an iteration of the basic systems theory. When seeking to explain the behavior of an individual, one must look also at the interrelationships of the individual's family. The assumptions of this theory are as follows:

- A family is a unique unit and is unlike any other family.

- A family is interactional, and its parts vary in their resistance to change.

- Healthy family development depends upon the family's ability to meet the needs of the family and the individuals comprising the family.

- The family undergoes changes that cause differing amounts of stress to each family member.

External Boundaries

External boundaries define the family and distinguish it from individuals and systems outside of the family. **Boundaries in systems theory** are not physical or tangible, but can be observed, in a sense, via a family's attitudes, rules, and use of space. Some families have **closed boundaries**. Families that

108

use closed boundaries are characterized by having many rules about associating with non-family, physical barriers used to limit access to the family, rigid rules and values, few connections with others, and are traditional and wary of change. Families that have **open boundaries** are characterized by having many connections to individuals outside the family, fluid rules and spontaneous decision-making skills, minimal privacy, Uniqueness is valued more than tradition, and there is no fear of change. Open boundaries may lead to the family experiencing more chaos.

Internal Boundaries

Internal boundaries are rules that develop and define the relationships between the subsystems of the family. A **subsystem** might include the parents, the males of the household, or members of the family who share the same hobby. **Role organization** within a family is influenced by the size of the family, its culture and history, lifestyle, and values. In a healthy, well-functioning family, roles should be both clear and flexible.

As a family grows, rules develop that define how family members relate both to each other and to the world around them. Rules may be explicitly stated or implicitly understood. Families vary greatly in the type of rules that they have, as well as regarding whether rules can be easily discussed or modified.

Distribution of power in a reliable manner is important to the functioning of a family, though this distribution may change over time in response to changing needs of family members. Effective communication is also necessary for the family system. Roles, behaviors, and rules are all established through some type of communication. Communication can be open (clear and easy to understand) or closed (confusing and unclear).

Family Life Cycle

Family life cycle theories assume that, as members of a family unit, individuals pass through different stages of life. Although various theories will break down the stages somewhat differently, the following is a common conceptualization of the stages:

- **Unattached Young Adult**: The primary tasks for this stage are selecting a lifestyle and a life partner. Focus is on establishing independence as an adult and independence from one's family of origin.

- **Newly-Married Couple**: The focus in this stage is on establishing the marital system. Two families are joined together, and relationships must be realigned.

- **Family with Young Children**: The focus in this stage is on accepting new family members and transitioning from a marital system to a family system. The couple takes on a parenting role. Relationships must again be realigned with the extended family (e.g., grandparents).

- **Family with Adolescents**: The focus here is on accommodating the emerging independence of the adolescents in the family. The parent-child relationship experiences change, and the parents may also begin to take on caregiving roles with regard to their own parents.

109

- **Launching Family**: The focus in this stage is on accepting the new independent role of an adult child and transitioning through the separation. Parents also must face their own transition into middle or older age.

- **Family in Later Years**: In this stage, spousal roles must be re-examined and re-defined. One focus may be the development of interests and activities outside of work and family. Another focus is on navigation of the aging process and losses that may occur.

The basic family life cycle can vary significantly as a result of cultural influences, expectations, and particular family circumstances (e.g., single-parent family, blended family, multi-generational family).

Family Dynamics

Family dynamics are the interactions between family members in a family system. Each family is a unique system. However, there are some common patterns of family dynamics. The following are common influences on family dynamics:

- the type and quality of relationship that the parents have
- an absent parent
- a parent who is either extremely strict or extremely lenient
- the mix of personalities in the family
- a sick or disabled family member
- external events, particularly traumatic ones that have affected family members
- family dynamics in previous generations or the current extended family

The following are common roles in the family that may result from particular family dynamics:

- **The problem child**: child with problematic behavior, which may serve as a distraction from other problems that the family, particularly the parents, do not want to face

- **Scapegoat**: the family member to whom others unjustly attribute problems, often viewed as "bad," while other family members are viewed as "good"

- **Peacekeeper**: a family member who serves to mediate relationships and reduce family stress

Effects of Family Dynamics on Individuals

There are many ways in which the family influences the individual socially, emotionally, and psychologically. All family systems have their own unique characteristics, with both good and bad functional tendencies. The family interactions are among the earliest and most formative relationships that a person has, so they define the relational patterns that the individual develops and utilizes with all subsequent relationships. Parenting styles, conflict resolution methods, beliefs and values, and coping mechanisms are just a few things that a person learns from their family of origin. It is also within the family that a person first develops an image of self and identity, often having to do with the role that they are given within the family system and the messages communicated by parents. If a child has a secure and healthy relationship with the family members, this will likely lead to overall wellbeing and emotional stability as an adult.

When it comes to physical or mental illness, the role that the family plays is critical in lowering risk factors and minimizing symptoms. A strongly supportive family will help a person function at the highest level possible. Oftentimes, family members can serve as caregivers or play less formal—but still critical—roles in supporting a person's health.

Exploring Religious and Spiritual Values

Religion is a potentially influential component of counseling that should be explored in the first sessions. A client's behaviors and values may be based on religious beliefs. Depending on the client's religion, their beliefs could either assist the client in creating change or they could hinder the process. Religion can be a valuable tool to help clients cope with stressful situations or to recover from lifechanging circumstances. Encouraging prayer or attendance to worship services as part of treatment can be beneficial for clients who find strength through their faith. It can be a reminder of the morals and values of their religion, which can motivate clients to commit to change. Although religion can be useful in counseling, it can also be part of the client's presenting problem. Exploring a client's religious beliefs and having knowledge of different religions can be crucial in developing a plan for treatment. For instance, if a client is struggling with an identity issue that is seen as a sin in their religion, an understanding of those beliefs will play a significant part in the counseling process. Respecting a client's religious beliefs and incorporating them into treatment will also help to build the therapeutic relationship.

Spirituality is sometimes mistaken for religion, but in fact, they are quite different terms. **Religion** is an organized system of beliefs that generally contain a code of conduct and often involve specific devotional or ritual observations. **Spirituality** is more abstract and includes participation in spiritual activities such as meditation, chanting, prayer, or unselfishly serving others. A spiritual person may or may not belong to a religious organization. Spirituality places emphasis on the growth and well-being of the mind, body, and spirit.

Studies have shown that persons who embrace spirituality tend to live both longer and happier lives. Several benefits of being a spiritual person include the following:

- Individuals are encouraged to strive towards being a better person.
- There is an increased likelihood of connections with others
- It offers hope to the hopeless through strong faith.
- It provides a path to heal from emotional pain.
- It helps reduce anxiety through meditation and other spiritual activities
- It leads to greater life commitment via the optimism spiritual persons tend to have.

Guiding Clients in the Development of Skills or Strategies

An important aspect of counseling is helping people work through challenging events in their life. The counselor's role is to facilitate awareness and help clients resolve their internal conflicts. There are various strategies a counselor can use to guide clients to develop their own strategies for problem resolution. The first step is to ask the client what they are trying to accomplish with counseling and how committed they are to creating change. Understanding the presenting concern is a crucial aspect in developing a treatment plan and setting goals. A model of assessment known as the **DO A CLIENT MAP** takes a broad range of variables into consideration before establishing a treatment plan.

The client map focuses on areas such as objectives, treatment models, resources, and timing. For example, a client dealing with anger issues will require certain steps in counseling to uncover the underlying cause of the rage, such as unprocessed trauma, sadness, or fear. One key component of anger therapy is **emotional regulation**, which includes relaxation techniques to maintain control of

111

uncertain situations. Other skills for anger management include skill development for crisis prevention and cognitive restructuring for balanced thinking patterns. Other examples include increasing self-awareness for clients with control issues, building trust in clients with paranoia, and cognitive restructuring for clients with social anxiety. Counseling strategies will be dependent on the client's overall goals, motivation, and readiness for change. For example, a client wanting to overcome codependency issues may seek treatment when feelings of resentment and emptiness overpower their daily activities. Counselors may initiate interventions, such as placing the client in a support group that follows a twelve-step model. **Co-Dependents Anonymous (CoDA)** helps clients learn self-compassion and set personal boundaries. Once clients learn to develop self-care and communicate needs clearly, counselors can progress to evaluating therapy goals.

Helping Clients Develop Support Systems

As part of the intake process and initial sessions, counselors need to explore and understand clients' existing support systems. All individuals have varying degrees of social support, which can include friends, family, and community. Counselors can help clients evaluate their level of support and determine how the support system can help during counseling and after it has ended. It may be necessary to help clients find ways to develop additional support, such as through groups or organizations. A support system is necessary to provide help, encouragement, and care.

Helping Facilitate Clients' Motivation to Make Desired Changes

Entering into counseling can provoke anxiety, fear, and resistance to change. Clients may have both internal and external reasons to want or need to change but exhibit some unwillingness to do so. Clients with internal or intrinsic motivation understand that they need to change to move forward, grow, and achieve personal goals. External factors, such as mandated counseling, can be motivating, but may create additional resistance. Clients will be more motivated and willing to change when they have a vested interest in the process and believe they will achieve a successful outcome. Commitment to the process is essential, especially considering that counseling may not seem enjoyable or even interesting but may be necessary.

Motivation and resistance impact a client's readiness to change behavior. These are two crucial components to examine when developing an intervention plan. High motivation is indicated by self-confidence and self-efficacy, as the client believes they are capable of change. High motivation is also characterized by a client's desire to correct an identified problem, work toward a goal, and reliably show up for sessions. High motivation also shows in the client's belief that implementing a change will improve their overall quality of life.

Resistance can refer to any behavior that indicates the client does not want to work with the counselor or improve their personal situation. Resistance may be indicated by a client's refusal to show up on time, or at all, for sessions. A client involuntarily coming to sessions (such as by a court order) may state that there is no tangible problem to work on, or the client may state they feel no changes are occurring. Counselors should examine resistance holistically to ensure they are not contributing to it. For example, clients may exhibit resistance to counseling sessions if they do not feel comfortable with the counselor, if they do not understand the counselor, or if they are expected to work on issues that they do not yet feel ready to address.

Readiness to change occurs in six stages: **pre-contemplation** (where an individual does not believe a need for change exists or is not self-aware), **contemplation** (where an individual recognizes a problem but is not ready to address it), **preparation** (where an individual recognizes a problem and

112

sets the stage for change), **action** (where an individual takes active, involved steps to stop a problem), **maintenance** (where the individual commits to the desired behaviors), and **termination** (where the individual is able to regularly sustain the desired behaviors without relapse).

Motivation and resistance pertain to the individual's readiness to acknowledge and change behaviors. Motivation is higher and resistance is lower when an individual feels ready to make a change. Some indicators of high motivation and low resistance include:

- Awareness and open acknowledgment of the presenting issue
- Willingness to list pros and cons of behavior change
- Willingness to make small steps toward and document outcomes of behavior change
- Acknowledgment that changing behavior is in the individual's best interest

Some indicators of low motivation and high resistance include:

- Lack of recognition of a present problem
- Hostility or apathy towards the counselor (which may be revealed by skipping sessions)
- Discussion of a presenting issue without openness to changing associated behaviors

Counselors can increase the client's motivation by discussing changes positively in terms that demonstrate benefit to the client's life, allowing the client to set his or her own goals and providing assistance only for those specific goals, highlighting the tools the client possesses to make changes, and acknowledging and respecting the client's fears about change.

Improve Interactional Patterns

Improving relationships for the client requires minimizing maladaptive interaction patterns. Interaction patterns that can harm a relationship include negative interpretations, shutting down, defending, complaining, and disapproving. A **validating style** of interaction is characterized by partners respecting each other's opinions and emotions, compromising, and resolving problems mutually. Volatile patterns lead to arguments and conflict, followed by reconciliation. The **avoiding style** is characterized by not dealing with problems at all. An example of a therapy method that attempts to improve interactional patterns is the Gottman Method. The **Gottman Method** includes assessment of the relationship and the development of a therapeutic framework with primary interventions. The areas addressed include conflict management, creation of a shared meaning, and development of friendship. The interventions assist with replacing negative conflict patterns with positive interactions to strengthen a relationship. The overall goal of this method is to achieve a sense of understanding, awareness, empathy, and interpersonal growth.

Providing Crisis Intervention

In 1964, psychiatry professor **Gerald Caplan** defined the recognizable phases of a crisis:

- Phase 1. This first phase consists of the initial threat or event, which triggers a response. The individual may be able to employ coping skills or defense mechanisms to avoid a crisis.

- Phase 2. This second phase is the escalation, during which initial attempts to manage the crisis are ineffective and the individual begins to experience increased distress.

113

- Phase 3. The third phase is the acute crisis phase, during which anxiety continues and may intensify to panic or a fight-or-flight response. There are still attempts to problem-solve during this phase, and new tactics may be used.

- Phase 4. The fourth phase is the climax of the crisis when solutions have failed; the individual may experience personality disorganization and become severely depressed, violent, and possibly suicidal.

A crisis situation requires swift action and specially trained mental health personnel and can occur at any time in any setting. **Albert Roberts** proposed a seven-stage model to deal with a crisis and provide effective intervention and support. Roberts's stages are as follows:

- Stage 1. Conduct thorough biopsychosocial assessments of client functioning, and identify any imminent danger to self or others.

- Stage 2. Make contact, and quickly establish rapport; it is important that the counselor is accepting, nonjudgmental, flexible, and supportive.

- Stage 3. Identify specific problems and the possible cause of crisis; begin to prioritize the specific aspect of the problem most in need of a solution.

- Stage 4. Provide counseling in an attempt to understand the emotional content of the situation.

- Stage 5. Work on coping strategies and alternative solutions, which can be very challenging for an individual in crisis.

- Stage 6. Implement an action plan for treatment, which could include therapy, the 12-step program, hospitalization, or social services support.

- Stage 7. Follow up, and continue to evaluate status; ensure that the treatment plan is effective and make adjustments as needed.

Critical Incident Stress Debriefing

Designed to support individuals after a traumatic event, **Critical Incident Stress Debriefing (CISD)** is a structured form of crisis management. Specifically, it is short-term work done in small groups but is not considered psychotherapy. Techniques used include processing, defusing, ventilating, and validating thoughts, experiences, feeling and emotions. CISD is best for secondary trauma victims, not primary trauma victims. For example, in cases of workplace violence, any employees who witnessed an event or who were indirectly impacted could benefit from CISD. Employees who were first-degree victims would need more individualized, specialized care and therapeutic intervention. It is important that CISD is offered as quickly as possible after an event; research has indicated it is most effective within a 24- to 72-hour time frame and becomes less effective the more time lapses after the event. CISD can be managed by specially trained personnel and could include mental health workers, medical staff, human resources, or other professionals. Trained Crisis Response Teams can be ready or quickly available to provide support directly following a traumatic situation.

Educating Clients About Transference and Defense Mechanisms

Transference is a concept from psychoanalysis that refers to the process of the clients transferring any feelings toward others onto the counselor. These feelings are likely unconscious, as they arrive from childhood experiences and relationships. For example, the counselor may remind clients of their distant parent, and the clients will project feelings about that parent onto the counselor. Transference can be very powerful, although both positive and negative forms exist. Positive or **good transference** allows clients to work through issues with the counselor, who is safe and nonreactive. Clients can project negative feelings or emotions onto the counselor, thus being able to resolve them in the absence of the parent or individual. Negative or **bad transference** exists when clients project negative emotions and become angry or hostile toward the counselor. This type of transference can create a blockage and diminish the effectiveness of therapy. It is the role of the counselor to understand and manage transference as it arises in the relationship. Transference can also occur for the counselor with clients. Supervision and consultation are both helpful and necessary should this occur.

Sigmund Freud's **psychoanalytic theory** focused on the conflicts, drives, and unacceptable desires in the unconscious mind and how they affect a person. One method of dealing with unconscious conflicts is through *defense mechanisms*, which are the mind's way of protecting a person from unacceptable thoughts. Here are some of the most common defense mechanisms:

- **Repression** is when a person suppresses thoughts or memories that are too difficult to handle. They are pushed out of the conscious mind, and a person may experience memory loss or have psychogenic amnesia related to those memories.

- **Displacement** takes place when someone displaces the feelings that they have toward one person, such as anger, and puts it on another person who may be less threatening. For example, someone may express anger toward a spouse, but the person that they are truly angry at is their boss.

- **Sublimation** is when the socially unacceptable thought is transformed into healthy, acceptable behavior in another direction. Pain may become poetry, for example.

- **Rationalization** is when unacceptable feelings or thoughts are rationally and logically explained and defended.

- **Reaction formation** occurs when the negative feeling is covered up by a false or exaggerated version of its opposite. In such a case, a person may display strong feelings of affection toward someone, though internally and unconsciously hate that person.

- **Denial** is refusing to accept painful facts or situations and instead acting as if they are not true or have not happened.

- **Projection** is putting one's own feelings onto someone else and acting as if they are the one who feels that way instead of oneself.

Facilitating Trust and Safety

The nature of the counseling relationship necessitates that clients trust and feel safe with their counselors. Clients reveal personal information to their counselors, and they must be able to trust that the counselor will not spread that information. They should also feel confident that their counselor is reliable, responsible, knowledgeable, and competent to handle their innermost thoughts, feelings, and experiences. Counselors can facilitate trust with their clients by explaining that they are bound by confidentiality (with some exceptions having to do with harming others or themselves). This allows clients to feel secure when disclosing information that they would not share elsewhere. Additionally,

115

counselors gain their clients' trust when they respond appropriately to the disclosure of difficult material. When counselors show compassion, care, and concern instead of judgment and condemnation, clients are more likely to develop trust and feel safe.

Building Communication Skills

An individual can communicate verbally and non-verbally through body language or silence. Interviews, two-way casual conversations, and written or verbal standardized assessments can help the counselor determine the individual's communication skills. **Role-playing** a specific situation can help the counselor determine how an individual communicates in certain contexts. Assessing the individual's personal, family, social, or cultural context can also provide valuable insight to communication skills and help validate an assessment.

Counselors use verbal and nonverbal communication techniques to engage clients in completing treatment goals. **Verbal communication** is vital to the counselor/client relationship, and counselors should be skilled at greetings, summarization, reflection, and the conveyance of new information to the client. The client may misconstrue a counselor's body language if it does not represent openness and trust. Likewise, the counselor needs to be adept at analyzing the client's body language in order to move forward. Clients use both verbal and nonverbal communication to convey their story to the counselor, and communication techniques used by the counselor can be modeled to teach the client improved communication. Clients should be instructed to recognize their own communication techniques in the context of the relationship with the counselor. Clients who are withdrawn or isolated may need especially sensitive communication with the counselor in order to better communicate verbally and nonverbally.

In order to build a strong helping relationship with the client, the counselor must learn to use effective verbal and nonverbal techniques. These skills are necessary throughout the treatment process and especially during assessment and engagement.

Developing and Facilitating Conflict Resolution Strategies

Counselors may engage in conflict resolution with clients by acting as a mediator or advocate. Mediators work with clients to intervene in the conflict and develop helpful solutions that reflect all parties involved. For example, the counselor may act as a mediator in family or couples therapy conflicts. Counselors may also work with clients on developing their own conflict resolution skills through methods such as reflection, role-playing, and empty chair techniques. Counselors may also encourage clients to practice the use of **metacommunication**, which is communication about the behaviors and reactions of their regular and possibly dysfunctional method of interactions or communication. Sometimes the client is in conflict with the counselor and transference issues must be resolved before progress can be made. Counselors and clients need to be in collaboration concerning treatment goals and modalities so that conflict is reduced.

In some cases, agencies contract with mediation services outside the agency to assist clients in resolving conflicts. Professional mediators are trained in mediation techniques and are paid by the agency for their services. They can be the final step of resolution when the agency cannot resolve client conflict. Child protective services agencies sometimes use professional mediators to reduce or eliminate conflict in cases involving juveniles.

Developing Safety Plans

Safety plans are problem-solving tools clients can follow when they are unable to think clearly or care for themselves. Counselors can help clients identify tasks to perform when crisis intervention is needed. Safety plans will be dependent on the reason clients require them. Clients with suicidal ideation, victims of domestic violence, and individuals with mood disorders can benefit from establishing a safety plan. There are a couple of components to a safety plan that should be created in collaboration with the client. Counselors and clients must first be able to recognize the signs of danger.

Clients who verbalize intent to self-harm or harm others are exhibiting signs of a crisis and require intervention. It is also important to be able to identify what the client is able to do on their own to mitigate the negative thoughts and manage stress. Initiation of coping strategies, such as meditation, music, and exercise, that can de-escalate harmful thoughts should be included. Another component to incorporate is the identification of resources. Clients and counselors can work together to create a list of friends, family, or professional resources to be contacted in crisis situations. The goal of a safety plan is to be client-centered, realistic, and achievable.

Facilitating Systemic Change

Counselors can apply the principles of systems theory to create change when working with families. An important concept of this theory is the idea that one part of a family system affects and changes other parts of the system. Homeostasis is a concept that refers to families' resistance to change and their pressure to maintain balance and the status quo. Counselors must use techniques to disrupt the homeostasis of a family in which problematic behaviors exist. For example, in a family with a parentified male child, a counselor might physically move the boy away from his mother and father and place him across the room, while placing the mother and father next to each other. This maneuver has the potential to disrupt the system. It is designed to help the married couple create stronger boundaries around their marriage, thereby excluding the child from the husband-wife dyad. Counselors can also facilitate systemic change by having clients draw genograms to show generational patterns. These diagrams visually depict family patterns of marriage, substance use, violence, divorce, etc. across multiple generations. They are designed to show families' negative and positive patterns and may give them motivation to begin intentionally creating new patterns.

Providing Distance Counseling or Telemental Health

Telemental health is an evolving form of counseling. Since the COVID-19 pandemic, telemental health services have become more prevalent, but the rules and regulations are not firmly established and may differ from state to state. While some insurance companies have started to pay for these services due to no-contact regulations during the pandemic, it is not certain if this will continue to be a covered practice post-pandemic. **Telemental health** includes video conferencing, phone calls, chat, text messages, and emails. Individuals, couples, families, and even groups can benefit from these services. Counselors who utilize telemental health must ensure that their devices and software are secure and do not allow recording.

Providing Education Resources

One of the major roles of a counselor is to act as a mediator and advocate for clients seeking therapy. Clients will often require additional resources outside of counseling sessions. For example, clients with

117

substance addiction issues can benefit from resources that provide education on common addictions, locate rehabilitation centers near their area, or provide intervention hotlines in case of a crisis. Websites such as addictionresource.com and drugabuse.gov provide an array of information for clients seeking education and additional resources. Clients who experience depression can benefit from outside engagement when counseling sessions do not occur. These clients are at a high risk of suicide and may require multiple resources. Organizations such as the **National Alliance on Mental Illness (NAMI)** provide support groups, advocacy, and educational articles to bring awareness and help clients experiencing emotional distress. Clients whose safety is at risk due to domestic violence also require a vast amount of resources. The **National Domestic Violence Hotline** offers pathways to creating a safety plan, education on recognizing the signs of domestic violence, and a list of regional organizations to help those in need.

Providing Psychoeducation for Clients and Groups

Psychoeducation refers to any form of training or instruction that is provided to clients and the client system as a part of understanding mental health or psychological issues and treatments. Its goal is to support clients experiencing mental illnesses, their families, and their networks while eliminating the stigma that has been associated with mental health issues for decades. Psychoeducation methods include explaining potential causes for specific mental health issues, understanding the challenges of specific mental health issues, explaining how support systems can acknowledge and cope with not only a client's mental health condition but also their own caregiving stress, teaching coping skills, building resiliency, and overcoming in ways that are accessible. This form of education can occur in group settings, seminars or webinars, and in individual or family sessions. It can also be presented through newsletters, other media, and formal courses.

It may be offered in home, online, in hospitals or other healthcare facilities, in community centers, or at conference venues. It is not considered treatment, but it is a beneficial complement to clinical care. It promotes positive and inclusive language, eliminates shame and fear around mental illnesses, creates educational value, fosters network support and understanding, and acknowledges a variety of feelings and responses to mental health conditions. Psychoeducation techniques are associated with reduced inpatient and hospitalization rates for clients with mental health conditions. Psychoeducation is correlated with clients' self-reported feelings of acceptance and increased family support. Family and friends self-report a better understanding of their loved one who may have a mental health condition, a better understanding of their role in providing positive support and care, the ability to draw healthy boundaries for themselves, and relief from learning and utilizing self-care techniques that reduce caregiver stress.

Summarizing

Summarizing is another active listening and rapport-building technique. The counselor listens to the content provided by the clients and summarizes the essential points of the conversation. This process can help isolate and clarify the essential aspects of issues and ensure that both the client and the counselor can focus on the most critical tasks. Additionally, summarization can be helpful in goal setting or at the end of a session.

Reframing/Redirecting

A technique used by counselors to help clients create a different way of looking at a person, situation, or relationship is known as **redirecting** or **cognitive reframing**. This technique helps clients look at

118

situations with a different perspective. For example, reframing thought processes can be effective in counseling teenagers who do not always agree with parental decisions. Anger that results from imposed curfews or punishments for underperforming academically can be redirected by having the client empathize with their parents and analyze the reasons for the restrictions. Effective reframing should acknowledge the client's feelings and help interpret the situation in a different manner. For example, clients who experience fear of failure can use that emotion to reframe their thought process into a positive one. Encouraging them to use fear as a form of awareness as opposed to a paralyzing emotion can help clients look at their situation with a different mindset.

Facilitating Empathic Responses

Empathy is considered an essential counseling skill. It is used not only to initially build trust but also throughout the counseling process. The process of empathy is used to help the counselor understand the client's viewpoint. It is more complex than sympathy, which is somewhat passive and a sense of feeling bad for another person. Empathy focuses on gaining insight into the client's experience to offer effective means to deal with any issues or concerns. Although psychologist Edward Titchener was the first to use the term, it is strongly associated with the client-centered approach of Carl Rogers. Rogers believed empathy extended beyond understanding a person's situation; it involved the counselor imagining him or herself in that situation. This level of empathy requires genuineness, acceptance, and a small measure of vulnerability on the part of the counselor.

Using Self-Disclosure

In rare cases, it may be appropriate for counselors to self-disclose to clients. It is important to remember that the therapeutic process is to help clients, not indirectly benefit counselors. First and foremost, counselors should consider the intent and who will benefit from their **self-disclosure**. It is not appropriate for clients to be burdened with counselors' emotions, as it could shift the atmosphere and power dynamic of therapy. Counselors can disclose an emotional reaction to content from clients, provided it is for the benefit of the clients. Counselors should be cognizant of their clients' level of functioning and issues prior to any purposeful self-disclosure to ensure professional boundaries are maintained.

Using Constructive Confrontation

For many clients, there comes a point when goals aren't being reached in counseling. The counselor needs to recognize when progress isn't being made and observe (through active listening) any inconsistencies that are holding the client back. This means listening for any contradictions the client makes regarding their behaviors or feelings. These inconsistencies may be the cause of conflict in the client's life. The client may say one thing but do another, or they may say two opposing things. The counselor will need to confront the client about these inconsistencies, but it needs to be done carefully. It is important that a therapeutic and trusting relationship is established before the counselor attempts any confrontation. The client could interpret the counselor's questioning or comments as criticism. The client needs to be approached with empathy and a sincere interest in revealing and understanding their conflicting actions and/or words. When pointing out contradictions, it is best to reflect back what the client has said and delicately inquire about discrepancies. If the client is open to analyzing how this affects their ability to make changes, they may reach a new level of self-awareness and begin to move forward in therapy.

119

Counselors should be sensitive to the needs of clients they work with. Some clients will respond better than others to confrontation, and the counselor needs to have the skills to identify how and when confrontation should occur. Culture and gender may be a factor in how confrontation will be received. The counselor should also be mindful of the language that is used. Accusatory or harsh language will be met with resistance, while encouraging and positive words are more likely to aid in the therapeutic process. If the confrontation is met with denial, the counselor will need to approach the problem in a different manner at a different time.

Facilitating Awareness of Here-and-Now Interactions

Here-and-now in counseling refers to using the present interactions between the counselor and client or between group members to resolve issues and change behaviors in clients. The idea behind this technique is that interactions or feelings that clients experience during counseling sessions reflect interactions and feelings that occur outside of counseling and that, by addressing them at the present moment, new behaviors and methods of interaction can be learned. In order for here-and-now interactions to be therapeutic and effect change, the counselor has to be aware of these opportunities for working through issues as they arise. After addressing the problem and working through it together, the counselor must summarize what has happened and make the client aware of how this interaction was handled and how this more productive and healthy method can be used to change behaviors and interactions in their daily life.

Counselors who follow the theory of **Gestalt therapy** place an emphasis on the present as opposed to the past or the future. Past experiences are not ignored but are used as milestones for change and growth. For example, clients who are unable to fulfill their interests due to unfinished business can benefit from incorporating the Gestalt method. The counselor can assist the client with redirecting their energy in a positive manner and creating adaptive ways to function despite negative past experiences. Examples of positive energy include optimistic statements, compassionate actions, and self-care. The **Empty Chair Technique** is an exercise that encourages dialogue between the client and an empty chair beside them. The chair should symbolize another person in the client's life, themselves, or a part of themselves in order to engage thoughts, behaviors, and emotions. Role reversal is essential so that the client is able to focus on immediate experiences and work through different aspects of conflicting situations.

Linking and Blocking

Blocking is the act of the group leader stopping unwanted behaviors from members that may be harmful or hurtful or violate confidentiality. This helps to set appropriate standards for how the group should behave. With linking, the group leader relates members' stories or situations to enhance interaction and cohesion of the group.

Management of Leader-Member Dynamics

Broadly speaking, anything that impacts the group can be considered dynamic. The word **dynamic** means change, activity, or progress. Thus, a group is constantly adapting and evolving. **Dynamics** are the interrelationships between the members, which include the leadership style, decision-making, and cohesiveness. **Cohesiveness** is the degree to which the group sticks together. There are two types of cohesion: task and social. Task is the level at which the group works to achieve a common objective. Social cohesiveness refers to the interpersonal relationships within the group.

120

There are three main styles of leading groups:

- **Autocratic**: This leader is authoritarian and sets clear rules, boundaries, and goals for the group. This type can be beneficial in situations where there are time or resource limitations, constant changes to membership, or the need to coordinate with other groups. This type of leadership can create resentment and dissatisfaction, as it is unilateral and strict.

- **Democratic**: This leader is considered the fairest by taking into consideration ideas and choices of the group. Not to be confused with the political usage, these leaders do not wield specific power or prestige; rather, they work to maintain a participatory style and harmonious atmosphere.

- **Laissez-Faire**: This is the most relaxed style of leadership; group members are responsible for all aspects of decision-making. Laissez-faire is an absence of leadership, which works best with motivated, self-directed members.

Modeling Giving and Receiving Feedback

Clients can benefit from counselors not only by the specific techniques they use, but also by observing how their counselors interact with them. The interactions between counselors and clients within sessions can demonstrate appropriate ways for clients to give and receive feedback in their lives outside of counseling sessions. For example, a client who is shy and unassertive could benefit from receiving genuine feedback about her interactional style in a way that is non-critical yet straightforward. Her observations about how the therapist gently and honestly speaks truth to her could give her courage to accept feedback from others without taking offense. The counselor could also demonstrate how to receive feedback by asking the client if she is satisfied with the progression of therapy. The openness of the counselor to receive feedback could exemplify how to accept feedback from others.

Addressing Impact of Extended Families

Clients with extended families often have concerns with invasions of privacy, unsolicited advice, and frequent criticisms. It is important for counselors to guide clients toward responding positively to uncontrollable behaviors. Setting boundaries is an important part of maintaining privacy. For example, extended family members who often interfere with activities of daily living may cause a disruption in routine. Clients should be encouraged to voice their concerns and explain their emotions to the family member in order to reach an understanding. When conflicts between individuals arise, including a third person creates **triangulation**. Counselors should encourage clients to address their concerns directly with the person involved in the disagreement and avoid sharing frustrated feelings with a third person. Individuals who find themselves following routines they are unhappy with can become resentful and repress their anger. These clients should be encouraged to break the pattern and communicate alternative solutions that work for the entire family.

Containing and Managing Intense Feelings

When there is a difficult situation or crisis, extreme emotions are usually involved. If possible, a client should be guided through relaxation techniques to help calm them down. Oftentimes, a calm and neutral party who can facilitate a conversation or listen to the client empathetically, but without feeding the emotion, will automatically de-escalate the situation. Confrontation or matching the client's emotions will escalate the situation. Allowing the client to communicate the situation fully may help them to become less emotional and more focused on the facts. At this point the client may be able to focus on the next steps and specific tasks that need to be done. If possible, help the client to regain emotional control so that extreme options such as restraints are unnecessary.

Exploring the Influence of Family of Origin Patterns and Themes

The family that a person grew up with is considered to be that person's family of origin. This can be their biological parents and siblings, grandparents, aunts and uncles, adopted parents, or any other people who raised them and were part of the household that the person grew up in. Whether biological or not, every family has patterns of interactions that are passed on to the next generation and affect aspects of the family members' lives such as relationships, self-worth, and regulation of emotions. Everything from religious beliefs to how anger is dealt with are established early in life by the influence of the family of origin.

When working with a client to understand and change present behaviors and patterns, the counselor can explore the patterns and interactions of the family of origin to identify the source of any dysfunction. There are numerous issues, such as anxiety, intimacy problems, and abuse, that can be attributed to these patterns and interactions that occur early in life. By exploring behaviors learned from the client's family of origin, the counselor can help the client unlearn old family behaviors and learn new and acceptable habits and responses, form better concepts of self, and change the types of relationships that they tend to gravitate toward.

Addressing the Impact of Social Support Network

An individual's social support network consists of the family, friends, and community groups that the client can turn to when in need of any kind of support. Support can be provided in many ways, such as listening to problems, giving advice, sharing resources, assisting with financial responsibilities, or running errands. Having a social support network makes difficult circumstances easier to bear. Individuals who do not have a support system tend to suffer from more mental and physical health problems than those who have a support system. A positive network of support can alleviate feelings of loneliness and can provide motivation for healthy changes and continued progress towards goals. An important consideration when looking at a client's support system is whether the individuals in that system provide a positive or negative influence. Counselors should be aware of the possibility that the system of support that a client has may include friends or family who perpetuate the issue that the client is trying to overcome. Therefore, counselors should be aware of the impact that each client's social support network has on their progression through counseling.

Using Structured Activities

Counselors have many theoretical approaches from which to choose, and within those approaches is a vast assortment of structured activities they can utilize to help clients meet their treatment goals. Recent research reflects the positive benefits of journaling and gratitude exercises for clients struggling with different types of diagnoses. For instance, gratitude has demonstrated efficacy in treating depression; therefore, counselors can encourage their clients to write a list of things they are grateful for every day.

Counselors can also have their clients complete genograms. **Genograms** are diagrams of family structures that include several generations. Clients are instructed to draw "maps" of their family history that include information such as marriages, births, deaths, occupations, divorces, suicides, drug and alcohol abuse, child abuse, etc. These can show clients generational issues existing within their families. Therapists can then work with clients to uncover destructive patterns in their immediate families and find ways to stop them.

The **empty chair technique** is a common therapeutic activity. This technique requires the client to sit across from an empty chair and have a dialogue with a person in their life or with some part of themselves. The therapist then has the client switch chairs and speak from the other perspective.

Therapists can also have clients write letters that are not intended to be given to the recipients. These letters can be written to people who are living or dead. This technique allows clients the opportunity to express their thoughts and feelings without facing the intended recipients when it may be unsafe or impossible to do so.

Promoting and Encouraging Interactions Among Group Members

Members serve different roles in the group and can change their roles as the group progresses. There are both functional and nonfunctional roles. Functional roles assist the group and include the energizer, harmonizer, tension reliever, and gatekeeper. Nonfunctional roles can disrupt and hinder the group and include the interrogator, dominator, monopolizer, aggressor, and recognition seeker. Other roles include victim, scapegoat, and follower, who are not overtly negative but do not assist in positive group functioning. Counselors should encourage positive interactions between group members and guide and encourage members to assume positive roles that benefit themselves as individuals and the group as a whole.

Promoting and Encouraging Interactions with the Group Leader

Counselors should encourage their clients who are in group therapy to interact with the group leader. The leader is there to not only facilitate the group, but also to help the group members get as much out of the group as possible. Groups may have multiple leaders. Co-leadership is widely used in group therapy sessions and is found to have many beneficial aspects. **Co-leadership** may be used as a way to train therapists to lead groups and is found to have positive impacts, especially in larger groups. Having two leaders can help ensure that all members get attention, can actively participate, and assist the group in accomplishing more. Co-leadership can be detrimental if leaders do not get along or cannot form a cooperative and united management team for the group.

Phases in the Group Process

Several theories outline the developmental stages of a group. One of the most well-known is **Bruce Tuckman's four-stage model**: forming, storming, norming, and performing. **Forming** is the stage where the group members are just beginning to get acquainted and may be anxious and less vocal. **Storming** involves conflict, discord, and struggles to agree upon a leader. **Norming** is the agreement stage, during which a leader is chosen and conflicts begin to resolve. **Performing** is the point at which the group becomes effective at achieving defined tasks. A fifth stage, **Adjourning**, was added, which defines the point at which the group terminates. Other group development theories include that of **Irvin D. Yalom**, whose three-stage model included orientation, conflict/dominance, and development of cohesiveness. **Gerald Corey**'s stages included initial, transition, working, and termination. All three theories share similar progressions of the group process.

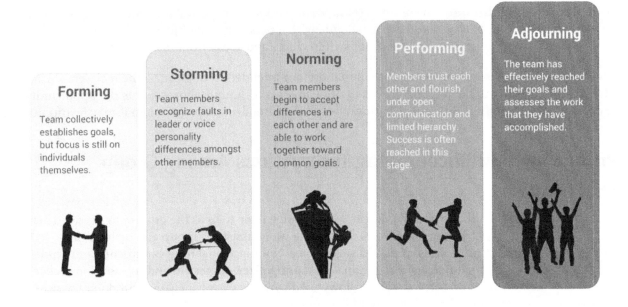

Other group development theories include that of Irvin D. Yalom, whose three-stage model included orientation, conflict/dominance, and development of cohesiveness. Gerald Corey's stages included initial, transition, working, and termination. All three theories share similar progressions of the group development. A general method of categorizing the group process uses stages—the beginning, middle, and end. Each stage is classified by different activities, processes, and tasks:

Beginning Stage
Counselors determine the group's purpose, members, objectives, and other logistical tasks (time, location, etc.). Group formation occurs at this stage as new members come together. The counselor fosters a safe and trusting environment by establishing acceptable group norms. As group members become more comfortable, conflicts arise as power and control behaviors emerge. Group roles and alliances begin to form. The counselor's role is to help guide the group through these challenges and process any conflicts that arise within the group.

Middle Stage
This stage is where most group work is done. Members share information, openly address issues, and work through conflicts. Some groups do not make it to this stage for several reasons, including member dynamics and a lack of investment by the group members. Group cohesion or the connectedness of the members is extremely important at this stage. The role of the counselor is to help members focus on methods and the meaning of communication, working through group differences and confronting members when necessary. Counselors should also help develop more intensive levels of cohesiveness while building on member individuality.

End Stage
Group members come to resolutions on the issues addressed during the group process. Members may have strong reactions to termination, especially if there was a high level of cohesion developed during the group process. The counselor should lead the group in discussing feelings about termination and

124

be aware of negative reactions that may surface. When these types of emotions occur, counselors should address any challenges that arise with members. The counselor should also help group members identify and reflect on the skills learned in the group process and how those skills can benefit the members with future challenges.

Working with Individuals in the Group Context

It is the role of the counselor to encourage all members to participate in the group process. The counselor can solicit feedback from each member of the group throughout the group process. Clients typically take on various roles during group treatment. **Roles** can be defined as functions that the individual members of the group are fulfilling or performing that facilitate the group process. Some roles include that of a clown, scapegoat, mediator, etc. The counselor must be aware of the roles of each individual and how those roles are affecting the group so interventions can be made when necessary.

Identifying and Discussing Group Themes and Patterns

Groups can take on characteristics that are often seen in families. As group members become comfortable with one another, their true personalities emerge and behavioral patterns from their families of origin tend to surface. Counselors can take note of these dynamics and use them within the group setting in a way that helps members see their familial patterns and make changes in line with their treatment goals. For example, if there is one person in a group who is viewed as everyone's favorite and who can do no wrong, then this person likely played the role of favorite child at home or as teacher's pet in school. Another example is a person who wants to be the leader's favorite; these individuals vie for the counselor's attention and attempt to curry favor by the way they respond to the leader. The counselor must be sensitive to all types of themes appearing in the group and be sure not to succumb to the subtle pressure to keep members in the roles they have played all their lives. Instead, the counselor's job is to identify these patterns and use them as therapeutic tools for transformation.

Creating Intervention Based on the Stage of Group Development

Groups have different stages of development, but not all groups go through every stage. The stages are:

1. Forming/pre-affiliation
2. Storming/power and control
3. Norming/intimacy
4. Performing/differentiation
5. Adjourning/termination

In each stage, the leader is responsible for creating certain elements that will help the group function productively and transition successfully to the next stage. For example, in the forming/**pre-affiliation stage**, a group leader could help a group function properly by actively easing members' concerns about being part of the group. The leader would also intervene if any conflict arose because conflict would be counterproductive in the early stage of group formation. Another example of group leader intervention can be found during the performing/**differentiation stage**. In this stage, the group is more productive, has established a sense of security and trust in the leader and in each other, and members are more willing to engage in honest feedback. A group leader in this stage might encourage member-to-member empathy by directing one person to talk with another member who is angry to try and understand why the person is feeling that way.

125

Challenging Harmful Group Member Behaviors

For a therapy group to be successful, leaders must fill crucial roles that change depending on the stage of the group's development. One important duty of the leader is ensuring that group members are safe from harmful group interactions. Sometimes a group member will behave in a destructive manner or say hateful things to other members. The **therapeutic group** is one in which the potential for conflicts exists, and leaders know that some conflict is productive and necessary when diverse people share intimate details about their lives. However, when a group member becomes aggressive or hostile to another member in a damaging way, the leader must confront the member. This must be done in a way that is straightforward, caring, and professional. The leader must stop the aggressive behavior and also attend to the offended member.

Potential Interaction of Members Outside of the Group

Groups are designed to fulfill different tasks. **Supportive groups** (those used for severe mental illness or medical conditions) sometimes encourage interaction outside of the group. Forming genuine friendships outside of the group could be beneficial for members. **Psychodynamic groups** (those designed to affect personality changes while focusing on relationship issues and interpersonal dynamics) often prohibit outside group involvement. This is done to prevent interference with therapy goals. **Cognitive behavioral groups** (designed for treating symptoms of psychiatric conditions or for acquiring new coping skills) also discourage members from interacting outside the group. **Self-help groups** (designed around themed life issues such as AA or grief support groups) often encourage members to interact outside of the group. The therapeutic purpose of the group determines whether members are allowed to have contact outside of the group.

Practice Quiz

1. Traditionally, a nuclear family consists of which of the following?
    a. One man, one woman, and their immediate children
    b. A single female head-of-household and her children
    c. A heterosexual or homosexual couple without any children
    d. Any type of family that has at least one domesticated pet

2. What are the four phases of a crisis as defined by Gerald Caplan?
    a. Threat, escalation, resolution, follow-up
    b. Threat, intervention, climax, resolution
    c. Threat, rapport, strategy, treatment
    d. Threat, escalation, acute crisis, climax

3. Dynamics deal with the interrelationships between the members, which include the leadership style, decision-making, and cohesiveness. Which of the following defines the dynamics of a group?
    a. Positive leadership
    b. Anything that impacts the group
    c. Lack of cohesiveness
    d. Norming

4. The empty chair technique is used by what type of group therapy and for what reason?
    a. Person-centered, to put oneself in another's situation and build empathy
    b. Gestalt, to resolve emotional issues with another person
    c. Psychoanalytic, to resolve issues with parents or authority figures
    d. Transactional analysis, to understand and edit life scripts

5. Conflict resolution requires a mutual agreement by both parties. Which of the following is required for successful conflict resolution?
    a. Assertive opinions
    b. Defining the solution
    c. Good communication
    d. Giving advice

See answers on the next page.

Answer Explanations

1. A: One man, one woman, and their immediate children. Nuclear family is a term that is widely considered to be narrow in its definition of a family unit. The other family types listed are examples of alternative families.

2. D: Caplan's phases are threat, escalation, acute crisis, climax:

- Initial threat or event, which triggers a response. The individual may be able to employ coping skills or defense mechanisms to avoid a crisis.

- Escalation, during which initial attempts to manage the crisis are ineffective and the individual begins to experience increased distress.

- Acute crisis phase, during which anxiety continues and may intensify to panic or a fight-or-flight response. There are still attempts to problem-solve during this phase, and new tactics may be used.

- Climax of the crisis when solutions have failed; the individual may experience personality disorganization and become severely depressed, violent, and possibly suicidal.

3. B: The word *dynamic* means activity, change, or progress; thus, dynamics are anything that affect (or change) the group. Group dynamics refers to any interactions and processes of the group. Choice A, positive leadership, can be part of a leadership style of a group, but it does not define group dynamics. Choice C, lack of cohesiveness, is the inability to form a united whole, and is incorrect. Choice D, norming, is one of the stages of group development and involves the time where the group becomes a cohesive unit.

4. B: The empty chair technique is used in Gestalt to help resolve feelings toward another person. The other choices are merely the goals of those types of therapies. In person-centered therapy, Choice A, the goal of the counselor is to put himself or herself in another's situation and have empathy toward that person. One goal of psychoanalytic therapy, Choice C, is to resolve issues with parents or authority figures. Finally, in transactional analysis, Choice D, therapists work with clients to understand their life scripts and how they may be edited to have a more functional life.

5. C: Conflict resolution is dependent on good communication; both parties should respect each other's opinions and eliminate negative verbal obstacles. Choices A and D are considered obstacles for effective communication and conflict resolution; forceful statements and unsolicited advice can disrupt rapport. Choice B is incorrect; conflict resolution involves defining the problem before reaching a solution.

Core Counseling Attributes

Awareness of Self and Impact on Clients

The process of acquiring values is important for counselors to keep in mind when working to understand where their own values and their clients' values originated. Counselors should be aware of their own moral codes, values, biases, and prejudices to avoid conflict with the treatment they are providing to clients. The process of acknowledging and controlling personal values in counseling practice is called **value suspension**. **Self-awareness** is a vital part of ensuring that one's personal values and beliefs do not intrude on the counselor/client relationship. It may be necessary to seek consultation from a supervisor or colleague in situations where one's personal values or beliefs conflict with those of the client and when those feelings cannot be resolved. In extreme cases where consultation and self-reflection cannot remedy the conflict, termination of the counselor/client relationship and referral to another therapist may be necessary.

Genuineness and Congruence

The term congruence is associated with the person-centered work of **Carl Rogers**. **Congruence** can be defined as genuineness on the part of counselors, in that there is agreement on their words and actions. Counselors display congruence when their body language, affect, and words correspond to demonstrate genuine concern for the client. Lack of congruence is revealed when counselors express concern but at the same time seem bored, disinterested, or use language that does not indicate a true understanding of the client. Counselors who are nonreactive or act as a blank screen for clients are not expressing congruence. Rogers considered congruence to be essential for effective counseling.

Knowledge of and Sensitivity to Gender Orientation and Gender Issues

The term **gender** refers to a range of physical, behavioral, psychological, or cultural characteristics that create the difference between masculinity and femininity. **Gender identity** is a person's understanding of his or her own gender, especially as it relates to being male or female. **Sexual orientation** is a more complex concept as it refers to the type of sexual attraction one feels for others. This is not to be confused with **sexual preference**, which refers to the specific types of sexual stimulation one most enjoys.

Types of Sexual Orientation
- **Heterosexual**: An individual who is sexually and emotionally attracted to members of the opposite gender, also known as "straight"

- **Homosexual**: An individual who is sexually and emotionally attracted to members of the same gender, sometimes referred to as "gay" or "lesbian"

- **Bisexual**: A male or female who is sexually attracted to both same and opposite gender sex partners

- **Asexual**: An individual who has a low level of interest in sexual interactions with others

Types of Gender Identity

- **Bi-gender**: An individual who fluctuates between the self-image of traditionally male and female stereotypes and identifies with both genders

- **Transgender**: A generalized term referring to a variety of sexual identities that do not fit under more traditional categories, a person who feels to be of a different gender than the one he or she is born with

- **Transsexual**: A person who identifies emotionally and psychologically with the gender other than that assigned at birth, lives as a person of the opposite gender

Those who are transgender or transsexual may be homosexual, heterosexual, or asexual. Being transgender can be defined as identifying as a gender other than the gender one was assigned at birth. Publicly sharing that one is transgender can be difficult for some individuals. Transgender individuals may live in a community where their identity is not positively accepted or is misunderstood, and they may feel shamed or ridiculed. It may be a difficult experience for close family members to understand the perspective of a transgender individual, which can affect the cohesiveness of family relationships and the family unit. Transgender individuals may also feel a lack of acknowledgement when others fail to use the correct pronouns or respect other identity wishes.

Some transgender individuals choose to medically transition to the gender they identify as. This is a procedure that requires physical, emotional, and psychological support. Individuals not receiving support during their transition can experience extreme feelings of sadness, isolation, and lack of belonging. Medically transitioning individuals also undergo hormonal changes in addition to surgical procedures, and these can cause unexpected feelings and reactions in the individual. There are also medical risks that go along with both the surgical and hormonal procedures of transitioning that the individual has to be aware of and manage. Finally, after the transition is complete, individuals may struggle with living as someone who is relatively unfamiliar to their friends, family members, and colleagues. The transgender person may or may not experience support and acceptance in these groups and relationships, and some group members may even act aggressively toward the transgender person. If this is the case, it may be helpful to find support groups where transgender individuals can find not only friendship and community, but also guidance on how to navigate their new life, society, friends and relationships, and medical recovery.

Knowledge of and Sensitivity to Multicultural Issues

Counselors must be adept at working with diverse populations. **Diversity** includes race, culture, gender, ethnicity, sexual orientation, socioeconomic status, religion, and age. As part of the profession, counselors will provide services to individuals and families with whom they have no cultural similarity. Thus, it is essential for counselors to develop and maintain a level of cultural competence. The first step is for them to engage in self-awareness and gain an understanding of their own identity, including their belief systems and biases. As part of the counseling process, counselors should be able to acknowledge differences and communicate to clients with trust and credibility while demonstrating mutual respect. They should engage in ongoing professional development to gain skills and awareness of differing cultural needs and, from an ethical standpoint, to ensure they are providing competent services. To maintain credibility and trust, counselors must clearly define issues and goals for counseling, taking into consideration cultural variations.

It is important not to use information about culture, race, and ethnicity in a stereotypical or overgeneralized manner. There are vast differences within groups. For example, group members holding a traditional viewpoint are likely to identify very strongly with their group and to reject the practices of other groups. In contrast, other individuals may be acculturated into a dominant group culture and may not identify with their culture of origin. With that caution in mind, some broad statements may be made to help counselors gain a better understanding of the ways in which race, culture, and/or ethnicity can influence behavior and attitude:

Native Americans

Core values include sharing, honor, respect, interdependence, obligation to family, group cohesion, and co-existence with nature.

Latinos

There is enormous variability among the various Latino groups due to the differences in their histories and cultural experiences. Values include family, avoidance of conflict, respect for others, religiosity, and patriarchy.

Asian Americans

Great diversity among groups should be noted, as this is a very broad category. Typically shared values across Asian cultures include family honor, deference to authority and to elders, humility, and avoidance of confrontation.

White Americans

Personal preferences and individualism are typically held in high regard. Values may include capitalism, individuality, and freedom.

African-Americans

Extended family is held as very important; women are viewed as the center and strength of the family unit. Church and the extended church community may play a large role in an individual or family's life. There is a distrust of government and authority figures.

Pacific Islanders and Native Hawaiians

Values include the interconnectedness between all people, not just family, that is related by blood, community, and sharing. They are often polytheistic, with a belief that spirits exist in animals and in objects.

Demonstrate Conflict Tolerance and Resolution

Helping clients deal with conflict requires resolution of negative emotions that result when individuals do not agree on a topic. Emotional detours, such as dominating or avoiding a situation, the inability to make decisions, and overaccommodating, can lead to emotional disturbances, including anger, anxiety, compulsions, and depression. Clients should be encouraged to express their initial positions, explore their underlying core concerns, and create a mutually agreed-upon plan that meets the expectations of all people involved. Conflict resolution is dependent on good communication. Obstacles such as threats, forceful opinions, and unsolicited advice can block effective communication. Counselors should also assess patterns of interaction, mediate effective dialogue, and block negative communication. The conflict resolution process begins with identifying concerns and establishing the importance of the confrontation. Taking turns defining the problem and acknowledging others' opinions can help build alternative solutions that satisfy conflicting ideals.

Empathic Attunement

Empathy is being able to relate to client circumstances and direction without the counselor actually experiencing it themselves. **Sympathy** differs from empathy in that sympathy is compassion for the client without having experienced the client's state of being. Empathy involves "being with" the client in their time and frame of mind. It involves connecting to the client on a visceral level while still maintaining some objectivity. **Attunement** occurs through listening to and watching the client. By tuning in to the client's words and body language, the counselor begins to experience empathy. The client's body language may reveal emotions that aren't being verbally communicated.

These emotions are usually subconscious, but sometimes they are emotions that the client doesn't feel safe sharing. Attunement to these unarticulated emotions, when expressed back to the client, can be a powerful way of showing the client they are in a place of safety and understanding. While working with a client, it is important to stay attuned to the changes in emotion and to pick up on the degree of comfort that the client has with moving forward and examining the emotions. In addition to feeling what the client is feeling, attunement can help the counselor guide the client through therapy at the rate that is most comfortable and effective for the client. Because empathy is the framework on which the counseling practice is built, it is imperative that counselors be empathetic with their clients. Those who cannot be empathetic should seek additional supervision or counsel in order to do their work effectively or refer the client to another counselor.

Empathic Responding

One of the most effective skills for encouraging clients to share and explore their emotions in counseling is **empathic responding**. The goals of empathic responding are for the client to know that the counselor understands exactly how they feel and to ultimately uncover the real significance and roots of their emotions. The counselor must have a deep sense of self-awareness in order to recall their own emotions from past experiences that enable the empathic response. Empathic responding is more than the counselor merely hearing the client and feeling pity for them, letting them know that they feel bad or happy for them, or telling them how awful, confusing, or stressful a situation must be. Empathic responding involves reflecting the emotions that the client expressed back to them and explaining the reasons for those feelings in a way that shows that the counselor can imagine being in the client's place.

It is crucial for the counselor to use words that describe precisely what the client is experiencing. This is not a time for problem-solving or judging the client's emotions. This is a time for the counselor to step away from their own perception of the client's problems and to step into the client's frame of reference and feel the same thing the client is feeling. When a counselor can show that they are simultaneously feeling the same emotions as the client without any judgment, the client should have no fear of being correct or incorrect in their expression of emotions. In this environment of true understanding and acceptance, the client will be more open to sharing their feelings. As the client's emotions are labeled accurately, the counselor and the client can deeply analyze and pinpoint the origins of the emotions and begin therapeutic change.

Fostering the Emergence of Group Therapeutic Factors

Counselors can foster the emergence of therapeutic factors to help the group successfully accomplish its goals. One of the most important initial therapeutic factors in group therapy is the promotion of cohesion, and counselors can accomplish this in several ways. For example, group leaders can promote cohesion by responding well when someone challenges their authority. The leader might ask the group if they agree with the challenge and what they think could be done differently to help the group. This, in turn, can help members bond with each other. Group leaders can also encourage empathy among members by calling upon individuals to check in with those who become emotionally dysregulated during sessions.

Counselors can promote therapeutic factors by helping members deal with conflicts appropriately. Instead of fearing conflict, the group can learn how to disagree without violating relationships within the group. The leader is often an important figure during conflicts because they monitor and provide space for safe discussions.

Counselors can also facilitate the emergence of therapeutic factors by showing care for all group members. When the leader demonstrates equal care for everyone in the group, members will likely feel safe to disclose more personal information. Not only does this encourage deeper disclosure, but it also provides the group members with an example of how they should act towards one another.

Additionally, counselors can provide insight to members about their behaviors and interchanges with each other. Counselors can use the group setting as a microcosm of the members' real-life situations by bringing about changes within the group that will result in outside transformations.

Non-Judgmental Stance

Counselors should treat all clients of all backgrounds with open-mindedness, without judgment, and with the client's desired intervention outcomes at the center of all interactions. Counselors may work with clients of different cultures, and counselors should respect the opinions and boundaries that these differences bring to treatment.

Counselors can communicate support and a nonjudgmental attitude through an open posture and eye gaze that shows interest but not intimidation. They should use a caring verbal tone and facial expressions, which indicate attention to what their clients are saying and can be used in addition to silence to create a positive environment for counseling.

Positive Regard

Carl Rogers believed that clients can begin to make changes independently once they experience positive regard from the counselor. **Positive regard** means that the counselor puts aside any judgment and embraces the client as a person of worth, not defining the client by their actions or expressions of emotions or beliefs. Counselors can show positive regard by allowing clients to speak freely about their behaviors, feelings, or thoughts without responding critically to what the client has said. The counselor should be able to communicate an understanding that the client is behaving or experiencing emotions to the best of their ability. This freedom from judgment then allows the client to be more accepting of themselves and more confident in their decisions to create change.

Respect and Acceptance for Diversity

Clients may come from all backgrounds. It is important that counselors do not make any prior negative judgments regarding the personality or life of any client. Each individual has worth. It is essential for counselors to be mindful of any personal prejudices or biases and employ empathy and sensitivity when working with the client.

133

The client must be allowed to disclose details of a situation to determine influences from his or her culture. This can be done by conducting an interview with the client about his or her background, customs, personal beliefs, values, and relationships. Appropriate group interviews with key members in the client's life can also provide additional verbal and nonverbal information.

It is recommended that in order to be effective, counselors engage in ongoing professional development to gain skills and awareness of differing cultural needs and ethical standpoints and to ensure they are providing competent services. To maintain credibility and trust, counselors must honor the client's motives and goals for the session, taking into consideration cultural variations.

Foundational Listening, Attending, and Reflecting Skills

Active listening is crucial to the relationship and rapport building stage with clients. Counselors must be fully engaged in the listening process and not distracted by thoughts of what will come next or intervention planning. The counselor must not only hear the audible language the client is offering but must also look at the non-verbal behaviors and the underlying meaning in the words and expressions of the client. **Nonverbal behaviors** include body language, facial expressions, voice quality, and physical reactions of the client. Other aspects of active listening include head nodding, eye contact, and using phrases of understanding and clarity (e.g., "What I hear you saying is . . ." and "You (may) wish to . . .") Counselors may verify they understand the client's message by paraphrasing and asking for validation that it is correct (e.g., "What I hear you saying is . . .").

Attending is the act of the counselor giving clients his or her full attention. Attending to the client shows respect for their needs, can encourage openness, and can create a sense of comfort and support in the counseling process. There are several ways for counselors to attend actively to clients, including maintaining appropriate eye contact, using reassuring body language and gestures, and monitoring their tone and expressions.

Reflecting is a basic counseling skill designed to build rapport and help clients become aware of underlying emotions. Counselors "reflect back" what a client says, both to indicate they are attending and also to analyze and interpret meanings. Reflecting is more than simply paraphrasing a client's words, as it involves more in-depth understanding and an attempt to elicit further information. An example would be a client stating, "I'm not sure what to do about my current relationship. I can't decide if I should stay or leave." The counselor would reflect by stating, "It sounds like you are conflicted about what to do; this is a difficult decision to make," and follow up with a probing question or allow time for the client to process and react.

Reflecting is one of several active listening and rapport-building skills but should not be overused. It is essential that the counselor be able to offer back meaningful restatements and not simply repeat back what is heard. It is also important that the counselor accurately reflects any feeling and does not project or misinterpret. In some cases, misinterpretation can help the client further clarify and is not detrimental to the relationship. By using reflection and clarification, any errors can be corrected. Even when errors occur, when the counselor clarifies what the client means, it communicates that the counselor is invested in understanding the client. From a cultural awareness standpoint, the counselor should be sensitive to any differences and ensure there is a level of trust prior to engaging in more in-depth reflection.

Practice Quiz

1. Reflection is a practice where counselors acknowledge the meaning behind a client's words. Why do counselors use reflection in sessions?
   a. To help clients understand underlying emotions
   b. To provide advice
   c. To set goals for sessions
   d. To allow for silence

2. Carl Rogers believed three core conditions must exist for effective counseling. What are those conditions?
   a. Trust, empathy, and kindness
   b. Empathy, positive regard, and kindness
   c. Genuineness, trust, and congruence
   d. Empathy, positive regard, and congruence

3. Group counselors need strong interpersonal skills in order to lead groups. Which skill is NOT required for a group counselor?
   a. Encouragement
   b. Support
   c. Confrontation
   d. Crisis intervention training

4. When a counselor "steps into a client's shoes" to see their view of life, which of the following techniques is the counselor using?
   a. Reframing
   b. Restructuring
   c. Empathizing
   d. Grounding

5. Which of the following is NOT true about a client's relationship with their counselor?
   a. Transference is possible.
   b. The counselor is in a position of authority to the client.
   c. The counselor can educate the client.
   d. It is appropriate for the counselor and client to become friends during the therapeutic relationship.

See answers on the next page.

Answer Explanations

1. A: To help clients understand underlying emotions. Reflection is also referred to as "reflection of feeling" and is used for counselors to indicate that they both hear and understand the meanings and emotions behind a client's words. Counselors do not provide advice during reflection, but let the client know they are being heard, so Choice *B* is incorrect. There is also no goal setting during this time, because it's important for the client to know their emotions are being validated, making Choice *C* incorrect. When reflection happens, the counselor provides communication to the client, so silence has less to do with it than Choice *A*, making Choice *D* incorrect.

2. D: Carl Rogers developed the person-centered approach to counseling, which stressed the important of the counseling relationship, as well as the need to evaluate therapy for effectiveness. Carl Rogers's three core conditions for effective counseling were empathy, positive regard, and congruence (genuineness).

3. D: Crisis intervention training is not needed for a group counselor, but the ability to encourage, support, and confront are necessary skills. A group counselor needs to have all the skills and training that an individual counselor would require. Encouraging group members, being supportive, and the ability to confront behavior are all skills needed and utilized by counselors.

4. C: Empathizing is when counselors try to understand the client's point of view by considering who they are and their life experiences that contribute to their perspectives. The remaining choices are incorrect.

5. D: Choice *D* is correct because it would be considered a dual relationship and would therefore be an ethical violation. Choice *A* is incorrect because it is possible for a client to have a reaction to their counselor based on earlier relationships. Choice *B* and *C* are also true.

NCE Practice Test #1

1. A counselor is teaching her client about gender differences that are evident in young preschool children's language skills. This is an example of which of the following?
   a. Racism
   b. Gender bias
   c. Psychoeducation
   d. Shaping

2. When working with a client who has a phobia, a counselor should NOT encourage the client to do which of the following?
   a. Talk about why they fear the object or situation.
   b. Progressively face the feared object or situation.
   c. Avoid the feared object or situation.
   d. Practice deep breathing.

3. A counselor has spent several months working with a woman who was initially diagnosed with anxiety. Her symptoms have greatly improved, and the counselor can see that the end of treatment is approaching. What would be the least appropriate action for the counselor to take?
   a. Have a discussion with the client about her progress and inform her that treatment is about to end.
   b. Ask the client if she has any other issues that she would like to address.
   c. Avoid talking about the end of treatment to prevent the client's anxiety from returning.
   d. Discuss how ending the counseling relationship may cause feelings of sadness or fear.

4. When a group counselor sees that members' conflict with each other is escalating to an unhealthy level, what is the most beneficial tactic for the counselor to use?
   a. Address the conflict between the group members, but let it run its course
   b. Address the conflict and help resolve it because it may cause damage to the group
   c. Stay out of the conflict entirely
   d. End the group

5. Which of the following refers to the perspective someone holds about society on a domestic and global scale?
   a. Worldview
   b. Cultural encapsulation
   c. Ethnicity
   d. Ethnocentrism

6. What is the main concern of a counselor when their client shows signs of hopelessness?
   a. The client may be suicidal.
   b. The treatment has been ineffective.
   c. The client needs a referral for medication.
   d. The client is depressed.

7. What is one of the most important tasks a counselor must accomplish within the first couple of sessions?
   a. Payment method
   b. Therapeutic alliance
   c. Diagnosis
   d. Treatment Plan

8. Which of the following indicates that a client is at high risk for suicide?
   a. The client has attempted suicide previously.
   b. The client is thinking about suicide but has no definite plan.
   c. The client has been diagnosed with depression.
   d. The client does not have a healthy support system.

9. Clients who distance themselves from others to prevent feeling dependent and getting hurt have an anxious-avoidant attachment style. What kind of practice will help prevent loneliness in these clients?
   a. Focusing on the future
   b. Personalizing situations
   c. Initiating a relationship with a partner who also has an avoidant attachment style
   d. Practicing empathy

10. Which of the following is a popular statistical software program?
   a. SPSS
   b. SAS
   c. Minitab
   d. All of the above

11. A client tells the counselor she has developed healthy coping mechanisms for her anger issues and is ready to terminate therapy. What strategy will the counselor perform next?
   a. Obtain client feedback prior to ending the therapy session
   b. Reflect on the client's progress and how they plan to continue growth
   c. Encourage the client to continue therapy to ensure progress
   d. Offer the client an opportunity to visit the office as desired

12. Fluid Intelligence refers to what type of abilities?
   a. Thinking and acting quickly, solving new problems
   b. Utilizing learned skills
   c. Adapting to new situations
   d. Developing opportunity from adversity

13. If a client reports that she has been eating soap for the past two months, the counselor should consider which of the following?
   a. Admitting the client to a hospital
   b. Diagnosing the client with pica
   c. Sending the client for a brain scan
   d. Diagnosing the client with anorexia nervosa

14. A 30-year-old client calls her counselor at 8:00 p.m. indicating that she is "at her wit's end." Upon further probing, the counselor learns that the client has a gun in her home, has thoughts of killing herself, and is feeling hopeless. The client lives alone. Which of the following would NOT be an acceptable step for the counselor to take?
    a. Call the police and give them the client's name, address, and phone number.
    b. Call the client's neighbor and ask him to check on the client.
    c. Ask the client to drive to the nearest hospital for an evaluation.
    d. Call the client's fiancé who has come to counseling on several occasions.

15. During couples counseling, one of the clients expresses that she rarely voices her opinions to her partner for fear of starting a conflict. What kind of communication style is characterized by this behavior?
    a. Aggressive
    b. Assertive
    c. Passive
    d. Obstructing

16. A client starts to consume an addictive substance more frequently after seeing a counselor for several months. The counselor should consider referring the client to a residential treatment facility if:
    a. The client is unable to perform their daily responsibilities.
    b. The client's family members keep contacting the counselor about the excessive consumption.
    c. The client receives a DWI.
    d. The client does not want to attend Alcoholics or Narcotics Anonymous.

17. Harry Harlow noticed that monkeys who did not receive consistent warmth or affection from a maternal figure were more likely to be which of the following?
    a. Less warm or affectionate to their own offspring
    b. Aloof and/or angry
    c. Socially impaired
    d. All of the above

18. A counselor is working with a married couple. Often, the husband speaks to his wife in a demeaning tone, moves his body aggressively toward her, looks down at her, and speaks loudly. The counselor demonstrates for the husband a different way to speak to his wife. This is an example of which of the following?
    a. Negative feedback loop
    b. Overstepping the husband's boundaries
    c. Confrontation
    d. Building communication skills

19. Tina is conducting a research study about underage drinking habits on college campuses on football game days. As she's scoring her collected data, she notices the test group is primarily made up of freshman students, and the control group is primarily made up of sophomore students. What does Tina realize about this distinction?
    a. It's to be expected.
    b. It may confound her results.
    c. It won't make a difference if she runs enough ANOVA tests.
    d. It should be tabulated in a chi-square cross section.

20. When is Critical Incident Stress Debriefing (CISD) most effective?
    a. When it is provided to individuals
    b. When it is provided by trained mental health professionals
    c. When it is provided within seven days of the incident
    d. When it is provided within 24 to 72 hours

21. Some issues that adults over 60 face and may want to discuss in counseling include what?
    a. Bereavement, ageism in the workforce, and unemployment
    b. The millennial generation, religion, and politics
    c. Sagging skin, hair loss, and cancer
    d. None of the above

22. Claudia is coming to therapy for the first time. She meets her therapist, Susan, a licensed clinical social worker, and Susan tells her what she can expect from treatment. Claudia says that she understands the process of therapy, as well as the risks, and that she is excited to begin. Susan makes a note of their discussion and begins her assessment. Has Susan satisfied the informed consent requirement? Why or why not?
    a. Yes. Susan discussed the process and risks of therapy, and the client agreed.
    b. No. Susan didn't ask Claudia if she understood everything fully.
    c. No. Susan did not have Claudia sign a consent form.
    d. Yes. Susan made a note that Claudia agreed as part of her documentation.

23. Which of the following Gestalt therapy techniques focuses on role reversal and engaging the client's thoughts and behaviors?
    a. The Hunger Illusion
    b. The Empty Chair
    c. The Miracle Question
    d. Virtual reality

24. When determining whether to give a diagnosis of enuresis or encopresis, the counselor should consider which of the following?
    a. Chronological age
    b. Whether the symptoms are voluntary or involuntary
    c. Developmental age
    d. Whether the symptoms occur during the day or night

25. Which of the following is NOT a central component of Carl Rogers's client-centered therapy?
    a. The counselor demonstrates unconditional positive regard.
    b. The therapist is congruent with the client.
    c. The counselor empathizes with the client.
    d. The counselor is a good listener.

26. A psychodynamic therapy group has been meeting for six months. Some group members have formed friendships and want to have dinner together. Is this possible in a psychodynamic group and, if so, under what conditions?
    a. Yes, if the group leader goes with them.
    b. Yes, with or without the group leader.
    c. No, psychodynamic groups cannot have outside contact.
    d. Yes, if all the group members go out together.

27. A counselor who has been working with an anorexic client arranges a session to discuss treatment progress. Which of the following would be the least beneficial in helping the client move toward her treatment goals?
   a. Asking the client to show the counselor her personal journal
   b. Showing the client her pre-treatment, mid-treatment, and current psychometric assessment scores
   c. Asking the client to bring her recent medical tests for discussion
   d. Asking the client if her family relationships are improving or declining

28. Client information is protected by confidentiality. However, in the instance where a client makes a threat against another individual during treatment, the social worker is required to warn the individual, thus breaking confidentiality. What court case established the duty to warn?
   a. *Tarasoff vs. Regents of University of California*
   b. *Regents of University of California vs. Bakke*
   c. *Blonder-Tongue vs. University of Illinois*
   d. *Fisher vs. University of Texas*

29. The cycle of violence follows which of the following sequences?
   a. Honeymoon, explosion, tension building
   b. Tension building, honeymoon, explanation
   c. Explosion, honeymoon, reunification
   d. Tension building, explosion, honeymoon

30. A counselor believes that a client's relationship with her fiancé is worsening her depression because he is emotionally abusive. Which of the following would NOT be an appropriate action for the counselor to take?
   a. Tell the client to stop seeing her fiancé.
   b. Help the client identify her fiancé's abusive treatment.
   c. Have the client bring her fiancé to counseling.
   d. Recommend a book about emotional abuse.

31. Which of the following is a reason client confidentiality may be breached without consent?
   a. A client expresses he wants to physically harm his partner.
   b. A client expresses feelings of sadness throughout the day.
   c. A client's friend calls the counselor to ask about the client's progress.
   d. The client states he wants to terminate treatment.

32. Which of the following is a holistic model that helps clients focus on the present and work toward personal growth and balance?
   a. Gestalt therapy
   b. Person-centered therapy
   c. Rational emotive therapy
   d. Jungian therapy

33. During an initial interview, counselors should ask questions pertaining to which of the following realms?
   a. Work, rest, play
   b. Scholastic, interpersonal, medical
   c. Biological, social, psychological
   d. Psychological, occupational, social

141

34. A counselor is working with a family and observes that whenever the father belittles the mother, the adolescent son corrects the father. This is an example of which of the following?
   a. Electra complex
   b. Parentification
   c. Paradoxical intervention
   d. Motivational interviewing

35. Which of the following is a valid reason for clients to terminate group counseling?
   a. A reduction in primary symptoms
   b. Regression of goal achievement
   c. Dependent coping
   d. An independent decision by a group leader

36. When does negative transference occur?
   a. When counselors project feelings onto clients
   b. When clients project feelings toward another person in the past onto the counselor
   c. When multiple roles exist between a therapist and a client
   d. When clients become angry or hostile toward counselors

37. What is one of the most important elements of an intake interview?
   a. Making an accurate diagnosis
   b. Obtaining a recent medical report from the client's doctor to rule out medical conditions that may masquerade as psychological conditions
   c. Asking open-ended questions
   d. Obtaining permission to break confidentiality if the client becomes suicidal

38. A counselor has been working with a client for the past nine months. The counselor first diagnosed the client with major depressive disorder after administering the Beck Depression Inventory (BDI), which resulted in a high score for depression. Three months into treatment, the BDI was administered again, and the client's symptoms were unchanged. In the ninth month of treatment, the BDI was administered again and at that time showed slight improvement in the client's symptoms. What would the counselor most likely conclude from these test results?
   a. The client was faking symptoms at the initial assessment.
   b. The BDI is an untrustworthy assessment tool because of its inconsistent results.
   c. The client should be referred to another counselor because he or she is not making adequate improvement, and the counselor is concerned about suicide risk.
   d. The treatment may be working, but alterations to the treatment plan may be needed.

39. What entity was responsible for supporting and expanding professional counseling services?
   a. The first mental health clinic in the United States
   b. The United States Department of Veterans Affairs
   c. The United States Army
   d. Carl Rogers' first privately funded organization

40. What is the approximate rate of divorce for second marriages in the United States?
   a. 65 percent
   b. 35 percent
   c. 50 percent
   d. 85 percent

41. A counselor has been working with a female client who has bipolar disorder for several months. Upon seeing no improvement in her symptoms, the counselor reminds her that completing the homework assignments is akin to taking medication; if she does not comply, she will likely not get better. Under what condition would this be appropriate?
    a. The psychiatrist agrees with the counselor.
    b. The counselor believes that the client is not complying with the treatment directives.
    c. A counselor should not make a comparison between medication compliance and homework assignments.
    d. The treatment has been occurring for more than six months.

42. Which of the following statements regarding sexual dysfunction is true?
    a. Sexual dysfunction only occurs during the orgasm phase.
    b. Sexual dysfunction is a medical problem, and the client should be referred to a physician.
    c. Sexual dysfunction only occurs in 10% of the population.
    d. Sexual dysfunction can occur during any of the four phases of the sexual response cycle.

43. What occurs during the pre-group preparation phase of group therapy?
    a. Informed consent is obtained, previous group experiences are discussed, and group members learn about each other's diagnoses.
    b. Alliance with the leader is established, informed consent is obtained, and client goals and limits of confidentiality are discussed.
    c. Informed consent is obtained, limits of confidentiality are discussed, and group members learn about each other's diagnoses.
    d. A waiver of confidentiality is signed, and the leader's role and client goals are discussed.

44. What are groups called that provide guidance, problem prevention, and skills building?
    a. Psychoeducational
    b. Structured
    c. Gestalt
    d. Psychodynamic

45. A 65-year-old male counselor is working with a 25-year-old male client. When the client comes to sessions, he is often short-tempered. Which of the following would be the most beneficial to the client?
    a. The counselor talks with the client about his short temper.
    b. The counselor overlooks the client's tone in an effort not to break the therapeutic bond.
    c. The counselor angrily replies to the client to demonstrate what it feels like to be treated in that manner.
    d. The counselor refers the client to another counselor.

46. In what year did the ACA launch the National Board for Certified Counselors?
    a. 1963
    b. 1973
    c. 1982
    d. 1993

47. A student receives daily threats from a classmate via text messages. Which of the following defines this kind of bullying?
    a. Cyberbullying
    b. Physical bullying
    c. Relational bullying
    d. Group bullying

48. Joe's parents divorced when he was six years old, and his father moved out of the house. He is now receiving therapy and has become very angry with his male therapist, fearing the therapist will abandon him. Joe's reaction is an example of what?
    a. Remorse
    b. Fixation
    c. Negative reinforcement
    d. Transference

49. A counselor is working with a client who has difficulty making and keeping friends. The counselor gives the client feedback about his inappropriate statements at various times to teach him social skills. Which of the following would NOT be an appropriate tool/technique for the counselor to use?
    a. EMDR
    b. Modeling socially appropriate statements
    c. Role-playing with the client
    d. Having the client watch a movie that demonstrates both appropriate and inappropriate social skills

50. A type II error _____ a _____ null hypothesis.
    a. rejects; true
    b. rejects; false
    c. fails to reject; true
    d. fails to reject; false

51. Positive interactions help develop the therapeutic relationship and encourage clients to meet their goals. What are the four stages of a positive interaction in counseling?
    a. Exploration, consolidation, planning, and termination
    b. Initiation, clarification, structure, and relationship
    c. Initiation, consolidation, planning, and termination
    d. Exploration, clarification, planning, and relationship

52. Social workers strive to consider cultural impact on individual values. How should cultural differences and values be addressed?
    a. Cultural values and differences should be pointed out so that the client knows the social worker is aware of them.
    b. Cultural values and differences should be learned by the social worker and worked around when issues arise.
    c. Cultural values and differences should be learned by the social worker and used as strengths to empower change.
    d. Cultural values and differences should be compared to the greater society to find similarities.

144

53. Under what conditions would it be inappropriate for a counselor to contact a client who was discharged from treatment six months ago?
    a.   The counselor cares about the client and wants to make sure they are still doing well.
    b.   The counselor remembers that the client had other issues that should be addressed.
    c.   It is the client's birthday.
    d.   It is the client's anniversary.

54. During which stage of the transtheoretical model is the client most motivated to create change?
    a.   Precontemplation stage
    b.   Contemplation stage
    c.   Preparation stage
    d.   Maintenance stage

55. The REACH model offers five steps to achieving forgiveness. Which of the following are components of that model?
    a.   Remember, Expect, Acquiesce, Consider, Harbor
    b.   Reflect, Examine, Acknowledge, Consider, Hold
    c.   Recall, Excel, Accept, Count, Happiness
    d.   Recall, Empathize, Altruistic Gift, Commit, Hold

56. Which of the following is an index that measures someone's ability to connect with others, develop relationships, and show empathy?
    a.   Intelligence Quotient
    b.   Emotional Quotient
    c.   Emotional Achievement
    d.   Emotional Handling

57. Why is depression a greater concern in older adults?
    a.   Older adults do not have coping mechanisms to deal with depression.
    b.   Depression does not happen in the older adult population.
    c.   Older adults are incapable of asking for help.
    d.   Symptoms of depression are often overlooked in older adults.

58. Counselors can help clients learn how to handle their negative emotions in a healthy way by having them acknowledge the emotions for what they are and then teaching them how to gain personal distance from the emotions so that they are not controlled by them. This technique is known as which of the following?
    a.   Cognitive defusion
    b.   Psychogenic fugue
    c.   Enmeshment
    d.   Differentiation

59. One fundamental difference between probability sampling and non-probability sampling is that probability sampling uses _____, while non-probability sampling does not.
    a.   convenience
    b.   randomization
    c.   volunteerism
    d.   referral

145

60. Blocking refers to what type of act in group counseling?
    a. A leader putting a stop to negative behavior
    b. Members being disruptive to the process
    c. A leader locking the door to prevent members from exiting
    d. Existing members not welcoming new members to the group

61. A practitioner is reviewing her appointment schedule and notices that her next client has a traditional Chinese name. The practitioner should assume _____.
    a. that the office translator will need to be present for the session and should be summoned immediately in order to ensure the client's comfort
    b. that the client is an only child
    c. that the client is male
    d. nothing

62. Which of the following is unethical?
    a. Referring a client to another counselor because the counselor does not have the proper training to treat the client's issues
    b. Referring a client to another counselor because the counselor does not like the client's religious preference
    c. Accepting a referral from another counselor because the other counselor does not like the client's religious preference
    d. Accepting a referral from another counselor because the other counselor has not been trained to treat the client's issues

63. Which of the following is a symptom of schizophrenia?
    a. Multiple personalities present in one individual
    b. Hallucinations
    c. Sleepwalking
    d. Night terrors

64. A large, multi-story building that serves as the primary office for a business corporation in the United States only has stairs available to access each floor and the main front door. There are no elevators within in the building, and there is no ramp anywhere outside of any of the external doors. Additionally, all of the doors that lead into the building are revolving doors, which the corporation cites as being more energy-efficient. This organization is in direct violation of _____.
    a. Individuals with Disabilities Education Act (IDEA)
    b. Americans with Disabilities Act of 1990 (ADA)
    c. Workforce Innovation and Opportunity Act
    d. The Hidden Job Market

65. Which of the following guidelines is endorsed by the American Counseling Association Competencies for Counseling with Transgender Clients?
    a. Refer to the client by whatever gender the counselor perceives them to be.
    b. Use nonsexist language when communicating with the client.
    c. Encourage the client to accept their biological gender.
    d. Avoid talking about gender-role stereotyping.

66. A small country like Denmark—where most people hold the same cultural beliefs, education status, dress, and traditions—is considered a/an _____; a larger country like the United States— where people come from many diverse backgrounds and many have emigrated from other countries— is considered a/an_____.
   a. narrow country; broad country
   b. ethnography; demography
   c. homogenous society; heterogeneous society
   d. heterogeneous society; homogenous society

67. A client indicates that she recently suffered from a blackout when drinking alcohol. What would be the most appropriate next step for the counselor to take?
   a. Have the client admitted to an inpatient alcohol treatment program.
   b. Ask additional questions about the client's alcohol consumption.
   c. Begin treating the client for alcoholism.
   d. Refer the client to an outpatient alcohol program such as AA.

68. Risky shift phenomenon refers to what aspect of group dynamics?
   a. Groups becoming increasingly risk-averse
   b. Groups becoming less risk-averse
   c. Leaders encouraging individual members to take risks
   d. Closed groups considering taking on new members

69. Maslow's hierarchy of needs is composed of five levels. Which needs are included in Level 4?
   a. Cognitive and aesthetic
   b. Food and shelter
   c. Safety and order
   d. Love and belonging

70. What is the main difference between persistent depressive disorder and major depressive disorder?
   a. Overeating/undereating
   b. Hallucinations
   c. Feelings of hopelessness
   d. The length of time that symptoms are present

71. A counselor is providing telemental health services to her clients via email. Under what condition(s) would this be ethical?
   a. The email server is secure and no one in the counselor's home has access to it.
   b. The counselor is in the same state as the client.
   c. The counselor tells her clients that the email service is insecure.
   d. Email communications are not allowed in telemental health counseling.

72. The phrase "neurons that fire together, wire together" describes which of the following?
   a. The process of repetition by which neural pathways in the brain are formed
   b. The process by which memories are formed in the brain
   c. The process by which neurotransmitters send chemical messages from one to another
   d. The process by which nuclei of brain cells send chemical messages within the cell body

73. Desensitization is a behavior modification technique designed to replace an anxiety-producing stimulus with a relaxation response. Which is NOT one of the stages of desensitization?
    a. Exposure to the object or action of fear
    b. Avoidance of the object or action of fear
    c. Creation of a fear hierarchy
    d. Learning relaxation techniques

74. Which of the following is NOT a factor of a mental status exam?
    a. Orientation to time
    b. Whether the client is guarded or unguarded
    c. Appropriate displays of emotion
    d. Authenticity

75. A young client who was adopted at age 12 has been skipping school, is verbally aggressive toward his adoptive parents, and does not follow house rules. The counselor should recognize that this may be occurring for which of the following reasons?
    a. The adoptive parents are setting house rules that are too strict.
    b. The client is going through a normal stage of development.
    c. Behavior issues are significantly more common in adopted children.
    d. The client is experiencing bullying at school.

76. A counselor is working with a client who suffers from anxiety. The client is a Buddhist who is considering dating a Muslim. Which of the following would NOT be a helpful focus for this client?
    a. Having the client go through a value-sorting card set
    b. Discussing the similarities and differences between the religions
    c. Having the client consider what the familial implications could be
    d. Discouraging the client from dating the person because it might escalate their anxiety

77. Which of the following is another term for horizontal interventions in group counseling?
    a. Interpersonal
    b. Intrapersonal
    c. Individual
    d. Organizational

78. Sixteen-year-old Jake is at his great-grandfather's 95th birthday party. Jake is talking with his great-grandparents, grandparents, parents, and siblings. Jake's great-grandparents, who have been married for over 70 years, believe couples should stick it out no matter what. Jake and his siblings believe most people will divorce once in their lifetimes. The grandparents believe divorce can usually be avoided, and the parents believe divorce is sometimes necessary. This is an example of which concept of Murray Bowen's family systems theory?
    a. Differentiation of self
    b. Family projection process
    c. Multigenerational transmission process
    d. Emotional cutoff

79. When parents disagree over a parenting issue, a counselor should instruct them to do all of the following EXCEPT:
    a. Disagree calmly in front of the child to display conflict resolution.
    b. Disagree in private where the child cannot hear what they are saying.
    c. Concede to each other at times.
    d. Set the issue aside until they can talk about it with the counselor at the next session.

80. When performing a mental status examination, a counselor asks their client what she would do if she found a wallet with money inside. The counselor is assessing which of the following domains?
    a. Short-term memory
    b. Abstract reasoning
    c. Spatial orientation
    d. Judgment

81. Which of the following is a major concern when providing counseling services electronically?
    a. Technology limitations cannot be discussed with the client.
    b. Rapport with the client cannot be established.
    c. There are limitations to client confidentiality.
    d. Counselors will need to establish a social media account.

82. When working with individuals in the LGBT community, it's important for a counselor to do what?
    a. Be an active member of the LGBT community.
    b. Assist the client in locating gender-neutral jobs.
    c. Consult with other professionals, and refer out when necessary.
    d. Reach out to employers to provide education about discriminatory hiring practices.

83. What are the stages for Kübler-Ross' five-stage model for grief?
    a. Anger, denial, bargaining, resolution, sadness
    b. Denial, anger, bargaining, depression, acceptance
    c. Denial, panic, sadness, anger, frustration
    d. Sadness, anger, bargaining, denial, acceptance

84. According to Erikson's stages of psychosocial development, in what stage is a five-year-old child?
    a. Initiative vs. guilt
    b. Trust vs. mistrust
    c. Autonomy vs. shame and doubt
    d. Identity vs. confusion

85. A 25-year-old, unemployed male who has recently returned from combat claims to experience reoccurring nightmares, angry outbursts, and feelings of depression. A counselor who wants to use a theory-based treatment method for this client would likely decide which of the following?
    a. The client has PTSD and should have psychoanalysis.
    b. The client has major depressive disorder and should have CBT.
    c. The client has PTSD and should have EMDR.
    d. The client is faking symptoms so that he will not have to find a job.

149

86. Which of the following is a method used in therapy to address sleep disorders?
    a. Tell the client how many hours of sleep he or she should be getting.
    b. Encourage the client to take a sleeping aid nightly.
    c. Have the client keep a sleep diary.
    d. Suggest the client change the sleep-wake schedule as needed.

87. A counselor is working with a client who is talking to other people who are not present during the session. The client is likely having what experience?
    a. Auditory hallucinations
    b. Delusions of grandeur
    c. Dissociative fugue
    d. Depersonalization

88. What are the differences between substantive advice and process advice?
    a. Substantive advice is nondirective; process advice is directive.
    b. Substantive advice is directive; process advice is encouraging.
    c. Substantive advice is directive; process advice is empowering.
    d. Substantive advice is fact-based; process advice is feeling-based.

89. According to Erikson's psychosocial model of development, what is the main task during the Generativity vs. Stagnation stage?
    a. Learning to trust others
    b. Finding oneself
    c. Contributing to the next generation
    d. Developing self-sufficiency

90. During the Strange Situation test, a counselor observes that the child becomes upset when the caregiver leaves the room and also avoids eye contact with strangers. What kind of attachment style does this behavior represent?
    a. Anxious-resistant insecure
    b. Depressed
    c. Secure
    d. Anxious-avoidant insecure

91. A counselor shares with her client that she was hospitalized for depression years ago. Which of the following is true?
    a. The counselor should not share personal information because it would derail the client's trust in her.
    b. This is appropriate if it would benefit the client.
    c. This is appropriate if the client had been previously hospitalized for a mental illness.
    d. This is appropriate if the counselor was about to hospitalize the client for depression.

92. What is the most difficult part of forgiveness called?
    a. Emotional
    b. Decisional
    c. Situational
    d. Conditional

150

93. Which of the psychologists below was a pioneer in humanistic theories?
    a. Wilhelm Wundt
    b. Sigmund Freud
    c. Carl Rogers
    d. Raymond Cattell

94. The Gottman Method is a type of therapy used for what kind of benefit?
    a. To enhance self-direction
    b. To incorporate a holistic view of people's environments
    c. To gain awareness of the present moment
    d. To strengthen relationships and improve interactional patterns

95. When a person with schizophrenia believes that the world is going to come to an end by a tsunami, that belief would be considered which of the following?
    a. Persecutory delusion
    b. Nihilistic delusion
    c. Grandiose delusion
    d. Referential delusion

96. A counselor has been using Adlerian therapy with a client for several months to help her overcome shyness but has not made significant progress. At this time, what should the counselor do?
    a. Refer the client to a psychiatrist for medication evaluation.
    b. Refer the client to another counselor.
    c. Use the empty chair technique.
    d. Consider using another treatment method.

97. A client tells her counselor, "I'm afraid that I'm going to die every time I have a panic attack. It feels like I'm having a heart attack." The counselor responds, "When you have a panic attack, you feel physical sensations in your heart that can make you feel like something is physically wrong." This is an example of which of the following?
    a. Modeling
    b. Reflection
    c. Congruence
    d. Unconditional positive regard

98. Under what conditions is it appropriate to discuss spiritual issues with clients?
    a. The client and the counselor are of the same faith.
    b. The client and the counselor do not attend the same church.
    c. The client and the counselor are of different faiths.
    d. The client has agreed to discuss spiritual issues in counseling.

99. What are the main components of the Cognitive Information Processing (CIP) career development theory?
    a. Communication and analysis
    b. Synthesis and valuing
    c. Valuing and executing
    d. Content and process

151

100. A male counselor is working with a group. One of the male group members has berated several of the other members at various times. On one occasion, the therapist yells at the belligerent group member to give feedback. Which of the following is true?
    a. If the group member and the counselor were both females, this would be appropriate.
    b. If the counselor was a female and the member was a male, this would be appropriate.
    c. This would be appropriate if it demonstrated protection of the group.
    d. This would never be appropriate.

101. When working with counseling clients online, one way to maintain the privacy section of the ACA Code of Ethics is to do which of the following?
    a. Encrypt all client intake information, communications, evaluations, and other related records.
    b. Use personal servers to store client information.
    c. Print all of the client's records, and store them in a filing cabinet.
    d. Let the client know before you begin treatment that you cannot guarantee any privacy when working virtually.

102. When a client is sleeping less than three hours per night, the counselor should consider all of the following EXCEPT:
    a. Referring the client to a sleep testing clinic
    b. Referring the client to a psychiatrist for medication
    c. Offering the client a bottle of melatonin since it is all natural
    d. Teaching the client progressive relaxation techniques

103. Albert Roberts designed a seven-stage model to deal with a crisis and provide effective intervention and support. What are the initial three tasks of Roberts's seven-stage model of crisis intervention?
    a. Assessments, identifying problems, and referring out
    b. Establishing contact, providing counseling, and referring out
    c. Assessments, establishing rapport, and identifying cause of crisis
    d. Intervention, assessments, and treatment

104. A study is considered to have strong external validity if the researcher can replicate and generalize its findings across multiple instances of what three factors?
    a. Population, time, and environment
    b. Gender, age, and height
    c. Animal studies, human studies, and non-living object studies
    d. Infant years, adolescent years, and adult years

105. According to Murray Bowen's family systems theory, a strong sense of self is associated with _____, while a weak sense of self is associated with _____.
    a. confidence and pragmatism; seeking approval from others
    b. only children; many siblings
    c. authoritative parenting styles; laissez-faire parenting styles
    d. physical strength; physical weakness

106. All end-of-life concerns are suitable for a counselor to work with a client on EXCEPT:
    a. Medication management
    b. Religious issues
    c. Financial matters
    d. With the client's written consent, communication with their family

152

107. In a group counseling session, the therapist asks, "Why didn't anyone say something about Samuel missing the last two meetings?" This is an example of which of the following?
    a. Giving interpersonal feedback
    b. Uncovering psychodynamic transference reactions
    c. Therapist transparency
    d. A therapist would not make this kind of remark.

108. Which of the following is NOT a physical symptom of anxiety?
    a. Feeling the need to urinate
    b. Having trouble sleeping
    c. Feeling weak or tired
    d. Sweating

109. An individual leaves early for their commute to work to avoid traffic. This is an example of what?
    a. Modeling
    b. Negative reinforcement
    c. Positive reinforcement
    d. Classical conditioning

110. Family units need guidance in dealing with problems and learning how to function more effectively, just as individuals do. Which is NOT a goal of family therapy?
    a. Resolving intrapsychic conflicts
    b. Increasing effective communication
    c. Creating more effective patterns
    d. Improving overall functioning and stability

111. A counselor is working with a client who is bothered by ruminating thoughts about losing his job two months ago. The counselor should consider all of the following EXCEPT:
    a. Working with the client using a five-column CBT chart
    b. Teaching the client progressive relaxation
    c. Referring the client to a psychiatrist for medication
    d. Using the empty-chair technique

112. Which of the following is an example of qualitative research?
    a. A counselor facilitates a discussion for a focus group of people claiming to experience hallucinations.
    b. A counselor conducts a survey over what type of hallucinations a group of people experience.
    c. A counselor compares and contrasts the type of hallucinations a group experiences.
    d. A counselor looks for patterns across the hallucinations a group experiences.

113. Which of the following is a focus area when counseling adult clients with attention-deficit hyperactivity disorder (ADHD)?
    a. Depression
    b. Conflict resolution
    c. Group therapy
    d. Dependency

114. If a counselor were to shame a client for disclosing hidden aspects of their life, the counselor would NOT be demonstrating which of the following?
   a. Congruence
   b. Unconditional positive regard
   c. Modeling
   d. Genuineness

115. A counselor is working with a combat veteran who was recently discharged. Which of the following is NOT likely to be a symptom that the veteran would display?
   a. Nightmares
   b. Avoidance of people he or she cares about
   c. Angry outbursts
   d. Psychosis

116. How does instrumental grieving differ from intuitive grieving?
   a. Instrumental grieving is thinking-based; intuitive grieving is feeling-based.
   b. Instrumental grieving is action-oriented; intuitive grieving is passive.
   c. Instrumental grieving is more feminine; intuitive grieving is more masculine.
   d. Instrumental grieving is anger; intuitive grieving is acceptance.

117. Which of the following often leads to preconceived notions, stereotyping, and unsupported assumptions of others who come from different backgrounds?
   a. Acculturation
   b. Assimilation
   c. Cultural encapsulation
   d. Worldview

118. According to the Substance Abuse and Mental Health Services Administration (SAMHSA), all of the following are considered protective factors against suicide EXCEPT:
   a. Membership in a place of worship
   b. Intact marriage
   c. Attendance in a 12-step group
   d. One year of sobriety

119. Symptoms of professional burnout include fatigue, headache, insomnia, depression, anxiety, boredom, and others. When does burnout in counselors and helping professionals occur?
   a. When countertransference is not managed
   b. When counselors become desensitized to client issues
   c. When counselors are overworked
   d. When clients regularly cancel or don't show

120. A counselor is meeting with a client for the first time. After hearing the client describe multiple issues, what is the best course of action for the counselor to take?
   a. The counselor should ask the client what he would like the focus of treatment to be.
   b. The counselor should tell the client what the focus of treatment should be.
   c. The counselor should send the client to a psychiatrist for a medication evaluation.
   d. The counselor should send the client to a psychologist to run a battery of psychological assessments.

121. A teenager receiving counseling for anger management discloses to the counselor that she is upset with her parents because they took away her car keys after she continually disobeyed curfew hours. What kind of technique can the counselor use to help the teenager understand the reasoning behind these actions?
   a. Cognitive reframing
   b. Reminiscence therapy
   c. Cognitive processing
   d. Ego state therapy

122. A counselor asks a client what methods they have previously used to overcome problems in their life. What type of treatment strategy is the counselor using?
   a. Identification of cognitive distortions
   b. A gestalt approach
   c. Strengths-based counseling
   d. Regression

123. When conducting an initial interview, counselors should rely most heavily on which of the following when formulating a diagnosis?
   a. Socioeconomic status
   b. Cultural background
   c. Client's self-report of symptoms
   d. Psychometric assessments

124. When counselors are preparing their clients for termination once treatment goals have been met, what would be the most beneficial information to convey?
   a. The counselor's enjoyment when working with the client
   b. The option of coming back in the future should the need arise
   c. The importance of the client remaining independent of the therapist so as not to create an unhealthy dependency
   d. A reminder that the client should focus on other problem areas even though the treatment goals were met

125. Which of the following would be an unhealthy coping mechanism for stress management?
   a. Progressive relaxation
   b. Avoidance of all stress-related thoughts and emotions
   c. Deep breathing practice
   d. Exercise

126. Susan has been seeing a client, Christine, for about six months. Christine has three young children and a previous drug addiction. Susan suspects that Christine may be using again and decides to confront her at their session. When Christine arrives, she appears to be under the influence, and she has her 2-year-old with her. Susan also notices that the two-year-old is covered in bruises. When she comments on the bruises, Christine becomes defensive. Christine has disclosed in the past that she sometimes gets so angry at her small children that she feels like she could beat them but that she never would. What is the ethical concern?
   a. Christine has disclosed past drug abuse and violent thoughts toward her children. Susan now suspects both are occurring, but she would have to break confidentiality to report her suspicions.
   b. Christine may be on drugs again, but she's already been defensive with Susan, so it will be difficult for Susan to bring it up without damaging their relationship.
   c. Christine has made disclosures in the past regarding drug use and also seems to need childcare so she can go to therapy. Susan knows a good babysitter who can help, but she also knows that would be establishing a dual relationship.
   d. Christine seems to be neglecting her children. Christine could possibly use education about parenting issues. Susan isn't sure if Christine would be open to a referral for parenting classes.

127. Which of the following symptoms is NOT part of the diagnostic criteria for attention-deficit/hyperactivity disorder (ADHD)?
   a. Inability to pay attention to teachers
   b. Inability to focus on video games
   c. Inability to follow instructions from parents
   d. Inability to stay organized

128. Counselors require feedback to gauge the effectiveness of therapy. Which of the following questionnaires is given to clients at the beginning of a counseling session?
   a. The Counselor Competencies Scale (CCS)
   b. The Session Rating Scale (SRS)
   c. The Outcome Rating Scale (ORS)
   d. The Group Session Rating Scale (GSRS)

129. When a person who has been diagnosed with cyclothymia experiences a major depressive episode with no manic or hypomanic episodes, what change should be made to the diagnosis?
   a. The cyclothymia diagnosis should be dropped, and the diagnosis should be changed to major depressive disorder.
   b. The cyclothymia diagnosis should be kept, and the secondary diagnosis of major depressive episode should be added.
   c. The cyclothymia diagnosis should be kept, and the primary diagnosis of major depressive episode should be added.
   d. The cyclothymia diagnosis should be kept, and the primary diagnosis of bipolar I should be added.

130. Trainee counselors who come from highly conflictual families of origin should consider all of the following EXCEPT:
   a. Getting personal counseling
   b. Taking courses in conflict resolution
   c. Not allowing families to argue during sessions
   d. Talking with a supervisor about highly conflictual families they are counseling

156

131. In which of the following stages of the family life cycle might parents experience empty nest syndrome?
   a. Independence
   b. Parenting
   c. Launching adult children
   d. Retirement

132. A client has disclosed to his counselor that he has been secretly viewing pornography for years. The counselor can do all of the following EXCEPT:
   a. Encourage the client to speak with his wife about it.
   b. Call the client's wife and ask her to come with her husband to his next session, without revealing anything about the pornography in the phone call.
   c. Allow the client to withhold the information from everyone in his life.
   d. Demonstrate a non-judgmental attitude toward the client.

133. Which of the following must the counselor determine to distinguish between bipolar I and bipolar II disorders?
   a. If the client has experienced a decreased need for sleep
   b. If the client has engaged in excessive shopping, gambling, or sexual activity during a depressive episode
   c. If the client has ever had a full manic episode
   d. If the client has ever had a full major depressive episode

134. Which of the following is an example of a third-party entity that requires the release of limited client records?
   a. The client receiving treatment
   b. The primary counselor providing treatment
   c. A client involved in group therapy
   d. The client's insurance provider

135. Which of the following needs to be considered when determining the usefulness of an evaluation tool?
   a. The cost of the test
   b. The technology used to administer the test
   c. The validity of the test
   d. The time it takes the client to take the test

136. Critical Incident Stress Debriefing (CISD) is short-term work done in small groups and is not considered psychotherapy. Techniques used include processing, defusing, ventilating, and validating thoughts, experiences, feelings, and emotions. CISD is designed for which of the following?
   a. Primary trauma victims
   b. Human resources professionals
   c. First responders
   d. Secondary trauma victims

137. One of the three main styles of leadership for managing a group is autocratic leadership. What are autocratic leaders most likely to lead with?
    a. Consensus and belonging
    b. Little to no structure
    c. Empathy and goal setting
    d. Control and power

138. A client is experiencing obsessive thoughts about a recent relationship breakup. The counselor could do all of the following EXCEPT:
    a. Use CBT to help the client adjust his perspective on the relationship.
    b. Use EMDR to help the client overcome his sadness.
    c. Have the client journal his thoughts and feelings about the breakup.
    d. Encourage the client to get together with friends.

139. How does negative reinforcement encourage specific behaviors?
    a. By removing unwanted stimuli
    b. By adding desired stimuli
    c. By punishing clients for unwanted behavior
    d. By extinction of stimuli

140. What do Yalom's stages of group development include?
    a. Forming, norming, storming, and performing
    b. Orientation, storming, working, and adjourning
    c. Orientation, conflict/dominance, and development of cohesiveness
    d. Initial, transition, working, and termination

141. A marriage counselor is working with a couple experiencing a lot of conflict. The counselor encourages the couple to have arguments and yell at each other during the session so that he can analyze their conflict. This is an example of which of the following?
    a. Cognitive behavioral therapy for marriage
    b. Gottman's marriage therapy
    c. Reality therapy for married couples
    d. This is not part of any specific marriage therapy.

142. A school-aged child is constantly being bullied and has presented with signs of depression and anxiety. The counselor realizes that the child is displaying which stage of development?
    a. Mistrust
    b. Shame and doubt
    c. Guilt
    d. Inferiority

143. Which of the following clients would benefit from a safety plan?
    a. A 7-year-old boy who is being bullied at school
    b. A 39-year-old man with anger issues who uses meditation as a coping skill
    c. A 25-year-old female who occasionally binge-drinks with her friends
    d. A 36-year-old female in a physically abusive relationship

144. A client tells her counselor that she thinks her life is over because of her recent breakup. The counselor says, "You feel like this breakup has many negative ramifications for you." This is an example of which of the following?
    a. Confronting
    b. Reframing
    c. Mirroring
    d. Underestimating

145. Which of the following is part of good sleep hygiene?
    a. Exercising for 30 minutes before bedtime
    b. Staying away from screens at least 20 minutes before bedtime
    c. A regular sleep routine
    d. Eating chocolate left on one's pillow

146. What are the five stages of change in Motivational Interviewing?
    a. Motivation, contemplation, preparation, action, change
    b. Considering, contemplation, preparing, action, behavioral change
    c. Precontemplation, contemplation, preparation, action, and maintenance
    d. Motivation, preparation, reconsideration, action, change

147. Research studies have indicated which of the following?
    a. Males develop language earlier than females.
    b. Males and females develop language at the same rate.
    c. Females develop language earlier than males.
    d. No determination for rate of language development has been made.

148. Who is associated with the concept of birth order and the influence that sibling position has on personality?
    a. Abraham Maslow
    b. Alfred Adler
    c. Albert Bandura
    d. Anna Freud

149. Which of the following affective tests can measure personality traits?
    a. Myers-Briggs Type Indicator (MBTI)
    b. Beck Depression Inventory (BDI)
    c. Connors 3 Rating Scales
    d. Child Behavior Checklist

150. When does modeling occur in the counseling process?
    a. When counselors model clients' feelings back to them
    b. When clients provide counselors with an ideal image of themselves to achieve
    c. When clients are told how to behave by counselors
    d. When counselors demonstrate appropriate reactions and behaviors for clients to follow

159

151. According to Dr. John Gottman's theory of marital distress, what are the four communication styles that can predict the end of a relationship?
    a. Contempt, controlling, belittling, stonewalling
    b. Contempt, stonewalling, confronting, scapegoating
    c. Contempt, criticism, stonewalling, defensiveness
    d. Criticism, confronting, belittling, controlling

152. What are some specific issues cited as commonly discussed by women in counseling?
    a. Infertility, marital conflict, and eating disorders
    b. Balancing a career and family, self-esteem, and mitigating societal expectations and pressures
    c. Exhaustion, joint pain, and postpartum depression
    d. Anxiety, work-life balance, and finances

153. When required by law to disclose confidential information about a client, the social worker should always discuss the disclosure with the client before the disclosure occurs. Is this true or false? Why?
    a. False. At the time of the informed consent, the client should have been told about legal requirements that cause the social worker to break confidentiality, and therefore, the social worker never needs to discuss a specific disclosure with the client.
    b. True. The social worker must get the client to sign a new informed consent form stating that the client understands the disclosure will be made.
    c. False. The social worker should assess any threat to their personal safety, or the safety of others, and should only discuss the disclosure with the client if no one appears to be at risk of harm.
    d. True. The social worker has a duty to tell the client that a disclosure is being made and that confidentiality is being broken.

154. Vertical interventions occur when the group leader focuses on which of the following?
    a. Individuals rather than the group
    b. The group rather than individuals
    c. Both the individuals and the larger group
    d. Group dynamics

155. Studies on gratitude have found that it is correlated with all of the following EXCEPT:
    a. Decreased levels of depression
    b. Stronger relationships
    c. Greater optimism
    d. Decreased psychotic episodes

156. A counselor is working with an adult who has anger management issues and minor cognitive impairment due to methamphetamine abuse. Which of the following would be the most appropriate method of treatment?
    a. Psychoanalysis
    b. Cognitive behavioral therapy
    c. Group therapy
    d. Gestalt therapy

160

157. Which term refers to how well a person can maintain a sense of identity and acknowledge/accept their own feelings and thoughts?
    a. Ego identity
    b. Emotional capitulation
    c. Superego formation
    d. Differentiation

158. Which of the following is NOT reason a counselor would administer a test or assessment to a client?
    a. To aid the counselor in sharing pertinent information with the client's loved ones
    b. To ensure a client's needs are within the counselor's scope of practice
    c. To help the client gain a better understanding of themselves
    d. To evaluate the effectiveness of counseling interventions

159. A client is using marijuana to the point where it interferes with his ability to get up and go to work every day. What should the counselor do?
    a. Encourage the client to begin an addictions program like Narcotics Anonymous.
    b. Not consider this a problem since marijuana is legal in the state where the client lives.
    c. Call the police since marijuana use is illegal in the state where the client lives.
    d. Refer the client to a psychiatrist who can prescribe medication to treat the addiction.

160. All of the following could help the development of a healthy support system EXCEPT:
    a. Encouraging church attendance
    b. Encouraging participation in a self-help group like AA
    c. Helping the client heal broken family relationships
    d. Encouraging the client to engage in regular exercise

161. How does group therapy help clients develop outside social interactions?
    a. Members act on the instincts of others within the group.
    b. Group therapy requires members to participate in free-form dialogue.
    c. Clients no longer have issues with conflict resolution after group therapy.
    d. It allows members to practice open expression of thoughts and feelings within a group.

162. During a session, the counselor is silent and notices the client speaking to himself. When prompted, the client tells the counselor he is responding to the questions he heard from a voice in his head. What follow-up question is important for the counselor to ask?
    a. "Are the voices telling you to harm yourself?"
    b. "When did you start hearing the voices?"
    c. "Is there an activity you would like to perform to distract you from the voices?"
    d. "Are you experiencing emotional distress at the moment?"

163. A counselor is working with an adult female client who suffered continuous sexual abuse from ages six to 14 by a male relative. To establish safety and trust, the counselor should do all of the following EXCEPT:
    a. Allow her to express feelings of rage about the abuse.
    b. Hug her when she is crying.
    c. Allow her to sit near the door.
    d. Express empathy when she describes the abuse.

164. Genograms are useful tools that help clients understand which of the following?
    a. The influence of generational patterns on present familial functioning
    b. The impact of past trauma on current behavioral patterns
    c. Psychodynamic influences on present relationships
    d. Intrapsychic influences on present behaviors

165. The statistically most common and normative behaviors of a society are referred to as what?
    a. Culture
    b. Modal behavior
    c. Tripartite
    d. Ethnology

166. Which of the following activities can help increase the mental and emotional stability of a client who just retired?
    a. Call the client's children and suggest the client be placed in a nursing home.
    b. Have the client wake up at the same time every day to establish a routine.
    c. Encourage the client to continue working a high-stress job to avoid mental instability.
    d. Tell the client to perform the same activities every day.

167. Sometimes in group counseling, group members may think of the leader as an authority figure in their lives, such as their father or mother. This is an example of which of the following?
    a. Resistance
    b. Countertransference
    c. Transference
    d. Role reversal

168. What are the main components of a safety plan?
    a. Initiation of coping strategies and identification of resources during crisis
    b. Mitigation of negative thoughts and group-centered interventions
    c. Recognition of danger signs
    d. Goals that are community-centered, realistic, and achievable

169. Which type of psychological group deals with long-standing pathology?
    a. Tertiary
    b. Secondary
    c. Primary
    d. Psychoeducational

170. During an initial interview with a client, counselors should consider all of the following when formulating a diagnosis EXCEPT:
    a. Mental health history
    b. Length of time that symptoms have been present
    c. Cultural background
    d. Occupation

171. A counselor sees signs of abuse in a child with whom she is working. Which of the following would be unethical for her to do?
    a. Report the abuse to the local authorities without the parents' knowledge.
    b. Let the parents know she is going to report the abuse while she is reporting the abuse.
    c. Talk to the child's teacher to confirm that she is seeing the same signs.
    d. Ask the child questions about the suspected abuse.

172. Which of the following signs indicate that a client needs to be hospitalized?
    a. The client is homeless.
    b. The client is hallucinating.
    c. The client scored high for depression on a psychometric test.
    d. The client has recently beaten his wife.

173. A group member starts crying because of something another member just shared. The counselor encourages the person sitting next to her to explore these elicited emotions. This is an example of which of the following?
    a. The leader being too controlling in the group
    b. The leader trying to develop empathy between group members
    c. The leader trying to help the member to stop crying so he can attend to what the other member said
    d. The leader trying to form an artificial bond between members

174. A client confides in his counselor that he has been unfaithful to his wife for the past 15 years. The counselor may do all of the following EXCEPT:
    a. Call the client's wife since she has attended previous counseling sessions.
    b. Provide a non-judgmental attitude.
    c. Encourage the client to tell his wife.
    d. Ask the client to have his wife come to a future counseling session where he can confess to the affair.

175. For which of the following reasons must a counselor refer a client to another counselor?
    a. The client is suicidal.
    b. The counselor has a sexual history with the client.
    c. The client is threatening to harm the counselor.
    d. The counselor is closing his practice.

176. Which of the following stereotypes exist regarding older workers?
    a. The idea that older workers will take more absentee and sick days
    b. The idea that older workers are resistant to new technology
    c. The idea that older workers are slower to learn new information
    d. All of the above

177. Robert Carkhuff wrote *Toward Effective Counseling and Psychotherapy*, a book wherein he discovered that therapeutic interventions did not always have a long-term positive impact on clients. Carkhuff also created a five-point empathy scale, designed to measure what?
    a. A counselor's ability to accurately reflect
    b. Effectiveness of a counselor
    c. Defensiveness of a counselor
    d. Adequate structuring of sessions

178. Dr. John Gottman's predictors of marital distress take the form of which of the following?
   a. The Wind and The Rain
   b. The Four Love Languages
   c. The Four Horsemen of the Apocalypse
   d. The Seven Stages of Marital Decline

179. A human resources manager who only reviews applications from individuals that are between twenty-two and thirty years of age, regardless of any other credentials or experience, is demonstrating which of the following?
   a. Sexism
   b. Millennial-leaning bias
   c. Ageism
   d. Classism

180. A counselor tells her client, "I understand how the divorce has hurt you. It has caused you many years of pain and loneliness." The counselor is demonstrating which of the following?
   a. Empathy
   b. Selective attunement
   c. Congruence
   d. Sympathy

181. Which of the following is NOT a symptom of Post-Traumatic Stress Disorder (PTSD)?
   a. Intrusive thoughts or images of the traumatic event
   b. Efforts to avoid thoughts of the traumatic event
   c. Duration of symptoms for longer than one week
   d. Reckless or self-destructive behavior

182. The storming phase of group development refers to which of the following?
   a. Anxiety from some members of the group and difficulty opening up
   b. Group termination and moving on
   c. The use of role-play
   d. Vying for leadership and group conflict

183. When processing difficult emotional issues with a client, a counselor can do all of the following EXCEPT:
   a. Be aware of the time left in the session so he can wrap things up with the client by the end of the session.
   b. Allow for periods of silence during the session so the client can experience his emotions.
   c. Cancel all afternoon clients so the counselor can spend the rest of the day with the client.
   d. Offer homework so the client can continue to work through his emotions between sessions.

184. Counselors should use all of the following methods to formulate their diagnoses EXCEPT:
   a. Psychometric tests
   b. Client's neighbor's report
   c. Mental status exam
   d. Client's self-report

185. When two individuals with children from a previous marriage get married, what is the best way to begin the parenting process?
    a. Allow the biological parent to discipline his or her own children until the new family unit has bonded.
    b. Allow the father to be the main disciplinarian so the mother can be seen as the nurturer in the home.
    c. Adapt a style of permissive discipline so the children will feel accepted and loved.
    d. Adapt an authoritarian style of discipline so the children will feel secure and protected.

186. Which of the following entities publishes the International Classification of Diseases (ICD)?
    a. The World Health Organization
    b. The United Nations
    c. The International Journal of Health Sciences
    d. The United States Agency for International Development

187. A married couple has been in counseling for four months, and the counselor believes that they are not making enough progress. The couple are first generation Mexican immigrants. The couple will likely NOT respond well to which of the following treatment methods?
    a. Referral to group therapy
    b. Inclusion of their parents, who live with them, in the counseling process
    c. Encouragement of spiritual practices
    d. Education about Gottman's Four Horsemen of the Apocalypse

188. During couples counseling, the counselor discovers that the wife is unhappy with the mother-in-law's suggestions for disciplining the couple's children. The wife shares these thoughts with the husband and expects him to address the issue with his mother. What tactic is the wife displaying?
    a. Strategizing
    b. Pattern interruption
    c. Separation
    d. Triangulation

189. Payment that is based on the client's income is known as which of the following?
    a. Private pay
    b. Sliding fee scale
    c. Health savings account
    d. Private insurance

190. Psychoanalytic groups focus on what specific solution?
    a. Decreasing anxiety
    b. Resolution of childhood issues
    c. Resolution of current relationship issues
    d. Increasing daily functioning

191. A client verbalizes experiencing shortness of breath and heart palpitations every time they meet a new group of people. The counselor recognizes that the client is displaying physical signs of anxiety. Which of the following counseling techniques can be used with the client during therapy sessions?
    a. Exposure therapy
    b. Interplay
    c. Positive psychology
    d. Reality therapy

165

192. Which theorist developed ideas on fluid and crystallized intelligence?
    a. John Ertl
    b. Alfred Binet
    c. Sir Francis Galton
    d. Raymond Cattell

193. A researcher is grouping participants into sample sets by gender. In this instance, gender is an example of what type of measure?
    a. Interval
    b. Nominal
    c. Ordinal
    d. Ratio

194. A client verbalizes to the counselor that he plans to commit suicide by jumping off a building that night. What action should the counselor perform next?
    a. Perform an in-depth suicide risk assessment, and contact the crisis team if the client has clear intent.
    b. Contact the client's family, and let them know the client plans to end his life.
    c. Tell the client to go home and rest and return in the morning.
    d. Ignore the client's statement, and change the subject to help the client forget about his plan.

195. When should the therapeutic alliance between a counselor and a client be established?
    a. During the first couple of counseling sessions
    b. When the counselor notices the client is not a good match for therapy sessions
    c. At the end of all counseling sessions
    d. The time when the alliance should be established is not important.

196. A counselor is working with a client diagnosed with bipolar disorder who was recently hospitalized after having a psychotic episode. Which of the following should the counselor do first?
    a. Refer the client to a psychiatrist for medication.
    b. Have the client take several psychological assessments to ensure the correct diagnosis was given.
    c. Begin working with the client on their history of childhood trauma.
    d. Have the client sign a HIPAA form, and then contact the hospital to obtain information about the psychotic episode, how it was treated, and the hospital's recommendation for future treatment.

197. According to Murray Bowen's family systems theory, the concept of the nuclear family emotional system refers to four different relationship dynamics. These are which of the following?
    a. Conflict, distance, child-adult interactions, and proximity
    b. Marital conflict, dysfunction in one spouse, impairment in one or more children, and emotional distance
    c. Happy, conflicting, grieving, and joyous
    d. Parent-child conflict, spousal conflict, full-family conflict, and sibling conflict

198. What is the function of the helping relationship in the counseling process?
    a. It works by giving advice to the client.
    b. It allows the counselor to set goals for the client independently.
    c. It helps create a climate for change.
    d. It helps counselors maintain power in the counseling relationship.

166

199. A counselor is working with a client who is suffering from grief after the loss of her mother. The counselor can do all of the following EXCEPT:
   a. Encourage the client to connect with her religious organization for support.
   b. Encourage the client to create a memory book of her mother.
   c. Encourage the client to join a grief support group.
   d. Agree to meet weekly for lunch with the client until her grief has passed.

200. A client verbalizes that she is unable to forget negative experiences in her past and they are interfering with her new relationship. What kind of theory-based therapy might benefit this client?
   a. Adlerian psychotherapy
   b. Gottman Method
   c. Humanistic psychology
   d. Gestalt therapy

Answer Explanations #1

1. C: The counselor is describing research on language differences in young children, which is an example of psychoeducation. Choice *A*, racism, and Choice *B*, gender bias, are not evident here. Choice *C*, shaping, is not what the counselor is attempting to accomplish since they are not slowly changing the client's behavior.

2. C: Avoiding the feared object or situation will only solidify the fear in the client's mind. The remaining choices are all components of helping a client overcome a phobia.

3. C: Avoidance would not be an appropriate way to handle impending termination because it does not address the emotional and psychological issues that may arise for the client when she completes treatment. Choice *A* would be appropriate because it would remind the client that she has met her treatment goals. Choice *B* would be appropriate because it would allow the client to bring up any issues that have not been addressed in treatment yet. Choice *D* would be appropriate because the counselor should prepare the client for the variety of potential feelings that might arise after treatment ends.

4. B: When a conflict reaches an unhealthy level, it is important for the counselor step in and help the members successfully resolve it; otherwise, the members may lose trust in the effectiveness of the group and may even leave the group. Choice *A* is not a good option because the conflict has already reached an unhealthy state. Choice *C* would not help the group navigate to a healthy resolution. Choice *D* is not warranted and could cause psychological harm to the members.

5. A: One's worldview is typically comprised of personal beliefs, values, and attitudes about the world around them and beyond. Choice *B*, cultural encapsulation, refers to a viewpoint wherein the individual refuses to take into account other beliefs and cultures that differ from their own. Choice *C*, ethnicity, is belonging to a certain group that has a common cultural tradition. Choice *D*, ethnocentrism, is a belief that one's culture is superior to another's.

6. A: Signs of hopelessness, when accompanied by other warning signs, may indicate that the client is suicidal. The remaining choices are all possibilities, but the greatest concern for the counselor would be the potential for suicide.

7. B: The therapeutic alliance is critical to the client's decision to stay in treatment. Choice *A*, payment method, is not one of the most important tasks in the first session; it should be agreed upon prior to the beginning of treatment. Choice *C*, diagnosis, might not be possible to formulate in the first couple of sessions. Choice *D*, treatment plan, may or may not be established in the first couple of sessions.

8. A: Previous suicide attempts put a person at a higher risk for suicide than someone who has never attempted suicide. Choice *B* is incorrect; if a client is thinking about suicide but has no definite plan, this alone does not put them at high risk for suicide. Choice *C* is incorrect. A client who has been diagnosed with depression is not necessarily suicidal. Choice *D* is incorrect; the lack of a healthy support system does not by itself make the client a suicide risk.

9. D: Clients with an anxious-avoidant attachment style who practice empathy and increase their closeness with others can experience decreased feelings of depression and loneliness. Choice *A* can cause more anxiety in the client; anxious-avoidant attachment styles are encouraged to practice mindfulness and focus on the present. Choice *B* will worsen the negative attachment style; taking

168

everything personally will damage social relationships. Choice *C* will result in a toxic relationship; communication is important for healthy interactions.

10. D: SPSS, SAS, and Minitab are all popular statistical software programs. These programs make it easier to analyze and run tests on large datasets. Choice *A*, SPSS, stands for Statistical Package for the Social Science and is one of the most popular packages that performs complex data manipulation with easy instructions. Choice *B*, SAS, stands for Statistical Analysis System, and is a software developed for advanced analytics, data management, business intelligence, multivariate analyses, and predictive analytics. Choice *C*, Minitab, is an all-purpose statistical software created for simple interactive use.

11. B: Reflecting on the client's growth and plan for progress can help ease the transition. Choice *A* is important for the counselor but not a priority in transitioning the client out of therapy. Choice *C* is incorrect; the client's choice to terminate therapy due to progress should be respected. Choice *D* crosses the professional boundary; clients should only return when they need therapy again.

12. A: Fluid intelligence refers to the ability to think and act quickly and solve new problems. It is independent of education and culture, making the other choices incorrect.

13. B: Eating non-nutritive substances for at least one month is a sign of pica. Admitting the client to a hospital is not warranted based on this information alone, nor is sending the client for a brain scan. Therefore, Choices *A* and *C* are incorrect. The client is not showing symptoms of anorexia nervosa, so Choice *D* is also incorrect.

14. B: Choice *B* is not an appropriate course of action because the counselor cannot break confidentiality with the client's neighbor; they can only break confidentiality with the appropriate authorities (e.g., the police) in the event of possible self-harm by the client. The remaining choices are all possible steps the counselor could take, depending on the situation, such as consent having been given to contact the fiancé if a situation like this should arise.

15. C: Passive communicators do not openly express their opinions and can be taken advantage of by others. Choice *A* is a communication style characterized by an inappropriate expression of feelings that violates the rights of others. Choice *B* is a communication style that is clear, direct, and honest. Choice *D* is not a type of communication style.

16. A: If the client is unable to perform their daily responsibilities, this may indicate a need for intensive treatment in a residential facility. Choice *B* is incorrect because a counselor should not talk with a client's family members (unless the client has signed a HIPAA form for each member of their family). Choice *C* is incorrect because receiving a DWI does not necessitate residential treatment. Choice *D* is incorrect because there are other forms of outpatient addiction groups that the client could attend instead of going to a residential facility.

17. D: Harlow, a theorist in mother-offspring attachment, noticed all of these qualities in monkeys who were given a wire mother substitute and were not shown warmth and affection. He theorized that newborns of many species, including humans, had an innate need to bond in this way in order to develop healthy personalities and attachment bonds.

18. D: This is an example of building communication skills, as counselors sometimes educate their clients by demonstrating appropriate behaviors. The remaining choices are incorrect.

19. B: Tina realizes that this distinction may confound her results. Confounding occurs when any results found correlate with multiple variables, therefore preventing a clear correlation between a particular independent variable and a particular dependent variable. In this instance, the fact that a majority of the test group and control group are each made up of a particular year of students may influence the presence of any habits that Tina is trying to study.

20. D: Critical Incident Stress Debriefing (CISD) is most effective when offered within 24 to 72 hours of an event. It can be provided by any trained individual, including HR or mental health professionals, and is intended for groups of secondary trauma victims.

21. A: Bereavement, ageism in the workforce, and unemployment are some issues older adults face and report discussing in counseling as they begin to lose friends and family or if they are forced into retirement or made redundant in their workplace.

22. C: No, informed consent has not been satisfied. Susan did not have a document outlining what counseling would entail, including the risks and limitations. She also did not have Claudia sign such a document to become part of the chart. Documentation of informed consent protects both the client and the counselor.

23. B: The Empty Chair Technique allows a client to use the chair as a symbol of a person in their life or a part of themselves; the dialogue encourages conflict resolution. Choice A is used for clients who want to overcome habitual behavior; the technique is a simple process that involves noticing automatic motivations, stopping the action, and keeping track of the resulting emotion. Choice C is a solution-focused technique that helps clients envision the future and focus on achievable goals. Counselors ask the client a question that describes what the perfect situation for them would be like. It assists the counselor with determining what the client wants out of therapy. Choice D is used in clients requiring exposure therapy for anxiety or fear disorders; clients are introduced to a virtual world that increases exposure to negative stimuli in a controlled setting.

24. C: Developmental age is a more appropriate consideration than chronological age since babies cannot control their elimination and yet are not diagnosed with either condition. Choice B is incorrect since the diagnosis can be given whether the symptoms are voluntary or involuntary. Choice D is not a relevant factor; the diagnosis can be appropriate whether the elimination occurs during the day or night.

25. D: Choice D is not a central component of Carl Rogers's therapy model. The remaining choices list the three main components of his method.

26. C: Under no circumstances do members participating in psychodynamic therapy meet outside of group time. Therefore, Choice C is correct, and the remaining choices are incorrect.

27. A: Asking the client to show the counselor her personal journal could possibly harm the client because she may not want to share this personal record with anyone. Choice B could show the client the progress she is making progress toward her treatment goals. Choice C could help the client see her physical progress. If the tests show improvement, she can see how her body is recovering from her past food deprivation. Likewise, if the tests show no improvement, the client can see that she has more work to do. Choice D would be beneficial when evaluating the effectiveness of treatment, especially if the eating disorder has caused tension between the client and her family members.

28. A: *Tarasoff vs. Regents of University of California* is the correct answer. In this 1976 case, the therapist failed to notify the intended victim of the threat of harm. After the client had stopped seeking treatment, he then attacked and killed Tarasoff, prompting her family to sue the university and therefore establishing the duty to warn. None of the other cases directly relate to duty to warn.

170

29. D: The cycle of violence follows the sequence of tension building, explosion, and honeymoon. First, the tension escalates, leading to a violent altercation, after which the abuser showers the victim with kindness, affection, and/or gifts. Choice A presents the phases in the wrong order. Choice B is incorrect because it leaves out the explosion phase. Choice C is incorrect because the honeymoon phase includes reunification.

30. A: Choice A would be inappropriate because counselors do not give advice. The remaining choices are appropriate actions that the counselor could take.

31. A: Professional counselors are legally and ethically required to report matters pertaining to harm of self or others. Choice B is symptomatic information that can be used for assessment and diagnosis. Choice C violates the client's privacy unless the client has provided written consent. Choice D is incorrect because clients are free to terminate the relationship at any time while maintaining confidentiality of their records.

32. A: Gestalt therapy is a holistic model that helps clients focus on the present and work toward personal growth and balance. Person-centered therapy, Choice B, is a group method designed to help members increase self-awareness, self-acceptance, and openness, and decrease defensiveness. These groups have less structure and focus on listening and reflecting. Rational emotive group therapy, Choice C, is based on cognitive behavioral theories. The focus is on the present with the goal of improving cognitive, emotional, and behavior functioning. Group members focus on adaptive behaviors. Jungian therapy, Choice D, is a form of therapy but not a specific group therapy. In Jungian therapy, the therapist is an analyst who works with the client to merge the unconscious parts of the psyche with the conscious parts of the self.

33. C: Biological, social, and psychological are known as the biopsychosocial realms of functioning, and they encompass the areas that counselors should assess to obtain a holistic view of their clients. The remaining choices do not adequately cover the entirety of the human condition.

34. B: Parentification occurs when a child fulfills a parent's role within a family system. Choice A, Electra complex, is the Freudian term describing a daughter's competition with her mother for her father's affection. Choice C, paradoxical intervention, is when a counselor encourages continuation of a negative symptom, therefore showing the client their ability to control it. Choice D, motivational interviewing, is a form of therapy.

35. A: A reduction in the primary symptoms that initially led the client to seek counseling is a positive outcome of group therapy. Choice B is incorrect; group therapy aims to help clients advance toward their goals. Choice C is the opposite outcome; group therapy encourages independent client coping. Choice D is incorrect because termination of group therapy should be a joint decision by its members.

36. D: Negative transference can result in clients becoming angry and hostile toward the counselor. Although transference is an essential part of psychoanalytic counseling, negative transference can be difficult to manage and must be dealt with in order for therapy to progress. Choice A, when counselors project feelings onto clients, is called countertransference. Choice B, when clients project feelings toward another person in the past onto the counselor, is known as transference. Choice C, when multiple roles exist between a counselor and client, is known as a dual relationship.

37. C: Asking open-ended questions is important because it encourages clients to clearly describe what brought them to counseling and what their presenting symptoms are. Choice A may not be possible in the initial interview because more data may need to be gathered in future sessions before a diagnosis

171

can be established. Choice *B* is important but likely would not occur in the first meeting. Choice *D* is not correct because permission to break confidentiality is not required when a client becomes suicidal.

38. D: The treatment may be working, but alterations to the treatment plan may be needed because the client's progress is insufficient. Choice *A* is not something that a counselor could conclude based on these test results. Choice *B* is incorrect because the BDI has empirically established validity. Choice *C* is incorrect because suicide risk is not indicated by the information given. Furthermore, counselors should only refer clients to other counselors under special circumstances due to the risk of emotional abandonment and feelings of rejection.

39. B: The United States Department of Veterans Affairs helped expand services after World War II in order to help returning servicemen transition back into civilian life and the civilian workforce.

40. A: Approximately 65% of second marriages end in divorce. The remaining choices are incorrect. Approximately 50% of first marriages and 75% of third marriages end in divorce.

41. B: This would be appropriate if the counselor believes the client is not complying with the treatment directives. The client needs to understand that compliance is required for progress to be made. Choice *A* is incorrect because whether the psychiatrist agrees with the counselor has no bearing on the decision to speak with the client about treatment compliance. Choice *C* is incorrect because compliance with the counselor's directives is vital to symptom improvement, just as medication compliance is essential. Choice *D* is incorrect because the length of treatment is irrelevant in this case.

42. D: Issues with sexual satisfaction can occur during the desire, arousal, orgasm, and resolution phases. Choice *A* is incorrect because sexual dysfunction can happen during any phase of the sexual cycle. Choice *B* is incorrect because sexual dysfunction may be a result of psychological concerns. Choice *C* is incorrect; more than 40% of women and 30% of men experience some form of sexual dysfunction.

43. B: Choice *B* correctly describes what occurs during pre-group preparation. Choices *A* and *C* are incorrect because clients are not always told what other group members' diagnoses are. Choice *D* is incorrect because clients do not sign a waiver of confidentiality; instead, they are told about the limits of confidentiality in group counseling.

44. A: Groups that provide guidance, problem prevention, and skills building are psychoeducational and may also be called guidance groups. Structured groups, Choice *B*, refers to how the group is set up—whether it is rigid in how it operates or more fluid. Gestalt groups, Choice *C*, are an alternative to intense psychoanalytic groups. Group members work on emotional awareness, freedom, and self-direction. Psychodynamic groups, Choice *D*, are long-term therapeutic groups made up of individuals who all have similar mental health diagnoses.

45. A: The counselor should talk with the client about his short temper. This would help the client learn how he comes across to others, and he can begin to work with the counselor on that matter. Choice *B* would not be the most beneficial option because the client may lack self-awareness in this area or he may falsely believe that it is appropriate to talk this way. If the counselor handles the interchange appropriately, the therapeutic bond will likely not be damaged. Choice *C* would be an unhealthy way for the counselor to teach the client how to change his temper, and it may recapitulate childhood traumas. Choice *D* would be inappropriate because it could send a message of abandonment to the client.

46. C: In 1982, the ACA launched the National Board for Certified Counselors. The establishment of this credential was key in defining fundamental standards for the counseling profession.

47. A: Cyberbullying includes the use of electronic media and technology. Choice *B* would include physical assaults or property damage. Choice *C* is the intent to discredit another person's reputation. Choice *D* is not a defined form of bullying.

48. D: Joe's reaction is an example of transference. Joe is transferring feelings toward his father onto his therapist, which may be beneficial in resolving his childhood issues. Choice *A* is incorrect; remorse is a feeling of deep regret for a wrong committed and does not make sense in this context. Choice *B* is incorrect; in Freudian theory, fixation occurs when a child is unable to progress from one psychosexual stage to the next. Choice *C* is incorrect; negative reinforcement is a learned behavior meant to avoid negative stimulus.

49. A: EMDR would not be helpful in teaching social skills. The remaining choices are all techniques or tools that the counselor could use.

50. D: A type II error in statistical testing occurs when the researcher fails to reject a null hypothesis that is false. This type of error in a test will indicate that there is no relationship between two variables when there actually is one.

51. A: The stages of positive interaction are exploration, consolidation, planning, and termination.

- Stage 1. Exploration of feelings and definition of problem: The counselor will use rapport-building skills, define the structure of the counseling process and relationship, and work with the client on goal setting.

- Stage 2. Consolidation: The client integrates the information and guidance from the counselor, allowing him or her to gain additional coping skills and identify alternate ways to solve problems.

- Stage 3. Planning: The client begins employing techniques learned in counseling and prepares to manage on his or her own.

- Stage 4. Termination: This is the ending of the therapeutic relationship, when the client feels equipped to manage problems independently and has fully integrated techniques learned in counseling.

52. C: Cultural values and beliefs should be researched and learned when working with clients from a different culture. These values should then be used as strengths during goal development to aid the client in making the changes they desire.

53. B: Choice *B* is correct because additional treatment should be initiated by the client. The remaining choices would be appropriate ways for a counselor to check in with a client and show care. Choice *D* would be especially appropriate if the client had done marriage counseling with the counselor.

54. C: Clients are motivated and ready for change during the preparation stage, so counselors are able to effectively work with clients in this stage. Choice *A* describes clients who are still in denial and not considering change. Choice *B* is when clients are only considering making a change. Choice *D* is the end stage after changes have been implemented.

173

55. D: Recall, Empathize, Altruistic Gift, Commit, and Hold are the five steps of the REACH forgiveness model. Choices *A, B* and *C* are not part of the model.

56. B: Emotional Quotient, also known as EQ, is less well-known than its IQ counterpart. People with high EQ tend to have better interpersonal and leadership achievements. Choice *A* is an index that measures someone's cognitive and critical thinking abilities, so this choice is incorrect. Choices *C* and *D* are too broad and do not refer to a measurement of emotional intelligence.

57. D: Depression manifests itself differently in older adults, and symptoms such as fatigue, loss of interest in sex, and pain often go unnoticed. Choice *A* is incorrect because older adults are still capable of developing coping mechanisms to deal with depression. Choice *B* is incorrect because depression occurs in every age group. Choice *C* may require a more in-depth assessment, but older adults are capable of seeking treatment.

58. A: Cognitive defusion is a term from Acceptance and Commitment Therapy. The remaining choices are incorrect.

59. B: Probability sampling uses randomization. In probability sampling, anyone who is eligible to be in the sample has an equal chance of getting randomly selected, whereas non-probability sampling may choose participants based on convenience, referral, volunteerism, etc., making Choices *A, C,* and *D* incorrect.

60. A: Blocking refers to a group leader blocking or putting a stop to negative behavior of a group member. This can be harmful comments or anything that violates confidentiality or group norms. Members being disruptive to the process, Choice *B*, would be an example of conflict within the group. The leader locking the door to prevent exiting, Choice *C*, is not a technique used in group therapy. Existing members not welcoming new members, Choice *D*, could be an example of scapegoating a group member.

61. D: Practitioners will serve clients from all backgrounds and should not make any assumptions from intake information. Practitioners should be aware of any personal biases they may hold and make all inferences about the client's situation from information that comes directly from their sessions.

62. B: Choice *B* is correct because it is unethical to refer a client to another counselor based on religious preference. Counselors must demonstrate acceptance and respect for their clients' religious preferences. The remaining choices describe ethical practices.

63. B: Hallucinations (both auditory and visual) are symptoms of schizophrenia. Choice *A* refers to dissociative identity disorder. Choices *C* and *D* are not common diagnostic symptoms of schizophrenia.

64. B: Americans with Disabilities Act of 1990 (ADA) requires that workplaces in the United States provide the necessary accommodations and structures for access, unless doing so places an unreasonable burden on the entity. In the building above, there are no accommodations for individuals with physical handicaps to enter the building or access any offices. Choice *A*, Individuals with Disabilities Education Act, was enacted in 1975 and also provides communities with extra funding to provide resources for disabled children. Choice *C*, Workforce Innovation and Opportunity Act, is designed to streamline training programs in the workforce. Choice *D*, the Hidden Job Market, is a term used for jobs that aren't advertised.

174

65. B: Using nonsexist language and gender-sensitive skills while counseling is encouraged by the ACA. Choice *A* will not build trust and rapport with the client. Choice *C* displays counselor bias toward a specific belief. Choice *D* is incorrect because counselors should facilitate client knowledge about how gender-role stereotyping and sexism affect their physical and mental health.

66. C: A homogenous society is one where the people are very similar in background, attitudes, and beliefs; a heterogeneous society embodies a great deal of diversity within its people.

67. B: The counselor should ask additional questions about the client's alcohol consumption to determine what the client needs. The remaining choices are all potential options after the counselor has ascertained more information.

68. B: Risky shift phenomenon refers to groups becoming less risk-averse or riskier in their decisions. The act of sharing the risk among others makes individuals less conservative in their actions. Group leaders encouraging members to take more risks, Choice *C*, would fall under therapeutic techniques. Closed groups considering taking on new members, Choice *D*, would involve completely changing the type of group from closed to open.

69. A: Maslow's hierarchy of needs is composed of five levels. The fourth level is esteem needs and was updated to include cognitive and aesthetic needs. This includes the need for self-esteem, status, prestige, knowledge, and an appreciation for beauty and balance. Level 1 is the need for food, shelter, warmth, air, sex, and sleep. Level 2 is the need for safety, personal security, stability, laws, and social order. Level 3 reflects the need for love and a sense of belonging. Level 5 of the pyramid is self-actualization.

70. D: The length of time that symptoms are present is the key difference between major depressive disorder (MDD) and persistent depressive disorder (PDD). In PDD, the symptoms must occur on most days over at least a two-year period. For an MDD diagnosis, the symptoms must be present on most days for at least two weeks. The remaining choices could all be present in either PDD or MDD.

71. A: Communicating via email is ethical so long as the email server is secure and no one in the counselor's home has access to it. Choice *B* is incorrect because a counselor may hold licenses in multiple states, allowing them to counsel clients across state lines. Choice *C* would not be an ethical safeguard against potential violations of confidentiality. Choice *D* is incorrect because email communications are allowed.

72. A: Neural pathways in the brain are formed through repetition (this is also known as the Hebbian principle). This describes the process by which behaviors and thoughts become ingrained. The remaining choices are not described by the given phrase and are incorrect.

73. B: Avoidance of the object or action of fear is NOT one of the stages of desensitization. Exposure to the object, creating a fear hierarchy, and learning relaxation techniques while being exposed are stages of systematic desensitization.

74. D: Authenticity is difficult to determine in a mental status examination because the counselor may not be able to verify the report's truthfulness. The remaining choices contribute to the overall picture of the client's functioning and are pertinent to a mental status exam.

75. C: Studies show that, due to previous abuse, a lack of security, caregiver deprivation, or early trauma, adopted children are almost twice as likely to develop behavior problems as those who are not adopted. Choice *A* is not the sole contributing factor to the client's behavior. Choice *B* is incorrect because extreme behavioral issues are not a normal trait of development. Choice *D* is not indicative of adoption issues.

76. D: Choice *D* would be inappropriate because counselors do not give advice. The remaining choices are appropriate measures the counselor could take with the client.

77. A: Horizontal interventions in group counseling are referred to as *interpersonal* and define when the leader works with the group as a whole rather than as individuals. Intrapersonal, Choice *B*, is another term for vertical interventions, which occurs when the group leader focuses on individuals rather than the group.

78. C: Multigenerational transmission process explains how the variance in differentiation of self between parents and children over time leads to a widespread difference in beliefs between the oldest generation and the youngest generation of the family. Choice *A* is incorrect; differentiation of self refers to how much an individual's personal beliefs differ from that of his or her group's beliefs, and Jake is identifying with his peers here. Choice *B* is incorrect; family projection process refers to how parents project emotional conflict onto their children. Choice *D* is incorrect; emotional cutoff is the act of failing to resolve issues between family members by reducing or eliminating contact with one another.

79. A: Choice *A* is not a good strategy because this allows the child to see where the alliance has broken down between the parents, and the child will possibly take sides. The remaining choices are all possible solutions that the counselor could offer.

80. D: The counselor is evaluating the client's judgment. Choice *A* is not being evaluated because the question does not address memory. Choice *B* is incorrect because the question relates to a concrete, hypothetical situation. Choice *C* is incorrect because spatial orientation involves identifying objects or oneself in a point of space/environment; this is not the focus of the question.

81. C: The ACA Code of Ethics addresses technology and its limitations with maintaining confidentiality; encryption methods should be used to minimize data breaches. Choice *A* should be addressed in the informed consent prior to delivering services. Choice *B* can still be established virtually through verbal and nonverbal communication. Choice *D* is not a requirement; professional or personal social media accounts are optional and must be kept separate.

82. C: It's important for a counselor to consult with other professionals if they feel they're outside the scope of their practice area. Being in the LGBT community is not necessary, although awareness and respect for the culture is.

83. B: Denial, anger, bargaining, depression, and acceptance are the five stages of grief according to Kübler-Ross. Sadness, panic, frustration, and resolution are not part of her stages, making Choices *A*, *C*, and *D* incorrect.

84. A: Initiative vs. guilt occurs between the ages of three and five. Choice *B*, trust vs. mistrust, occurs in the first year of life. Choice *C*, autonomy vs. shame and doubt, begins around 18 months and lasts until about two or three years of age. Choice *D*, identity vs. confusion, occurs between the ages of 12 and 18.

85. C: The client's symptoms are all common to PTSD, and EMDR is an empirically established method of treatment for that condition. Choice *A* would be inappropriate because psychoanalysis is not an empirically established treatment method. Choice *B* is incorrect because reoccurring nightmares are not a typical symptom of major depressive disorder. Choice *D* is incorrect because there is no indication that the client is faking symptoms.

86. C: Sleep diaries can pinpoint triggers that cause disturbances in sleep and assist in developing positive sleep hygiene practices. Choice *A* can give the client more anxiety if he or she is not able to meet a certain goal. Choice *B* should be a collaborative intervention with the client's medical doctor if needed. Choice *D* is incorrect; sleep-wake schedules should remain as consistent as possible to encourage healthy sleep hygiene.

87. A. The client is likely experiencing auditory hallucinations. The remaining choices are not evident in the given situation.

88. C: Substantive advice can be considered directive and may involve the counselor imposing his or her opinions onto clients. Process advice is more empowering and helps clients navigate options for solving their own issues. In some situations, it may be appropriate for the counselor to offer process advice; it is less likely that substantive advice should be given.

89. C: Contributing to the next generation is the goal of individuals in the Generativity vs. Stagnation phase. Choice *A* is part of the Trust vs. Mistrust phase. Choice *B* is part of Identity vs. Identity Confusion. Choice *D* is part of Autonomy vs. Shame and Doubt.

90. C: A healthy attachment will result in distress when the caregiver leaves the room; this is a normal response with a secure attachment style. Choice *A* is a type of attachment style in which children are wary of strangers and will become highly distressed when the caregiver is not in the room. Choice *B* is not a type of attachment style. Choice *D* will result in no distress; children with an anxious-avoidant attachment style do not seek closeness and will not show preference for caregivers over strangers.

91. B: Ethical guidelines regarding counselor self-disclosure indicate that it should occur only when beneficial for the client. Choice *A* is too broad of a statement. Choices *C* and *D* may or may not be true, depending on the client.

92. A: Emotional forgiveness is akin to forgiving someone from the heart and requires an emotional release of the wrongdoing. Choice *B*, decisional, is the first type of forgiveness; it is an intellectual move toward forgiveness. Choice *C*, situational, and Choice *D*, conditional, are not components of the forgiveness paradigm.

93. C: Carl Rogers was responsible for developing and influencing many of the theories related to understanding humans holistically. Choice *A*, Wilhelm Wundt, was a German physician who founded the Institute of Experimental Psychology. Choice *B*, Sigmund Freud, is considered the founder of psychoanalysis. Choice *D*, Raymond Cattell, is known for his exploration into empirical psychology and is known for developing theories on fluid and crystallized intelligence.

94. D: The Gottman Method is a type of therapy that identifies and addresses the natural defenses that hinder communication and bonding. The technique enhances a sense of understanding, empathy, and interpersonal growth by practicing conflict management and positive interactions between couples. Choices *A*, *B*, and *C* are all characteristic of Gestalt therapy, which is designed to help clients increase mindfulness, focus on the present, and understand the different aspects of an experience, mental health issue, or conflict.

95. B: Nihilistic delusions are beliefs that a major catastrophic event will occur. Persecutory delusions are beliefs that one is being or will be harmed by another person or agency. Grandiose delusions are

177

beliefs that one possesses talents, beauty, or power that are not supported by objective evidence. Referential delusions are unwarranted beliefs that impersonal gestures or things occurring in the environment are directly related to oneself.

96. D: The counselor should consider using another treatment method because the Adlerian therapy method has not proven successful with this client. Choice *A* would not be appropriate because shyness is not treatable with medication. Choice *B* could possibly harm the client since she might interpret the referral as a rejection, further entrenching her fear of being with people. Choice *C* is incorrect because the empty chair technique would be an insufficient method to improve shyness after several months of treatment.

97. B: Reflection is when a counselor restates the client's words so the client knows that the counselor is listening and understands. The remaining choices are incorrect.

98. D: It is appropriate to discuss spiritual issues when the client has agreed to discuss them. The remaining choices are irrelevant when determining whether spiritual issues can be discussed in counseling.

99. D: Cognitive Information Processing (CIP) asserts that content and process are the main components of the career decision-making process. The content is what an individual must know to make a decision (such as self-assessment and knowledge of careers and options). The process is what an individual needs to do to make a decision.

100. D: It would never be appropriate for a counselor to yell at a counselee. It would be appropriate (and necessary) for the counselor to address the belligerent group member but not in a hostile, demeaning way. The remaining choices are incorrect.

101. A: When working with counseling clients online, you must encrypt all client intake information, communication, evaluations, and other related records. Encryption works by securing messages sent online so that only the sender and the target audience are able to see the information. Choices *B, C,* and *D* won't help maintain the client's privacy.

102. C: Counselors should never offer medication or supplements of any kind to clients since it is out of their scope of practice. The remaining choices are all suitable options for counselors to explore.

103. C: Briefly, Roberts's seven phases of crisis management are:
- Biopsychosocial assessments
- Making contact and quickly establishing rapport
- Identifying problems and possible cause of crisis
- Providing counseling
- Working on coping strategies
- Implementing an action plan for treatment
- Creating a follow-up plan

104. A: Population, time and environment. If a research design can produce the same outcomes across multiple types of people, multiple seasons or temporal periods, and across a variety of settings and situational contexts, it is considered to have high external validity. Any results are likely generalizable to the target population.

105. A: Bowen discusses the idea that a strong sense of self is associated with confidence and pragmatism, while a weak sense of self is associated with seeking approval from others under the

178

concept of "Differentiation of Self." This refers to how much an individual's personal beliefs differ from that of his or her group's beliefs and plays an important role in whether someone develops a strong or weak sense of self.

106. A: Medication management is not within the counselor's scope of competence. The remaining choices are all appropriate and within the counselor's scope of practice.

107. A: This kind of statement would be made by a counselor to model appropriate feedback. The remaining choices are incorrect.

108. A: Feeling the need to urinate is not a symptom of anxiety. The remaining choices are all symptoms of anxiety.

109. B: This is an example of negative reinforcement. This type of behavioral technique involves changing a behavior by removing its unwanted consequence. It intends to teach that the behavior (leaving late for work) is associated with an unfavorable experience (being stuck in traffic). The negative aspect is the act of removing, as opposed to positive reinforcement that adds a consequence, such as a reward for a desired behavior, which makes Choice *C* incorrect. Choice *A*, modeling, is when a counselor models a behavior for a client so they can behave in a similar fashion. Choice *D*, classical conditioning, is when two stimuli are paired repeatedly, and the response to the first stimulus eventually becomes the response to the second stimulus by itself. This is shown in Pavlov's dog, where eventually the dog salivates to the sound of a bell, even if there is no food paired with it anymore.

110. A: Choices *B*, *C*, and *D* are all goals of family therapy. Resolving intrapsychic conflicts is a function associated with psychoanalysis and not family therapy.

111. C: Based on the information given, referring the client to a psychiatrist for medication is not warranted. Choice *A* would be helpful because he could learn to counter his thoughts with realistic or alternative appraisals of his situation. Choice *B* is a good option because it would teach the client to notice how his thoughts are impacting his physical stress and how to calm his body and thoughts. Choice *D* could be helpful for the client to process with his former employer (in an imaginary way) how he feels about losing his job.

112. A: Qualitative research typically focuses on the analysis of a group without many rigid parameters in place. A discussion within a focus group provides the counselor an opportunity to gain perspective on personal experiences from participants in the group. Surveys and more analytical approaches take the candidness out of the research and focus more on concrete numbers and data.

113. B: ADHD in adults can affect personal relationships and workplace success as a result of mood swings, short temper, and difficulties coping with stress; interpersonal conflict can result from being off-task, having trouble paying attention, or struggling to control impulses. Choice *A* is a possible condition that develops from having ADHD but is not a focus area when providing therapy. Choice *C* is a type of counseling intervention. Choice *D* is not characteristic of ADHD.

114. B: Unconditional positive regard is when a counselor accepts all aspects of a client, whether good or bad. The remaining choices are incorrect.

115. D: A combat veteran is not likely to display psychosis as a symptom. The remaining choices are common symptoms of PTSD, which is common among combat veterans.

116. A: There are thought to be two types of grieving: instrumental grieving and intuitive grieving. Instrumental grieving is more thinking-based and focused on solving problems rather than feeling and is viewed as a more masculine approach to grief. Intuitive grieving is more emotional and focused on sharing and processing feelings and is considered a more feminine approach to grief.

117. C: Cultural encapsulation refers to a narrow viewpoint of global cultures or any culture differing from one's own. Choice *A*, acculturation, refers to the process of group-level change that can occur when two or more cultures meet. Choice *B*, assimilation, refers to the process of one or several people from a minority group accepting and modeling characteristics of a larger group. Choice *D*, worldview, refers to the set of basic presuppositions that someone holds about the nature of reality, the world, culture, and society on a domestic and global scale.

118. D: One year of sobriety is not a protective factor against suicide; in fact, recent addiction may put the person at a greater risk for suicide. SAMHSA considers the remaining choices to be protective factors against suicide.

119. C: Although challenges with clients (Choices *A, B,* and *D*) can contribute to counselor burnout, the main reasons for burnout are overwork and lack of appropriate supervision.

120. A: The counselor should ask the client what he would like the focus to be because clients control their treatment goals. Choice *B* takes the power away from the client, which is detrimental to treatment. Choices *C* and *D* may or may not be warranted; the counselor would need more information before taking either of these actions.

121. A: Cognitive reframing is a technique that helps clients identify and change the way ideas, emotions, and experiences are viewed; clients are encouraged to look at situations from a different perspective and empathize with the decisions made by others. Choice *B* is incorrect; reminiscence therapy is used to treat severe memory loss and would not prove helpful in this situation. Choice *C* is incorrect because cognitive processing helps clients process traumatic events and is beneficial for clients with posttraumatic stress disorder. Choice *D* explores the different roles and identities that can impact behavioral patterns; the given situation does not depict this behavior.

122. C: Strengths-based counseling can help the client identify positive attributes they have used in the past and apply them to present problems. Choice *A* refers to cognitive behavioral therapy. Choice *B* is not implied here since the gestalt approach would focus on awareness of current situations, not methods used in the past. Choice *D* refers to looking into one's childhood issues to resolve present problems.

123. C: A client's self-report of symptoms is one of the main considerations when formulating a diagnosis. Choice *A* (socioeconomic status) is not a diagnostic criterion. Choices *B* and *D* (cultural background and psychometric assessments) can contribute to the formulation of diagnoses, but they are not central factors.

124. B: It is important for counselors to give clients the option of coming back in the future should the need arise because clients should know that they can return to counseling without feeling any sense of failure. Choice *A* is something that the counselor could disclose, but it is not necessary. Choice *C* is incorrect because clients should know that they are welcome to return if any other issues arise. Choice *D* would be unhelpful and potentially harmful to clients. Instead, they should be congratulated on meeting their treatment goals.

125. B: Studies have demonstrated that avoiding painful thoughts and emotions is not an effective long-term solution and may create bigger problems; therefore, Choice *B* is correct. The remaining choices are all healthy coping mechanisms.

126. A: Susan has knowledge that Christine has a history of drug abuse. Christine has shown signs of possible relapse. Susan also has safety concerns for Christine's children based on what she has seen and the way Christine has behaved. Due to her concerns, a good faith report is warranted, which will require that Susan break confidentiality to report the suspected child abuse and neglect.

127. B: The inability to focus on video games is not part of the diagnostic criteria for ADHD. In fact, although individuals with this condition are unable to focus on many activities, they are sometimes able to focus on video games. The remaining choices are all elements of the diagnostic criteria.

128. C: The Outcome Rating Scale (ORS) should be introduced at the beginning of the session to obtain the client's sense of well-being in regard to therapy. The scale assesses areas of life that can change as a result of therapeutic interventions. The four items assessed are interpersonal well-being, symptom distress, social roles, and overall well-being. Choice *A* assesses the counselor's skills development and professional competencies; clients are not involved in rating a CCS. Choice *B* is a feedback tool that should be given to the client at the end of the counseling session. Choice *D* is for clients in group therapy to report their experience in relation to overall cohesion, approach, and goals; it helps to measure group therapy alliance.

129. A: If an individual diagnosed with cyclothymia has a major depressive episode, then their diagnosis of cyclothymia should be dropped. The remaining choices are incorrect because they indicate that the original diagnosis should be kept while another is added.

130. C: Choice *C* would not be a healthy way for a trainee counselor to counsel families. The remaining choices are possible ways that a trainee counselor could manage a highly conflictual family.

131. C: Empty nest syndrome is characterized by feelings of sadness and purposelessness that parents may feel when their children leave the family home and begin adult independence. Choice *A*, independence, occurs when the individual leaves the family unit into which he or she was born to establish independence. Choice *B*, parenting, is when a couple adds children to the family unit and raises them. Choice *D*, retirement, is the stage that focuses less on caretaking and professional work.

132. B: Choice *B* would be unethical because the counselor cannot break confidentiality under this circumstance. Choice *A* would be appropriate because it provides the client with support without pressure. Choice *C* is acceptable because, even though a counselor can encourage a client to break the cycle of shame by sharing with appropriate people, it is ultimately the client's decision when to share and with whom. Choice *D* is appropriate because it would allow the client to speak freely about it.

133. C: The distinguishing characteristic between bipolar I and II is whether the client has ever had a full manic episode. Individuals with bipolar I have experienced a full manic episode while those with bipolar II have experienced only a hypomanic episode. Choice *A* (a decreased need for sleep) can be present in both bipolar I and II. Choice *B* (excessive shopping, gambling, or sexual activity during a depressive episode) would occur during a manic episode, not a depressive one. Choice *D* (a full major depressive episode) is not a distinguishing feature because it can occur in both bipolar I and II.

134. D: Third-party payers such as insurance companies may request basic client information, diagnosis, and treatment for billing purposes. Choices *A* and *B* are not considered third parties. Choice *C* is incorrect because client confidentiality is limited in group therapy.

135. C: The validity of the test ensures that the tool is measuring what it is intended to measure. Choices *A*, *B*, and *D* do not play a role in the worth of the test.

136. D: Critical Incident Stress Debriefing (CISD) is best suited to secondary trauma victims. First-degree victims need more direct assistance, making Choice *A* incorrect. HR professionals and first responders can provide needed help, making Choices *B* and *C* incorrect.

137. D: Autocratic leaders are most likely to lead with control and power. Democratic leaders use consensus and belonging, making Choice *A* incorrect. Laissez-faire leaders operate with little to no structure, making Choice *B* incorrect. Choice *C* is not a group of characteristics for any main style of leadership.

138. B: EMDR would be an inappropriate treatment method because it is primarily used for trauma recovery. Choice *A* would be appropriate because CBT (Cognitive Behavioral Therapy) entails rationally addressing and altering one's thoughts. Choice *C* would be appropriate since clinical studies have demonstrated effectiveness when using this method to treat emotional dysregulation. Choice *D* would be appropriate because social connectedness is often a good antidote for ruminations and sadness.

139. A: Negative reinforcement encourages specific behaviors by removing unwanted stimuli. An example of this is putting on a seat belt to remove the sound of the car dinging (reminding you to fasten your seat belt). Choice *B*, adding desired stimuli, is considered positive reinforcement. Negative reinforcement does not include punishment for unwanted behavior, which makes Choice *C* incorrect. Negative reinforcement also does not include extinction of stimuli (Choice *D*) but the removal of unwanted stimuli; the "unwanted" here is important.

140. C: Yalom's three-stage model includes orientation, conflict/dominance, and development of cohesiveness. Corey's stages include initial, transition, working, and termination, making Choice *D* incorrect. Forming, norming, storming, and performing are included in Tuckman's theory, making Choice *A* incorrect. Choice *B* is a mixture of all of these stages.

141. D: This is not part of any specific marriage therapy. There is not a specific form of marriage therapy that encourages clients to yell at each other during their sessions. The remaining choices are incorrect.

142. D: School-aged children establish either industry or inferiority in this stage of development; poor relationships in school can lead to feelings of inferiority. Choice *A* can potentially happen during infancy when needs are not being met. Choice *B* happens during early childhood when asserting independence. Choice *C* occurs during the preschool years when a parent's reaction impacts the child's attitudes and behaviors.

143. D: Safety plans are useful for clients who experience harmful thoughts or situations. Choice *A* does not provide enough information to determine if this client is in danger. Choice *B* is a healthy coping mechanism to alleviate the problem. Choice *C* is not displaying repetitive behavior that requires a safety plan.

144. B: The counselor is trying to reframe the client's perspective in less drastic terms. Choice *A*, confronting, is when a counselor challenges a client. Choice *C*, mirroring, and Choice *D*, underestimating, are not therapeutic techniques.

145. C: A regular sleep routine helps to establish a consistent cycle, making it easier to fall sleep and wake up on time. Exercising for 30 minutes before bedtime does not give the body time to relax and get ready for sleep, so Choice *A* is incorrect. Choice *B* is incorrect because staying away from screens that emit blue light for at least 20 minutes before bedtime is not long enough; it is recommended to turn off screens at least one or two hours before bedtime. Eating chocolate left on one's pillow might sound romantic, but chocolate contains caffeine and should be avoided before bed. Therefore, Choice *D* is incorrect.

146. C: Choice *C* lists the correct stages of Motivational Interviewing. The remaining choices are incorrect.

147. C: Choice *C* is correct because females develop language earlier than males. The remaining choices are all incorrect.

148. B: Adler believed that birth position and the context of one's sibling relationships played a pivotal role in shaping one's personality. Choice *A*, Abraham Maslow, created Maslow's hierarchy of needs, a pyramid that depicts biological and psychological needs. Choice *C*, Albert Bandura, was a psychologist who theorized that learning takes place socially through observation and imitation of others and that not all behaviors are conditioned. Choice *D*, Anna Freud, was a psychoanalyst that focused on the ego and child development.

149. A: The Myers-Briggs Type Indicator (MBTI) is an example of an objective personality test that evaluates multiple personality dimensions based on statistical analysis of client responses. Choices *B*, *C*, and *D* are all symptom checklists.

150. D: Modeling occurs in the counseling process when counselors demonstrate (or model) appropriate reactions and behaviors for clients to follow. Modeling is nonverbal and helps clients learn appropriate behavior through observation.

151. C: Contempt, criticism, stonewalling, and defensiveness are the four communication styles that can predict the end of a relationship. Choices *A*, *B*, and *D* are not part of Gottman's formulation.

152. B: Women commonly discuss issues related to balancing a career and family, self-esteem, and mitigating societal expectations and pressures. Men, on the other hand, are more likely to discuss work pressures, time commitment to family, work-life balance, and verbally expressing fears and concerns.

153. C: A social worker should always assess their own personal safety, as well as the safety of others, when deciding if a confidential disclosure should be discussed with the client. For example, a social worker is working with someone who has a history of violence toward women, and he discloses that he has been contemplating harming his neighbor who has turned down his advances. In this instance, it would be safer if the social worker didn't discuss the disclosure with the client. Given his history of violence, discussing the disclosure might put both the therapist and the neighbor at risk.

154. A: Vertical interventions occur when the group leader focuses on individuals rather than the group (also referred to as intrapersonal). Choice *B* is incorrect; when the group leader focuses on the group as a whole rather than individuals, this is known as horizontal interventions, or interpersonal.

155. D: Gratitude has not been clinically demonstrated to decrease psychotic episodes. The remaining choices have all been found to be associated with gratitude.

183

156. B: Cognitive behavioral therapy can be used with individuals who have some compromised intellectual functioning. The remaining choices are forms of therapy that would not be suitable for this individual.

157. D: Differentiation is the process whereby individuals maintain a sense of who they are in relation to those with whom they are in intimate or close relationships. Instead of losing oneself and conforming to others, one maintains their personal identity, thoughts, feelings, and behaviors. The remaining choices do not describe this phenomenon.

158. A: Choice *A* is incorrect; this violates counselor/client confidentiality laws. Ensuring the client's needs are within the counselor's scope of practice, helping the client gain a better understanding of themselves, and evaluating the effectiveness of counseling interventions are all reasons a counselor would administer a test to a client.

159. A: Choice *A* is correct since the client has developed an addiction and needs treatment. Choice *B* is incorrect because if a person's use of marijuana interferes with their daily functioning, then it is an addiction that requires treatment regardless of whether the substance use is legal. Choice *C* is incorrect because drug use is not a reportable issue for which the counselor can break confidentiality. Choice *D* is not a good treatment decision because the client should learn to break the addiction without medication.

160. D: Choice *D* is not a component of creating a healthy support system. The remaining choices describe potential places where clients can develop relationships that might become part of their healthy support system.

161. D: Groups help clients practice honesty and communicate their feelings openly. Choice *A* is incorrect; the goal is for members to act on their own instincts and not be dependent on others. Choice *B* is incorrect because clients should never be forced to participate; free-form dialogue allows members to willingly express their thoughts. Choice *C* is not a guarantee after clients attend group therapy.

162. A: Auditory hallucinations can often direct the client to self-harm or become homicidal; counselors should assess suicidal or homicidal intent. Choices *B, C,* and *D* are all important to ask to establish common occurrences, distraction methods, and aggravating factors; however, safety should be prioritized prior to establishing patterns.

163. B: Choice *B* would be inappropriate. Since she has suffered sexual abuse, she may feel threatened if the counselor initiates physical contact. The remaining choices would facilitate trust with the counselor.

164. A: Genograms are diagrams that display familial patterns across multiple generations. The remaining choices do not accurately represent the purpose of genograms.

165. B: Similar to the term mode, which indicates the number that occurs the most often in a dataset, modal behavior describes behaviors that occur most often within a group of people. Choice *A*, culture, refers to the beliefs, customs, and arts of a particular people. Choice *C*, tripartite, refers to awareness, knowledge, and skills of multicultural counseling. Choice *D*, ethnology, is a branch of anthropology that systematically studies and compares the similarities and differences between cultures.

166. B: Having a structured day allows for a sense of productivity and normalcy. Choice *A* is incorrect because clients should continue to feel a sense of independence. Choice *C* is incorrect; if clients decide

184

to continue working, they should be encouraged to work in a less stressful job. Choice *D* could to boredom and disillusionment.

167. C: Transference is the process whereby someone projects onto the counselor a previous relationship. Choice *A*, resistance, does not apply here as it pertains to reluctance to take part in the counseling process. Choice *B*, countertransference, is when a counselor has emotional reactions to a client based on a previous relationship. Choice *D*, role reversal, does not apply. This would involve the client swapping roles with the leader or another member of the group.

168. A: Safety plans are created for clients to use during crisis situations; clients should be able to initiate coping strategies, such as music, meditation, and exercise and be able to identify family, friends, or professional organizations that can help. Choices *B* and *D* are incorrect; interventions during crisis should always be client-centered. Choice *C* is only partially correct; the plan must incorporate interventions to perform during a crisis.

169. A: Tertiary groups deal with long-standing pathology; think of it as the third and most acute level. Tertiary groups are used to facilitate long-term personality change or rehabilitation. Primary groups are educational in nature, making Choice *C* incorrect. Secondary groups are focused on counseling, making Choice *B* incorrect. Psychoeducational group structure refers to a type of group designed to teach individuals to develop or maintain specific skills, making Choice *D* incorrect.

170. D: Occupations are not considered when formulating diagnoses, though some occupations may put individuals at greater risk for the development of certain diagnoses. Choice *A* (mental health history) provides clinicians with information about the type, length, and severity of symptoms; this information is necessary when formulating a diagnosis. Choice *B* (length of time that symptoms have been present) is a defining characteristic of certain conditions such as persistent depressive disorder. Choice *C* (cultural background) must be a consideration because symptoms occurring in the Western world may not be considered unhealthy in other regions of the world.

171. C: Talking to the child's teacher would be unethical because it violates confidentiality. The counselor is only required to report abuse to the local authorities. The remaining choices are all valid options.

172. B: If a client is hallucinating, then they are unable to make the rational decisions necessary to take care of basic needs; therefore, hospitalization is needed. Choices *A* and *C* are incorrect because homelessness and high levels of depression are not grounds for hospitalization. Choice *D* is incorrect; if a client has recently beaten his wife, then a report should be made with the police, but hospitalization is not necessary.

173. B: This is an example of the leader trying to develop empathy between group members. The remaining choices are incorrect.

174. A: Calling the client's wife would be unacceptable because it is the client's decision to reveal this information. The remaining choices are possible options for the counselor.

175. B: Choice *B* is correct. It is unethical for counselors to have sexual dual relationships with their clients. Choice *A* is incorrect. Suicidal clients should not be referred to another counselor but rather evaluated for possible hospitalization. Choice *C* is incorrect. A client who is threatening to harm the counselor should be reported to the police. Choice *D* is incorrect. Prior to closing a practice, counselors must prepare their clients for eventual termination. This may include referral to another counselor, but it is not mandatory.

185

176. D: All of these stereotypes exist toward older workers and are a form of ageism. These ideas include that older workers may need extra accommodations to work, may not understand new technologies, or may have health issues that lead to more absentee days or higher health insurance costs.

177. B: Carkhuff's scale measures the effectiveness of a counselor or the degree to which a counselor is providing empathy, genuineness, concreteness, and respect. Choice *A*, accurate reflection, is a counseling skill, but not one measured by Carkhuff. Defensiveness of a counselor, Choice *C*, is incorrect. The scale does refer to how defensive a counselor is toward the client, but its goal is to measure effectiveness. Choice *D*, structuring of sessions, is important, but it is not the correct answer.

178. C: The four horsemen of the apocalypse are contempt, criticism, stonewalling, and defensiveness. When partners communicate using these four styles, they increase the likelihood of the relationship ending. The remaining choices are not part of Gottman's theory.

179. C: Ageism. Ageism is discrimination against someone because of his or her age. In this situation, the manager is automatically filtering out older applicants even if they bring appropriate skills and knowledge for the position, simply because of age. Choice *A*, sexism, is when prejudice or discrimination is shown against someone on the basis of sex. Choice *B*, millennial-leaning bias is not an actual term. Choice *D*, classism, is prejudice against someone because of a certain socioeconomic class.

180. A: The counselor demonstrates empathy by seeing the client's perspective of the situation and displaying understanding. The remaining choices are incorrect.

181. C: For a diagnosis of PTSD, the symptoms must last for at least one month. The remaining choices are all criteria for PTSD.

182. D: The storming phase involves conflict, discord, and struggles to agree upon a leader. Choice *A* refers to the forming phase, where the group members are just beginning to get acquainted and may be anxious and less vocal. Choice *B* is adjourning, which is the point in which the group is terminated. Role-play is not relevant to group development but is a technique used in therapy to help clients work through how they would handle conflict with individuals.

183. C: Cancelling all afternoon clients so the counselor can spend the rest of the day with the current client is likely to foster unhealthy dependency and communicate that the client is unable to handle his emotions independently. Choice *A* is a healthy strategy aimed at helping the client re-enter the world when the session is over. Choice *B* provides opportunities for the client to learn how to manage his painful emotions. Choice *D* is important because much of the work of counseling is accomplished between sessions.

184. B: A report from the client's neighbor would not be considered when formulating a diagnosis because the counselor would not discuss the client with their neighbors. The remaining choices are useful sources when formulating a diagnosis.

185. A: Choice *A* allows the children to adapt to the new parent gradually. Choice *B* may cause the stepchildren to rebel against the father in the newly formed unit. Choices *C* and *D* are incorrect because permissive and authoritarian styles of discipline do not encourage stability or attachment to the new stepparent.

186. A: The World Health Organization publishes the International Classification of Diseases (ICD) as an international resource for medical and epidemiological data, health statuses, and other health information. The United Nations, Choice *B*, is a global union of members dedicated to confronting, managing, and solving world problems. The International Journal of Health Sciences, Choice *C*, is a peer-reviewed journal dedicated to all aspects of health. The United States Agency for International Development, Choice *D*, administers civilian foreign aid when needed.

187. A: Choice *A* is correct because the culture they come from does not generally encourage the disclosure of personal struggles to strangers. The remaining choices could be beneficial to them.

188. D: Involving a third person in a conflicting situation is known as triangulation; manipulating the third person to resolve the conflict is not beneficial for dealing with extended family issues. Choice *B* is a positive technique used to develop alternative solutions to stagnant routines. Choices *A* and *C* are not terms used in the management of extended family conflicts.

189. B: Sliding fee scale is a method of determining fees based on the client's income. Choice *A* is payment with cash or credit card. Choice *C* is a savings account that allows money to be set aside pre-tax. Choice *D* pays the counselor directly after a claim is reviewed.

190. B: Resolving childhood issues is the crux of psychoanalytic therapy, in individuals or in groups. Decreasing anxiety, Choice *A*, can be a goal of individual therapy as well as Rational Emotive or psychodynamic groups. Resolution of current relationship issues, Choice *C*, is the goal of family therapy. Increasing daily functioning, Choice *D*, would be a goal of Rational Emotive as well as psychodynamic groups.

191. A: Exposure therapy helps clients experience social situations progressively; it is done in time increments to lessen the physical effects of anxiety. Choice *B* is used to increase self-awareness and encourage better life choices; the client in the scenario is struggling with social anxiety. Choice *C* is not appropriate for the scenario because positive psychology is a theory that aims to help clients identify happiness from moment to moment. Choice *D* is a technique used to encourage problem solving and meet personal needs such as power, freedom, and survival.

192. D: Raymond Cattell proposed the concept of fluid and crystallized intelligence in the 1940s. John Ertl, Choice *A*, invented a neural efficiency analyzer that measured the speed and efficiency of electrical activity in the brain using an EEG. Alfred Binet, Choice *B*, developed the first test to determine which children would succeed in school. Sir Francis Galton, Choice *C*, believed that intelligence was genetically determined and could be promoted through selective parenting.

193. B: In this case, gender is an example of a nominal measure. A nominal measure describes variables that are categorical in nature. An interval measure, Choice *A*, describes variables that use equally spaced intervals (e.g., number of minutes, temperature). An ordinal measure, Choice *C*, describes variables that can be ranked (e.g., Likert scales, 1 to 10 rating scales). A ratio measure, Choice *D*, describes anything that has a true "zero" point available (e.g., angles, dollars, cents).

194. A: Direct suicide ideation statements should be taken seriously, and help should be obtained for the client promptly. Choice *B* may be an option after a suicide risk assessment has been performed and the client discloses his support systems. Choices *C* and *D* are dangerous interventions that may cause the client to harm themselves if not assessed properly.

195. A: In order to predict a positive counseling relationship, the therapeutic alliance should be established as early as possible. Choices *B* and *C* are later than desired; the alliance needs to be established early to improve counseling outcomes. Choice *D* is incorrect; the timing of a therapeutic alliance is crucial for a good counseling outcome.

196. D: The counselor should have the client sign a HIPAA form so they can contact the hospital. The hospital could provide the counselor with valuable information that would aid in treatment planning. Choice *A* is incorrect because the client is likely already on medication from the hospital. Choice *B* is incorrect; while psychological assessments might be helpful later, they should not be the first step. Choice *C* is incorrect because this approach may or may not be appropriate for this particular client.

197. B: Marital conflict, dysfunction in one spouse, impairment in one or more children, and emotional distance are four different relationship patterns in the nuclear family emotional system, and they affect how family units handle various problems.

198. C: Creating a climate for change generates opportunities for reflection and facilitates the client's awareness of possibilities. Choice *A* is incorrect because counselors should help clients uncover solutions to their own problems. Choice *B* is incorrect because setting goals should be a collaborative effort. Choice *D* is incorrect because clients should maintain power in the relationship while counselors use it to assist clients in developing strategies for change.

199. D: The counselor should not agree to meet weekly with the client for lunch because the client could interpret such interactions as the development of a friendship or more intimate relationship. The counselor should keep the relationship strictly professional. The remaining choices are acceptable methods of working with a client.

200. D: Gestalt therapy helps clients focus on the present as opposed to the past or future. Choice *A* focuses on values clarification, self-worth, and acceptance; the client in the scenario is experiencing different issues. Choice *B* is a type of therapy that identifies and addresses the natural defenses that hinder communication and bonding; the scenario does not depict communication issues. Choice *C* focuses on the hierarchy of needs and explores morality and ethics; the scenario does not speak to such issues.

NCE Practice Test #2

1. Sadie recently moved into a foster home. Her foster parents notice that she frequently complains of stomachaches, seems exhausted, and becomes disconnected when they try to talk to her about her recent move to their home. They are new to fostering children and express that they don't understand what is going on with Sadie. What would be helpful for these foster parents to know?
   a. The more they try to get her to talk about her experiences, the better Sadie will feel.
   b. The foster parents should change their household setup until Sadie seems comfortable.
   c. The foster parents should stop talking about Sadie's biological family and the home she came from.
   d. Trauma can manifest in children as somatic complaints, dissociation, and difficult sleeping.

2. A client who has been seen by the same counselor for a year is requesting an ADHD diagnosis to show their primary care provider to obtain medication management for their symptoms. The counselor does not have specialized training in this area, and this is the first time this client has mentioned symptoms of ADHD in a session. How should the counselor proceed?
   a. The counselor should ask more about the client's ADHD symptoms and offer methods of reducing their intensity and duration by providing mindfulness techniques.
   b. The counselor should offer to write a note regarding the diagnosis since a formal ADHD evaluation may not be covered by the client's insurance.
   c. The counselor should refer the client to an assessment center that can evaluate them for ADHD and provide a formal diagnosis.
   d. Both A and C

3. Which of the following is true regarding the dependent and independent ANOVA?
   a. The independent ANOVA is also called the simple analysis of variance or one-way analysis of variance, while the dependent ANOVA is also referred to as the repeated measures ANOVA or within-subjects ANOVA.
   b. The independent ANOVA is used for unrelated groups, while the dependent ANOVA is used for related groups.
   c. ANOVAs compare the means of two or more groups.
   d. All of the above

4. Which statement best describes the concept of out-group homogeneity?
   a. "No one else experiences things like I do."
   b. "We are diverse, but they are all alike."
   c. "You're so articulate for being of that race."
   d. "I wish I could be like everyone else."

5. Why is it beneficial for counselors to initiate open conversations with their clients regarding treatment plan compliance?
   a. The client is more likely to adhere to the plan if they understand the benefits and potential risks.
   b. There is no benefit to this; counselors should not discuss treatment plan compliance with their clients.
   c. The client will feel too intimidated to risk non-adherence to the plan.
   d. The client will understand how important the plan is to their counselor.

6. You are working with a parent who shares that every time their child fails a test at school, they must complete an extra chore at home. This is an example of _____.
   a. negative punishment
   b. positive punishment
   c. systematic desensitization
   d. extinction

7. How does a counselor demonstrate self-awareness and emotional stability?
   a. Through immediate self-disclosure of their own biases and faults when first meeting with a new client
   b. By showing congruence between their mood and affect
   c. By expounding on any incongruence between their mood and affect
   d. Through explaining how they maintain both self-awareness and emotional stability to clients

8. Which of the following is NOT especially useful when conducting an initial interview for a highly motivated, help-seeking client?
   a. Rapport-building
   b. Gentle redirection
   c. Motivational interviewing
   d. Open-ended questions

9. Ben notices changes in his partner, Hank. Hank has been attending family gatherings less often, is struggling to maintain social relationships, and has started muttering to himself quite often. Ben notices that the content of Hank's ramblings seems nonsensical, and Hank is quite defensive and tearful when Ben tries to ask him about it. Hank has also been insisting that their neighbor has been spreading rumors about him even though they've never had contact with each other. What is the most plausible explanation?
   a. Psychosis
   b. Anxiety
   c. Depression
   d. Paranoid delusions

10. Adolescent development of personal fables can be dangerous because:
   a. It can lead them to dream more about their future endeavors.
   b. It involves the adolescent's belief that others are constantly focusing on them.
   c. It is not healthy or normal for an adolescent to be egocentric.
   d. It can lead to an increase in risk-taking behaviors.

11. If you are a therapist who takes a(n) _____ perspective, you might treat a client with addiction by identifying their life goal and using that to help motivate the client in their recovery process.
   a. Adlerian
   b. cognitive behavioral
   c. dialectical behavioral
   d. psychoanalytical

12. Ursula has been immensely struggling with her journey to finish nursing school. She notes that she feels depressed and like she will never achieve her goals. As a logotherapist, you may use _____ to remind Ursula of the broader picture, including how much schooling she has completed so far, what she has overcome to get her where she is now, and what this achievement will mean for her and her family.
    a.   paradoxical intention
    b.   attitude modification
    c.   Socratic dialogue
    d.   dereflection

13. The result is significant at $p < .05$, and the value of p is $< .00001$. What does this indicate regarding the null hypothesis?
    a.   We cannot reject the null hypothesis.
    b.   We can reject the null hypothesis.
    c.   This tells us nothing about the null hypothesis.
    d.   We can accept the alternative hypothesis.

14. A counselor is working with a new couple. During their first session together, the counselor notices that one of the clients is hesitant to speak and has several visible bruises. The other client does all the talking, explaining that they are only in counseling because the other client's mother requested it and that nothing is really wrong. The counselor suspects abuse. What is the most ethical way for the counselor to proceed?
    a.   Suggest individual counseling to complete risk assessments with both clients, as couples counseling puts the potentially abused client at greater risk
    b.   Accuse the potentially abusive client of being abusive and defend the potentially abused client
    c.   Immediately decline to see either client again and refer the potential abuser to a domestic violence treatment program
    d.   Offer the potential victim of abuse information regarding the National Domestic Violence Hotline and cancel all future appointments

15. Tegan has developed an increased awareness of the importance of environmentally conscious decision making when it comes to shopping. She works for a large-scale retailer that does not adhere to good environmental practices. Although Tegan abhors this, she is dependent on this job for her livelihood. This is most likely to create _____ for Tegan.
    a.   rationalization
    b.   conformity
    c.   anxiety
    d.   cognitive dissonance

16. The transtheoretical model is also referred to as:
    a.   The Freudian model
    b.   The cognitive behavioral model
    c.   The stages of change model
    d.   The person-centered model

17. A counselor is working in an emergency department completing crisis assessments for patients reporting mental health concerns. The emergency department is especially full one day, and there are not enough rooms available for the assessment. A charge nurse requests that the counselor does the assessment in a somewhat crowded hallway so that they do not become more backed up with all the patients coming in. How should the counselor proceed?

   a. The counselor should complete the assessment in the hallway as the nurse has requested since they can assume this is just how the emergency department operates.
   b. The counselor should wait to do the assessment until a room becomes available.
   c. The counselor should complete the assessment in the hallway only if the hallway becomes less crowded so there is less chance of someone overhearing.
   d. The counselor should complete the assessment in the hallway's storage closet since it is the only space with a closeable door that is not currently occupied.

18. Seth is observational, analytic, and prefers to work independently and in his own direction. According to Holland, his career path might fall under the category:

   a. Enterprising
   b. Conventional
   c. Investigative
   d. Realistic

19. Amanda is in her initial therapy session. Her new therapist, Tessa, explains her therapeutic approach in the latter half of the session. Tessa states, "I am here to support you, but you are responsible for solving your own problems." This statement is most reflective of:

   a. Person-centered therapy
   b. Gestalt therapy
   c. Cognitive behavioral therapy
   d. Solution-focused therapy

20. Rebecca asks Harold to identify preferred focus areas for therapy. Which of the following is Rebecca asking Harold to identify?

   a. Diagnostic criteria
   b. Treatment goals and objectives
   c. Coping skills
   d. Triggers

21. What should a counselor do if a client comes to them with postpartum depression as a primary concern, and this is outside of the counselor's scope of expertise?

   a. The counselor should refer the client to a provider who specializes in treatment for clients with postpartum depression and seek training in this area.
   b. The counselor should move forward with the client's care since they have experience treating clients with major depressive disorder.
   c. The counselor should move forward with the client's care and seek training in this area at the same time.
   d. The counselor should continue to meet with the client unless the client expresses concern regarding the counselor's ability to treat them appropriately.

22. Trey is speaking with his counselor, Amanda, about his recent breakup. Which statement most effectively conveys empathy?
    a. "I'm so sorry that you are going through this. Breakups are always painful."
    b. "I just went through this last month; I know exactly how you feel."
    c. "People go through breakups all the time. Let me tell you the best way to deal with this."
    d. "Wow, I'm so sorry this is happening. I can hear how sad you're feeling."

23. Susie has been experiencing issues in her relationship and is talking about them to a friend. Susie notices lately that her husband has been putting her in the position of asking him directly for money despite the money being in a mutual account. Her friend points out that this is an example of:
    a. Emotional abuse
    b. Intimidation
    c. Economic control
    d. Coercion and threats

24. Wren finds that at the end of her workday, she feels worn out from being around people all day and struggles to readjust to being at home with her family. She finds herself trying to isolate when she gets home. As a new coping skill, she allots 30 minutes of alone time doing yoga at a nearby park before going home, which allows her to feel ready to interact socially again and lessens her desire to isolate when she gets home. This is an example of:
    a. Displacement
    b. Sublimation
    c. Rationalization
    d. Repression

25. Tracy is sharing her experiences with racism at work with a colleague whose behavior has been problematic recently. They respond with, "I could never be racist. My husband is black." What is this an example of?
    a. Objectivity
    b. Racial microaggression
    c. Transference
    d. Egotism

26. The career test with six occupational themes is also known as:
    a. Myers-Briggs type indicator
    b. Self-directed search
    c. Keirsey temperament sorter
    d. Vanderbilt rating scale

27. Elizabeth received a score of 14 on the PHQ-9. This reflects:
    a. A moderate level of depression
    b. A moderate level of anxiety
    c. An average IQ
    d. A likely diagnosis of ADHD

28. Which of the following is accurate in characterizing a typical patient with anorexia nervosa?
    a. They have a lack of preoccupation with food.
    b. They have no guilt associated with increased caloric intake.
    c. They are always engaged in regular binging and purging behaviors.
    d. They are most often in the age range of adolescent girls to young adult women.

193

29. When is a biopsychosocial interview typically conducted?
    a. At the beginning of counseling as part of the intake process
    b. Two months into counseling
    c. Six months into counseling
    d. Upon the discontinuation of counseling as part of the termination process

30. When are counselors required to break confidentiality for the safety of others?
    a. When a client is a danger to themselves
    b. When a client is a danger to others
    c. When they suspect a child is being abused or neglected
    d. All of the above

31. Ember is a client who has been working to achieve sobriety. She discloses that she has been spending a lot of time with her old friends who still use substances around her regularly. Ember shares that they have always been a source of support for her. Which statement would be a good use of confrontation?
    a. "That is a bad idea. You'll never get sober that way."
    b. "As long as they are supportive, I understand why you'd want to keep them around. Just be careful…"
    c. "When I was trying to get sober, that kind of scenario really did not work for me."
    d. "You value sobriety, but surrounding yourself with people who are still using doesn't seem to support that value."

32. In a counseling consultation, which of the following remains the same as in traditional counseling?
    a. The function of a counseling consultation remains the same as in traditional counseling.
    b. The role of a counseling consultant remains the same as in traditional counseling.
    c. The counseling skills utilized remain the same as in traditional counseling.
    d. The context of a counseling consultation remains the same as in traditional counseling.

33. You are leading a group therapy session. One group member named Greta raises her hand to share a story despite having shared one a few minutes ago. You say, "I am so glad that you want to share, Greta, but let's give other group members a chance to respond to the prompt." What is this an example of?
    a. Blocking
    b. Linking
    c. Confronting
    d. Active listening

34. As a child, your client struggled immensely with trying to ensure that "everything was perfect" for their parents. Now, they seem to struggle with being a "people pleaser" in their work environment, which is leading to burnout. This unhealthy interpersonal coping skill can be categorized as:
    a. Moving against people
    b. Moving with people
    c. Moving away from people
    d. Moving toward people

35. According to the Center for Disease Control (CDC), most victims of rape who are female have experienced rape before the age of:
   a. 18
   b. 35
   c. 25
   d. 45

36. Grace's grandmother recently passed away. Grace remembers a recent argument with her grandmother and is suddenly and frequently expressing the fear that she may pass away too. She resolves to always be agreeable and on her best behavior so that she "will not die next." Based on her conceptualization, what is her likely age group?
   a. Adolescent (12–18 years old)
   b. Preschool (3–5 years old)
   c. School age (6–11 years old)
   d. Toddler (under 3 years old)

37. A counselor has a severely underweight client diagnosed with anorexia nervosa who has recently been admitted to the hospital due to collapsing during a session. The client is stabilized and then transferred to inpatient care. What is the initial goal of inpatient treatment for this client?
   a. To verbalize self-acceptance
   b. To participate in groups regularly
   c. To be on bedrest
   d. To stop losing weight

38. Renee notices that her sister Chloe has been acting very out of character over the past few days. She has seemed very energetic, her moods have been shifting rapidly, she hasn't been eating, and her pupils have been dilated. Renee suspects that Chloe has been using:
   a. Amphetamines
   b. Heroin
   c. Alcohol
   d. Oxycodone

39. When should rapport-building begin?
   a. Around three sessions into the therapeutic relationship
   b. Whenever the client and counselor cross paths in public spaces
   c. During the initial meeting between client and counselor
   d. Around five sessions into the therapeutic relationship

40. Jane and her mother, Fredricka, are attending a day-long family event with out-of-town relatives whom Jane is unfamiliar with. For the entirety of the day, Jane is weepy, clingy, and often refuses to let Fredricka out of her sight. When Fredricka attempts to console Jane, she finds that Jane is difficult to comfort. This is reflective of a(n) _____ attachment style.
   a. insecure-avoidant
   b. secure
   c. insecure-ambivalent
   d. insecure-disorganized

41. Which theory supports the idea that people have all they need within themselves to succeed, but problematic thoughts and behaviors can be caused by a lack of problem-solving resources?
    a. Psychoanalytic
    b. Humanistic
    c. Behavioral
    d. Cognitive

42. A pro-life counselor receives an email from a prospective client who is seeking counseling after having an abortion. This is a primary concern related to her mental health. This is an emotionally charged topic for the counselor, and reading the email leaves them teary-eyed. How should the counselor handle this client's care?
    a. The counselor should ignore the appointment request.
    b. The counselor should respond with their personal opinion on the matter.
    c. The counselor should refer the client elsewhere.
    d. The counselor should ignore their feelings on the matter and move forward with scheduling the appointment.

43. How long should it take to conduct a diagnostic interview?
    a. Around two and a half hours
    b. Around five hours
    c. Around thirty minutes
    d. Around seven hours, including breaks

44. Molly has recently opened up to her family regarding her schizophrenia diagnosis with the support of her counselor. A hallmark of Molly's diagnosis is that she experiences vivid auditory hallucinations that she hears as multiple voices. Molly's family is seeking guidance for the most helpful way to respond when they notice that Molly is experiencing and interacting with her hallucinations. Which piece of advice correlates with best practices?
    a. When they notice Molly is engaged with the voices, Molly's family should join in responding to the voices as well.
    b. When Molly is hallucinating, Molly's family should empathize with the feelings the voices can elicit, such as fear and anxiety, and avoid challenging the validity of her experience.
    c. Molly's family should be encouraged to immediately reality test with Molly, reminding her that the voices are not real.
    d. Molly's family should take her to the hospital each time they notice she is speaking to the voices.

45. Which therapeutic model aims to help clients achieve self-acceptance, understand their emotions, and find alternative ways to regulate intense emotions that have led them to behave in destructive or harmful ways?
    a. Cognitive behavioral therapy
    b. Dialectal behavioral therapy
    c. Psychoanalysis
    d. Gestalt therapy

196

46. Opioid misuse impacts approximately 9.5 million people, according to a 2020 study by the Substance Abuse and Mental Health Services Administration (SAMHSA). Which opioid contributes to the largest percentage of opioid misuse?
   a. Heroin
   b. Cocaine
   c. Prescription pain medications
   d. Ketamine

47. Erikson's industry vs. inferiority developmental stage is denoted by the idea of competence, in that the child is seeking to identify what they excel at and to develop a sense of self-worth. The typical age range for this stage is:
   a. 5–12 years old
   b. 3–5 years old
   c. 12–18 years old
   d. 1.5–3 years old

48. What are the three elements of the ABC model?
   a. Assist, bolster, and collaborate
   b. Adversity, belief, and consequence
   c. Action, benefit, and closure
   d. Attitude, behavior, and condition

49. In adolescents, levels of the sleep hormone melatonin appear to rise later in the night and fall as the morning progresses. Generally, what might this cause?
   a. Teens present as sleepier in the morning and more awake at night.
   b. Teens are less likely to stay up late.
   c. Teens function best early to mid-morning.
   d. Teens need fewer hours of sleep per night than other age groups.

50. Which role in Karpman's triangle wants everyone to believe that they are "good"?
   a. Rescuer
   b. Victim
   c. Persecutor
   d. Observer

51. Brit and her partner Sara are navigating conflicts surrounding their communication style during disagreements. When they reach a topic that they struggle to communicate about, Brit will want to keep talking, while Sara will shut down and refuse to discuss it further. Sara's behavior could be classified under which of the Gottman Institute's "Four Horsemen"?
   a. Criticism
   b. Stonewalling
   c. Defensiveness
   d. Contempt

52. Christopher notices that twice over the last week, when his friend Regina did not listen to the teacher, she was assigned extra homework. He now always listens to the teacher. According to Albert Bandura, what is the best description of what is happening?
  a. Vicarious learning
  b. Modeling
  c. Intrinsic reinforcement
  d. Subliminal perception

53. Beatrice shares that when her child gets ready for school without needing significant redirection, they listen to the child's choice of music on the way to school. What is this an example of?
  a. Modeling
  b. Classical conditioning
  c. Praise
  d. Operant conditioning

54. Which therapeutic modality postulates that people are fundamentally motivated to work toward a positive framework and are experts on their own lives?
  a. Psychodynamic therapy
  b. Person-centered therapy
  c. Adlerian therapy
  d. Gestalt model

55. A client explains that they have experienced shame surrounding their need to take anti-anxiety medication to get through an especially challenging time. You reply, "I understand how you feel. When I was struggling during a difficult divorce, it was hard to admit that I needed help by using anti-anxiety medication too." This is an example of which therapeutic tactic?
  a. Self-disclosure
  b. Reflective listening
  c. Countertransference
  d. Transference

56. To what does the ABC model in reactive emotive behavioral therapy (REBT) refer?
  a. The therapeutic model of distress tolerance, core mindfulness techniques, problem solving, and emotional regulation skills
  b. The stages that a person goes through before successfully changing a behavior pattern
  c. A set of breathing and relaxation techniques
  d. The cycle in which a negative event occurs, we explain why it occurred, and we respond with feelings and behaviors

57. Which of the following reminds group members that their presenting concerns are NOT unique to them?
  a. Catharsis
  b. Congruence
  c. Altruism
  d. Universalism

198

58. The miracle question technique would be used in which therapeutic modality?
   a. Psychoanalysis
   b. Solution-focused therapy
   c. REBT
   d. Structural family therapy

59. A client has a substance use disorder and bipolar disorder. Which of the following is NOT a term a counselor could use to define this client's presentation?
   a. Dual disorders
   b. Co-occurring disorders
   c. Mixed diagnostic category
   d. Comorbid disorders

60. Your client believes that her anxiety is triggered when she encounters a former partner. Your client establishes a goal to abstain from contact with this person to gauge the potential impact to her anxiety. Which of the following actions could be a barrier to this goal?
   a. Journaling her feelings
   b. Making plans to do yoga
   c. Blocking his number
   d. Meeting his sister for dinner

61. A client struggling with self-injurious behaviors or suicidal ideation can benefit from having a(n) _____ in place.
   a. affidavit of guardianship
   b. sponsor
   c. hospital bed
   d. safety plan

62. You are facilitating a therapeutic group that addresses grief and loss. You are working with members to establish group rules for communication and expectations. Which stage in the group process is this?
   a. Adjourning
   b. Norming
   c. Forming
   d. Storming

63. The "Why Am I Telling?" (WAIT) method is a technique used by therapists regarding:
   a. Self-disclosure
   b. Confrontation
   c. Therapeutic silence
   d. Treatment planning

64. Reid's mom is asking him what happened in school today. He shares with her that he saw his principal in passing and noticed that she came back from the weekend with a tan. Reid says, "I bet she went somewhere sunny!" Reid is demonstrating:
   a. Moral reasoning
   b. Inferential reasoning
   c. Theory of mind
   d. Object permanence

65. Elaine is a 28-year-old client whom you are treating for depression and anxiety. She has a pattern of dependency and has been struggling with an unhealthy relationship with her mother. In a session, she talks about a recent fight with her mother. She asks, "What do you think I should do?" Which of the following responses would be most helpful?
   a. "I can't give you advice."
   b. "You need to cut off contact with her."
   c. "Wow, it sounds like your mother was in the wrong there."
   d. "Tell me more about what you think the best approach is here."

66. Yuri's therapeutic approach is based on the idea that although genetic and social factors influence a person's behaviors, there is still an element of free will. What concept does he likely adhere to?
   a. Environmental determinism
   b. Biological determinism
   c. Hard determinism
   d. Soft determinism

67. Your client is sharing a recent interaction with her mother. The client says, "I asked my mom what she used to make her chili, and suddenly she was irate. She accused me of criticizing her food! It was so surprising; I don't understand why she felt that way." Coming from a transactional analysis perspective, you theorize that this may have been a(n) _____ transaction.
   a. complementary
   b. duplex
   c. crossed
   d. angular

68. Wendy, a therapist born and raised in North America, ends her first session with Xu, a client who recently moved from China to attend graduate school in the United States. Wendy observes that Xu avoided eye contact while they spoke about suicidal ideation. She tells her supervisor that she believes he was intentionally evasive with her. Which of the following might Wendy be experiencing?
   a. Countertransference
   b. Unbiased approach
   c. Individualism
   d. Cultural bias

69. Co-occurring diagnoses may be the result of a shared risk factor. This means that the biological, environmental, social, or psychological factors which increase the risk of one diagnosis also increase the risk of the other. Which comorbidity hypothesis is this?
   a. The direct causal hypothesis
   b. The indirect causal hypothesis
   c. The genetic vulnerability hypothesis
   d. The common factors hypothesis

70. Taking the time to care for oneself, cultivating healthy levels of independence, and learning to contain one's emotional responses to express them in a helpful manner are all indicators of the healthy version of which interpersonal coping skill?
   a. Moving toward people
   b. Moving against people
   c. Moving away from people
   d. Moving with people

71. "Demonstrate marked improvement in impulse control" is a treatment goal best suited for a child diagnosed with:
   a. Attention-deficit/hyperactivity disorder
   b. Generalized anxiety disorder
   c. Body dysmorphia
   d. Post-traumatic stress disorder

72. During your second therapy session with Sev, a 26-year-old client who presents with post-traumatic stress disorder, you discuss mindfulness, positive relationships, and purpose. These are examples of:
   a. Diagnostic criteria
   b. Resiliency factors
   c. Risk factors
   d. Treatment goals

73. During a biopsychosocial interview, a counselor discovers that a client's outbursts at school are the result of a difficult relationship he has with his brother at home. Which of the following does the underlying issue stem from?
   a. The client's biological history
   b. The client's social history
   c. The client's psychological history
   d. None of the above

74. Your client, Ren, is a former runner who has experienced depression after a debilitating injury. She has identified a long-term goal of running a race again because she notices that her mental health is better when she exercises. Which of the following is the best example of a short-term goal that is within SMART goal parameters?
   a. Ren will run once per week for three months.
   b. Ren will run a race in two weeks.
   c. Ren will run for 30 minutes three times per week and reassess in three months.
   d. Ren will start running again.

75. What is the best way for a counselor to encourage a client's autonomy and help them develop a sense of independence?
   a. Give the client an outline of what their goals for counseling should be based on the presenting problem
   b. Offer solutions to problems the client presents so that the client can either choose to accept these solutions or not
   c. Allow the client to determine their own goals for counseling and listen while the client presents issues which arise throughout treatment, encouraging self-discovery without inserting ideas of right or wrong outcomes
   d. When the client gets off topic during a session, redirect the client to the issues that really matter

76. You are working with a parent who is struggling to get their child to comply with a bedtime routine. You suggest starting an incentive system in which the child gets to place a sticker on a chart each time they complete a step. The child earns a prize when the chart is entirely filled out. This is an example of _____.
    a. positive punishment
    b. praise
    c. shaping
    d. token economy

77. A counselor has been seeing a client for a year with no improvement regarding their mental health symptoms. The client has been seeing outpatient providers for the last 10 years and has experienced the same lack of change in their mental health throughout. The client also sees a psychiatrist regularly. What should the counselor recommend next regarding the client's level of care?
    a. The counselor should recommend partial hospitalization programming or intensive outpatient programming.
    b. The counselor should recommend the client continue to come to outpatient counseling, without recommending alternatives, for at least another year.
    c. The counselor should recommend that the client explore alternatives to traditional counseling, such as ketamine therapy.
    d. The counselor should recommend the client find a new psychiatrist since this is likely an issue that can be best addressed with proper medication management.

78. One criticism of Freud is that his theories about the unconscious are neither tangible nor measurable. Which phenomenon speaks to this criticism?
    a. Replication
    b. Occam's razor
    c. Projection
    d. Falsifiability

79. Your client is sharing about a party they attended last night. They perseverate on a moment of awkwardness that occurred while greeting the host when they first arrived rather than the few hours of good conversation they later had with various guests. They insist that this night was a failure. What is this called?
    a. Overgeneralization
    b. Personalization
    c. Selective abstraction
    d. Labeling

80. A counselor suspects a client has borderline personality disorder during their first session together. Which would be the most appropriate modality for treatment?
    a. Humanistic therapy
    b. Cognitive behavioral therapy
    c. Rational emotive behavior therapy
    d. Dialectical behavior therapy

81. The idea that children are more deeply motivated by future goals and possibilities than by past childhood experiences can be attributed to:
    a. Social learning theory
    b. Fictional finalism
    c. Freudian theory
    d. Attachment theory

82. A therapist who is strengths-based and primarily focused on incorporating past resolutions, looking for exceptions, and using present and future focused language is likely using which therapeutic model?
    a. Cognitive behavioral therapy (CBT)
    b. Solution-focused therapy
    c. Psychoanalysis
    d. Rational emotive behavioral therapy (REBT)

83. Ten-year-old Regina's dad drops her off at her mom's house. He tells Regina, "I'm not talking to your mom. Let her know that I would appreciate if she'd let me know in advance next time the schedule is going to be different." What is this called?
    a. Defensiveness
    b. Reality shifting
    c. Stonewalling
    d. Triangulation

84. A mental model that a person uses to organize their current fund of knowledge and prepare for future understanding is called a:
    a. Bias
    b. Schema
    c. Cognition
    d. Phobia

85. Which response might a therapist use to express doubt about something their client said?
    a. "Are you considering suicide?"
    b. "Are you using this word to mean _____?"
    c. "It seems like you are feeling frustrated."
    d. "That is unusual."

86. Like addiction to substances, a person can become addicted to a behavior/process (gambling, pornography, etc.), in part due to the release of the chemical _____ in the brain in response to the behavior/process.
    a. neurons
    b. serotonin
    c. dopamine
    d. oxytocin

87. You are providing outpatient counseling to a child with conduct disorder and his parents. Which of the following is an example of a short-term treatment objective?
    a. Eliminate all antisocial behaviors.
    b. Demonstrate empathy and understanding of how their behavior impacts others.
    c. Establish and maintain strong parent-child boundaries.
    d. Identify situations, thoughts, and feelings that trigger antisocial behavior.

88. A counselor is primarily passive in their sessions with a client. The client leads the conversation, and the counselor listens. Which therapeutic orientation is this counselor utilizing?
    a. Cognitive behavioral therapy (CBT)
    b. Rational emotive behavior therapy (REBT)
    c. Psychoanalytic or psychodynamic therapy
    d. Dialectical behavior therapy (DBT)

89. Three-month-old Kiki is laying in her pack and moving her arms and legs around while her parents watch. According to Mildred Parten, this type of play is called:
    a. Spectator play
    b. Associative play
    c. Solitary play
    d. Unoccupied play

90. Erikson theorizes that _____ reflects a person's need to develop a meaningful contribution to the world.
    a. initiative
    b. stagnation
    c. industry
    d. generativity

91. The phenomenon in which members of a group are unwilling to express a dissenting opinion and emphasis is placed on unanimity can be described as:
    a. Group polarization
    b. Deindividuation
    c. Groupthink
    d. Inoculation effect

92. A father calls his 23-year-old son's counselor requesting information regarding his son's sessions. He is paying for his son to go to therapy and wants to know how things are going. What is the best way for the counselor to respond to the father's request?
    a. Since the father is paying for the sessions, the counselor can provide him with information regarding his son's progress in therapy as long as they do not directly quote anything from the sessions.
    b. The counselor should explain that they are not able to provide any information regarding the client's counseling sessions. The client is his own legal guardian, and legally nothing can be disclosed even though the father is paying for the sessions.
    c. The counselor should praise the father for his interest in his son's mental health and provide a brief update with minimal information.
    d. The counselor should hang up the phone immediately and block the father's number since it is a conflict of interest to have any communication with him.

93. Which of the following best describes a counselor's role in providing gender-affirming care to a client who is beginning hormone therapy with a medical provider?
    a. The counselor should provide detailed, comprehensive medical information to the client.
    b. The counselor should inform the client of hormone therapy's risks and benefits.
    c. The counselor should learn about the impacts that hormone therapy can have on their client's mental and emotional health.
    d. Because the counselor is not a medical professional, this topic is off limits for counseling sessions.

94. In which type of transaction does a person receive a response that aligns with what they've said?
    a. Angular
    b. Complementary
    c. Crossed
    d. Duplex

95. Career development theorist _____ theorizes that someone can make the best career choice when they understand their individual traits, know the labor market, and recognize the relationship between the two.
    a. John Holland
    b. Albert Bandura
    c. Linda Gottfredson
    d. Frank Parsons

96. Betty is starting grief therapy with a new counselor, Kris. In their first session, Kris shared that she uses a cognitive behavioral framework to approach her work with clients. What might Betty expect in sessions?
    a. Kris will support Betty in accepting her negative feelings and thoughts surrounding her loss.
    b. Kris will focus on using creative self-expression to help Betty heal from her loss.
    c. Kris will help identify and reframe Betty's negative thought patterns regarding her loss.
    d. Kris will encourage Betty to participate in therapy sessions with other grieving clients.

97. Sammy is an outpatient counselor working with Bessie, a seven-year-old who is reported to be struggling with hyperactivity and attention issues in multiple settings. What would be the best assessment tool to determine Bessie's diagnosis?
    a. WAIS-IV
    b. WPPSI-IV
    c. NICHQ Vanderbilt Assessment Scales
    d. PHQ-9

98. _____ refers to a child's ability to understand the relationship between two people, objects, or concepts based on previously learned information.
    a. Classification
    b. Object permanence
    c. Transitive inference
    d. Conservation

99. Every Sunday, Jorge spends the day baking with his son. He has been focusing on teaching his son recipes that his own father taught him. Jorge remembers his own father sharing his memories about baking with Jorge's grandfather. This is best described by which type of generativity:
    a. Biological generativity
    b. Parental generativity
    c. Technical generativity
    d. Cultural generativity

100. An achievement test measures _____.
    a. maximum performance
    b. minimum performance
    c. typical performance
    d. unconscious traits

205

101. "Let's talk a bit more about identifying the primary issue you want to work on in therapy." This statement is an example of:
    a. Exploring
    b. Reflective listening
    c. Clarifying
    d. Empathizing

102. In the third session with a client, Erica, the counselor notices that Erica is bouncing her leg up and down, wringing her hands together, and biting her lip. The counselor infers that Erica is feeling anxious and starts the session with low music and a breathing exercise instead of the usual check-in. This is an example of which of the following?
    a. Empathic attunement
    b. Empathic listening
    c. Congruence
    d. Unconditional positive regard

103. Mario is processing his history with a new therapist. He discloses that he dropped out of college in his late teens after his father died to help his mother pay household bills. He shares that he didn't think twice about this decision, and his family has always supported each other in hard times. His therapist validates his thoughtfulness and determination, recognizing that Mario's family system likely subscribes to which of the following value systems?
    a. Collectivism
    b. Individualism
    c. Low context culture
    d. Acculturation

104. Yara's parents recently separated, and Yara is living in a new apartment. Yara had a set routine in her old house. Recently, Yara has been frequently waking up late for school and missing the school bus. According to Bandura's triadic reciprocal model of causality, what factor seems to be the cause here?
    a. Emotional factor
    b. Individual factor
    c. Behavioral factor
    d. Environmental factor

105. What is the process of adapting to a different culture while retaining elements of one's own culture?
    a. Assimilation
    b. Congruence
    c. Acculturation
    d. Immigration

106. Jackie notices that her three-month-old son Kirk is putting his thumb in his mouth to suck on it. According to Piaget, this is an example of a:
    a. Primary circular reaction
    b. Reflex
    c. Tertiary circular reaction
    d. Secondary circular reaction

107. Greta, an 11-year-old, refuses to attend school one morning after discovering that she has a pimple on her forehead. She insists to her parents that everyone will be staring at the pimple if she goes to school. This is best characterized by:
   a. Egocentrism
   b. Sublimation
   c. Rationalization
   d. Assimilation

108. A parenting style that is demanding in nature but low in responsiveness is referred to as:
   a. Authoritative
   b. Permissive
   c. Neglectful
   d. Authoritarian

109. Makala's outpatient practice is working to build a more inclusive atmosphere for a gender diverse population. Which of the following practices would NOT be beneficial to instill?
   a. Asking preferred pronouns
   b. Making gender and/or sexuality a topic of focus in therapy, even if it's not the presenting issue
   c. Offering gender-neutral restroom options
   d. Engaging in ongoing education surrounding LGBTQIA+ topics

110. A client comes to counseling with a diagnosis given by a previous counselor. The client disagrees with this diagnosis. How should the counselor ultimately determine the client's diagnosis moving forward?
   a. By consulting the client's previous counselor
   b. By allowing the client to decide based on what feels most accurate to them
   c. By consulting the client's family members
   d. By consulting the DSM-5

111. Which of the following is an example of a closed-ended question or inquiry?
   a. "Did you engage in binging/purging last night?"
   b. "Tell me more about your family."
   c. "How are you feeling?"
   d. "When did this behavior start for you?"

112. Lena is struggling with not listening when getting ready for bed. Each time that she is able to get her pajamas on the first time her parents ask, they respond with significant praise and high fives. Which tactic are Lena's parents using?
   a. Contingency contracting
   b. Negative reinforcement
   c. Modeling
   d. Positive reinforcement

113. Eliza is newly sober after completing a treatment program and is considering her support options. As her therapist, you encourage her to join a 12-step group, such as Narcotics Anonymous. What reasoning might support this suggestion?
    a. These group settings offer increased freedom of choice.
    b. Mutual support can help encourage healthy behaviors.
    c. There is no reasoning to support this suggestion; 12-step programs are not appropriate for newly sober clients.
    d. Such group settings are void of triggers for relapse.

114. Vera is working with Trent to process trauma from his childhood. Trent shares vivid memories of gradually becoming quiet and observant. He now understands that this was likely to anticipate and prepare for his mother's violent outbursts. What is the best description of this behavior?
    a. Autoplastic adaptation
    b. Alloplastic adaptation
    c. Individualism
    d. Collectivism

115. How many questions are included in the cultural formulation interview?
    a. 25
    b. 50
    c. 16
    d. 10

116. In a family therapy session, the child, Ricky, shared a conversation he had with his parents the night before. Ricky's father discovered that Ricky had failed his history exam and confronted him about it. Ricky remembers saying, "I don't know why I keep failing. I guess I'm just worthless." Which role in Karpman's triangle is Ricky playing?
    a. Rescuer
    b. Observer
    c. Victim
    d. Persecutor

117. A counselor works a second job in finance and has a co-worker in this sphere who often vents to them, asks for advice, or says they simply need a listening ear. The counselor tries to mitigate the frequency of these interactions but is also open to supporting their colleague while maintaining clear boundaries. One day, the co-worker shows up at the counselor's private practice requesting a session. The co-worker says that if they are going to request emotional support from them, they figure they might as well compensate the counselor for their time. What is the best way for the counselor to handle this situation?
    a. Agree to this arrangement and take compensation for the time they are already spending supporting their coworker
    b. Agree to this arrangement and offer their co-worker a discount since they know one another well
    c. Agree to this arrangement, but only if, moving forward, they can work together without discussing personal matters in the office
    d. Disagree, as this would be a dual relationship and an unethical way to practice

118. Patients who are struggling with terminal illness are at a high risk of developing depression, yet it is vastly under- or misdiagnosed. What best describes a prevalent reason for this?
    a. Lack of clinical training among providers treating these patients
    b. The patient is hiding the symptoms or being dishonest with the provider.
    c. The diagnosis and treatment of depression is irrelevant when a terminal illness is present.
    d. Issues separating physical symptoms related to terminal illness from those secondary to depression

119. Your client has been newly diagnosed with bipolar disorder. Which of the following would be the most appropriate focus in helping them understand how to best cope with their diagnosis?
    a. Understanding patterns of mood shifts and self-monitoring tools
    b. Analyzing the relationship between anxiety and avoidance
    c. Pinpointing the reason for unwanted and intrusive thoughts
    d. Reality-testing methods

120. Who theorized the idea that children develop a set of interpersonal coping styles in response to basic anxiety that has formed because of fractured parental relationships?
    a. Sigmund Freud
    b. Karen Horney
    c. Erik Erikson
    d. Carl Jung

121. Trent shares that when he is engaging in a stressful conversation with his boss, his mind will go blank, he has difficulty concentrating, and he wants to retreat into his office. What is the best description of this response?
    a. Hypoarousal
    b. Hyperarousal
    c. Trauma
    d. Grounding

122. Kohlberg's theory of moral reasoning proposes that an individual in the conventional morality stage:
    a. Follows societal rules in order to maintain law and order
    b. Begins to account for the varying values and beliefs of others
    c. Follows their individual rule of justice despite potential conflict with laws
    d. Obeys rules primarily to avoid punishment

123. A counselor's client has recently lost their job and insurance. Which is the most ethical option for the counselor to propose moving forward?
    a. The counselor should request that the client see them more often, providing the client with additional support during this difficult time. It would be too stressful for the client to switch counselors amidst these other hardships.
    b. The counselor should suggest they meet less often, so the client is able to afford their services.
    c. The counselor should recommend that the client take a break from counseling and return once they have regained employment.
    d. The counselor should refer the client to a provider who offers counseling services on a sliding scale fee basis.

209

124. Helen is meeting with her client, Roger, who has been diagnosed with major depressive disorder. He is experiencing a particularly challenging depressive episode characterized by suicidal ideation with a plan and access to means. He doubts his ability to keep himself safe and has expressed ambivalent intent to act. Helen determines that he needs the most intensive level of care. Which of the following is the most intensive level of care?
   a. Intensive outpatient program
   b. Group therapy
   c. Partial hospitalization program
   d. Inpatient treatment

125. Tiera applied to law school and recently discovered that she has been placed on the waiting list. According to Schlossberg's transition theory, this is considered a:
   a. Resultant nonevent
   b. Ripple nonevent
   c. Delayed nonevent
   d. Unanticipated transition

126. Two counselors must conduct several cultural formulation interviews. Without having any additional information regarding the clients, one of the counselors says that they would prefer to conduct an interview for a client named Sam and have their colleague conduct an interview for a client named Fudam. When their colleague asks why, the counselor is not sure. This example can be identified as which of the following types of bias?
   a. Explicit racial bias
   b. Social comparison bias
   c. Implicit cultural bias
   d. Affinity bias

127. What is the process of using approximate steps to help a client get closer to goal behavior?
   a. Operant conditioning
   b. Modeling
   c. Shaping
   d. Chaining

128. Which of the following is NOT a requirement to obtain valid informed consent?
   a. Disclosing any risks involved for the client throughout the counseling process
   b. Providing the client with their website address or business card as a way for the client to contact them with any additional questions
   c. Providing information regarding their credentials and experience
   d. Disclosing any other professionals involved in the client's care, including a supervisor or consulting provider

129. According to the transactional analysis model, the ego state that is rooted firmly in the present and appears to be the most rational part of one's personality is called the:
   a. Parent ego state
   b. Unconscious ego state
   c. Child ego state
   d. Adult ego state

130. Which of the following statements regarding bullying in childhood is the most accurate?
    a. Children ages 9–12 are more likely to experience bullying online rather than in school.
    b. Children who have experienced bullying are at increased risk for anxiety, sleep difficulties, and academic struggles.
    c. Children who have experienced bullying often overcome trust and self-esteem concerns more quickly, and these concerns are less likely to become prevalent in adulthood.
    d. LGBTQ students are less likely to experience cyberbullying than their non-LGBTQ peers.

131. Complete the following statement: The Davidson _____ Scale measures _____.
    a. Suicide; the severity of suicidal ideation and behavior
    b. Trauma; the frequency and severity of post-traumatic stress disorder symptoms
    c. Self-Harm; the frequency, severity, and duration of deliberate self-harm
    d. Self-Esteem; positive and negative feelings about oneself

132. Helena recently graduated from college and started an entry-level job in finance. According to Donald Super, which career development stage is Helena in?
    a. Maintenance
    b. Exploration
    c. Growth
    d. Establishment

133. Gretchen is typically a great student; however, she recently received a D– in her chemistry class. She now believes that she is going to fail out of college. The best description of this cognitive distortion is:
    a. Catastrophizing
    b. Emotional reasoning
    c. Fallacy of change
    d. Personalization

134. The ability to help others describes which of Dr. Irvin Yalom's group therapeutic factors?
    a. Instillation of hope
    b. Altruism
    c. Development of social skills
    d. Group cohesiveness

135. In most states, a counselor has _____ in cases that pose potential and imminent risk of harm.
    a. an obligation to protect their client's privacy
    b. a duty to warn and protect
    c. no legal obligation
    d. no ethical obligation

136. Which of the following names the process of encouraging interaction and connection between group therapy members by actively identifying common themes?
    a. Blocking
    b. Interpreting
    c. Linking
    d. Supporting

137. Complete the following statement: The Rosenberg _____ Scale measures _____.
    a. Suicide; the severity of suicidal ideation and behavior
    b. Trauma; the frequency and severity of post-traumatic stress disorder symptoms
    c. Self-Harm; the frequency, severity, and duration of deliberate self-harm
    d. Self-Esteem; positive and negative feelings about oneself

138. Emily shares that she feels sad because she doesn't have many friends. She concludes that people must not like her. Which of the following is a helpful example of reframing in this scenario?
    a. "You feel lonely."
    b. "What do you worry that people don't like about you?"
    c. "You have a few friends, but you'd like to make more."
    d. "That is a totally normal feeling to have at your age."

139. Allison shares that she feels like her life is a mess and that there is nothing to live for. You respond with, "It sounds like you are feeling hopeless." This is an example of:
    a. Clarification
    b. Cognitive dissonance
    c. Reflective listening
    d. Psychoanalysis

140. Which of the following refers to components of the established treatment plan that support the client in meeting their long-term treatment goals?
    a. Outcomes
    b. Barriers
    c. Objectives
    d. Therapeutic progress

141. Which of the following is NOT necessarily an aspect of conducting a mental status exam?
    a. Assessing behavior
    b. Assessing appearance
    c. Rapport-building
    d. Assessing cognitive functions and thought processes

142. Katie has been providing weekly counseling sessions for a 22-year-old client named Haley. After 15 weeks of treatment, Haley continues to struggle with self-injurious behaviors that have been occurring for several years. She is desperate to maintain her new job but is finding herself in need of significantly more therapeutic support. Katie is considering referring Haley to a different level of care. Which of the following would be the best treatment option?
    a. A DBT therapy program
    b. A different outpatient provider within Katie's practice
    c. A partial hospitalization program
    d. Short-term inpatient hospitalization

143. Compliance is to _____ as conformity is to _____.
    a. explicit; implicit
    b. fear; agreeability
    c. social norms; direct request
    d. rejection; legal consequence

144. What does the acronym SDQ mean?
   a. Suicide and Depression Questionnaire
   b. Symptoms of Depression Questionnaire
   c. Strengths and Difficulties Questionnaire
   d. Similarities and Differences Questionnaire

145. What do negative and positive Z-scores indicate about the mean?
   a. Positive Z-scores are below the mean, and negative Z-scores are above the mean.
   b. Negative and positive Z-scores indicate nothing about the mean.
   c. Positive Z-scores are above the mean, and negative Z-scores indicate nothing.
   d. Positive Z-scores are above the mean, and negative Z-scores are below the mean.

146. Helga is diagnosed with obsessive-compulsive disorder. One way this unhelpfully manifests for her is that she feels the need to check that her office door is locked precisely seven times before she can leave the building for any reason. This exemplifies a _____ reinforcement pattern.
   a. fixed interval
   b. variable interval
   c. fixed ratio
   d. variable ratio

147. Heather is feeling overwhelmed with her roommates, who are constantly leaving messes in shared areas and aren't respectful of Heather's need for quiet study time. This comes to a head one evening when there is an unscheduled party in the other room while Heather is trying to study. She feels dysregulated and wants to go out of her room and scream at her roommates. Instead, she takes 10 calming deep breaths before she works on a plan. Which emotion regulation strategy is she using?
   a. Distraction
   b. Tuning in to physical symptoms
   c. Seeking emotional support
   d. Cognitive reappraisal

148. In therapy, what is it called when the counselor uses a neutral attitude that allows the client to express their thoughts and feelings freely?
   a. Non-judgmental stance
   b. Transference
   c. Unconditional positive regard
   d. Reflective listening

149. Counseling professionals often engage in the discussion of nature vs. nurture to understand what impacts human cognition and behavior the most. For example, nature refers to _____, while nurture refers to _____.
   a. conditioning, societal impact
   b. parental behaviors, parental genetics
   c. genetic traits, environmental influences
   d. evolution, biological determination

150. A 15-year-old client is unwilling to state their presenting problem. If they are willing to complete the following, which would be most helpful for the counselor in assessing both the client's presenting problem and their current level of psychological distress?
- a. The Generalized Anxiety Disorder Scale (GAD-7) and the Mood and Feeling Questionnaire (MFQ)
- b. The Brief Symptom Inventory (BSI)
- c. The Emotional Avoidance Strategy Inventory for Adolescents (EASI-A)
- d. The Adverse Childhood Experiences (ACES) Questionnaire

151. You are working with a client who struggles with alcohol addiction. They share that they are considering entering a rehabilitation program to support them in achieving sobriety for the first time. When you start to discuss potential program options, the client interrupts and expresses that it "probably won't happen," and continues to share their frustrations with handling insurance, getting time off work, and explaining the program to family. They are likely in which stage of change?
- a. Precontemplation
- b. Contemplation
- c. Action
- d. Relapse

152. Someone on social media sends a counselor a friend request. The counselor accepts the request, thinking that the username reminds them of someone, and it must be someone they know. The counselor then receives vaguely threatening comments on every one of their posts from this person. The counselor looks again at the profile and recognizes the user as one of their clients. Which is the best way for the counselor to proceed?
- a. "Unfriend" the client on social media and let it go, not mentioning it in their next counseling session.
- b. Block the client and address the matter with them during their next session.
- c. Refrain from terminating the counseling relationship, even if the counselor is concerned that the client may follow through with their threats or in some way harm them, because the client would still clearly benefit from counseling.
- d. Laugh it off and send the client a funny message, letting them know it's no big deal, but report the threats to the police so the incident is on their radar.

153. You suggest a book for your client to read in between sessions. What is this therapy technique called?
- a. Mindfulness
- b. Bibliotherapy
- c. Art therapy
- d. Visualization

154. You are leading a support group for parents of early to late adolescents and providing psychoeducation on brain development. You explain that the part of teenagers' brains that support planning and reasoning are not fully developed until age _____.
- a. 25
- b. 13
- c. 16
- d. 18

155. _____ theorized that everyone is born with the notion that they are inferior to other people.
    a. Sigmund Freud
    b. Alfred Adler
    c. Fritz Perls
    d. Albert Bandura

156. Frida has started working with a new client, Bee, who is grappling with gender identity issues. Frida is worried that she won't be able to empathize with Bee since she has never had these issues personally. Which option is NOT an appropriate approach?
    a. Frida should ask Bee to continue describing her experience until Frida can relate to it.
    b. Frida should research gender identity and LGBTQIA+ culture so that she can increase her ability to provide gender-affirming care.
    c. Frida should focus on empathizing with Bee's emotions even if she doesn't yet understand Bee's experience.
    d. Frida should ask open-ended questions like, "What aspects of your exploration of your gender identity are important for me to understand?" and "What could help you feel supported in therapy as you learn more about your identity?"

157. You are working with a seven-year-old named Jimmy who is struggling with some acting out behaviors. In a recent session with his dad, you ask to spend some time with the family after school. You explain that you are hoping to get a better understanding of what this transition time looks like for their family and to observe how the family interacts with each other. This technique is reflective of which family therapy model?
    a. Transgenerational therapy
    b. Strategic therapy
    c. Narrative therapy
    d. Structural therapy

158. Which best describes symptoms of anxiety?
    a. Poor short-term memory and lack of sustained focus on non-preferred tasks
    b. Loss of pleasure and withdrawal from things one once enjoyed
    c. Muscle aches and tension, cardiovascular concerns, headaches, and digestion issues
    d. Delayed speech and communication skills and difficulty tolerating certain sights, smells, and sounds

159. Amber is two years old and is at a play group with her mother for the first time. Another child takes Amber's toy and throws it across the room, which startles her. She begins to cry and returns to her mother, who comforts and reassures her. Which feature of Bowlby's attachment theory is best represented here?
    a. Insecure attachment
    b. Separation distress
    c. Proximity maintenance
    d. Safe haven

160. You are an outpatient counselor working with a 36-year-old client. You receive a phone call from a social worker in a psychiatric inpatient unit and learn that the client has been admitted to a short term inpatient program. The social worker is calling to coordinate care with you. What is your next step?
    a. Immediately divulge your treatment goals with this patient since they have been admitted to an inpatient unit.
    b. Refuse to communicate with this social worker because it is not necessary to coordinate care in this case.
    c. Ask the social worker if the patient has given you permission to speak with them.
    d. Ensure that you receive informed consent signed by the patient that permits you to coordinate care with the social worker.

161. Piaget outlines four main developmental stages for children. The stage that is characterized by pretend play and the inability to distinguish between an object and the category it belongs to is:
    a. Formal operational
    b. Preoperational
    c. Concrete operational
    d. Sensorimotor

162. For which disorder is EMDR (Eye Movement Desensitization and Reprocessing) treatment most helpful?
    a. Post-traumatic stress disorder (PTSD)
    b. Schizophrenia
    c. Bipolar disorder
    d. Dissociative disorders

163. A support group is in the middle of an intense discussion, but they are struggling to transition to a resolution or another topic. One group member, George, makes a joke, causing the group to break out into laughter and allowing them to transition past the intense discussion. Which role did George take on?
    a. Tension reliver
    b. Harmonizer
    c. Energizer
    d. Supporter/encourager

164. Angie and her mom are talking about school when her mom brings up Angie's past experiences with a challenging teacher. Angie begins to speak about this teacher but states, "I don't want to talk about that anymore," and quickly changes the subject. Angie is exhibiting:
    a. repression.
    b. regression.
    c. displacement.
    d. suppression.

216

165. A counselor is seeing a client with a long history of addiction who is not a danger to himself or others. He has just left inpatient care where he spent one month due to suicidal ideation. Prior to being admitted, he received a chemical dependency assessment at the hospital. He has a support system and is safe at home. However, he feels he needs additional support beyond outpatient counseling and psychiatry. What should the counselor recommend for this client?
  a. Partial hospitalization programming
  b. Returning to inpatient care
  c. Another chemical dependency assessment
  d. A support group for addiction

166. You are seeking more information about a client's disruptive emotional reactions in school and at home. Which assessment tool would be most helpful for the client's parents and teachers to complete?
  a. DAST-10
  b. Vanderbilt Assessment Scales
  c. BASC-3
  d. GAD-7

167. Kübler-Ross developed a five-stage, non-linear model to help us better understand how patients process and adjust to grief and loss. In the _____ stage, there is often a struggle to find meaning in the recent or upcoming loss and can sometimes be characterized by feelings of guilt.
  a. denial
  b. bargaining
  c. depression
  d. anger

168. You are a counselor in a college health center. The nurse refers a student to you who is experiencing concerns with gender identity, homelessness, relationships, and depression. According to Maslow's hierarchy of needs, your initial goal with this student should address:
  a. Love and belonging
  b. Safety needs
  c. Self-actualization
  d. Physiological needs

169. Your client, Gary, is sharing a dream in which he was faced with difficult decisions that he struggled with. You practice Jungian therapy and therefore might respond with:
  a. "It sounds like you've had to make some really challenging decisions in the past."
  b. "You have to make difficult decisions quite often."
  c. "I wonder if there are decisions coming up for you that you're worried about making."
  d. "Often, dreams are of little importance and can distract us from what we need to focus on."

170. Gerald's client, Samuel, discloses that sometimes when he is unable to afford toiletries, he takes toiletry items from his work's office supplies. Which of the following responses displays unconditional positive regard?
  a. "This is something you should report to your boss."
  b. "Sometimes when you struggle to afford items, you seek them out at work."
  c. "You want to turn over a new leaf at this job, but this kind of behavior got you fired from your last job."
  d. "Thank you for sharing that. I imagine that it feels stressful when you don't have the means to purchase those items."

217

171. Resolving conflict and altering unhelpful individual patterns for more fulfilling relationships are most often the focus in which type of counseling?
    a. Couples counseling
    b. Guidance counseling
    c. Systemic counseling
    d. Psychodynamic counseling

172. Samuel presents with a faded complexion, has baggy eyes, and indicates that he has been sleeping more often than usual. These are common physical impacts of which mental health disorder:
    a. Depression
    b. Anxiety
    c. Trauma
    d. Oppositional defiant disorder

173. Which of the following statements accurately reflects commonalities in the adoptee community?
    a. The suicide rate is four times higher among adoptees, compared to non-adopted people.
    b. Adoptees do not often experience disenfranchised grief.
    c. Adoptees will always have mental health issues because of their adoption experience.
    d. Adoptees go to therapy at half the rate of non-adoptees.

174. Why is random sampling utilized in psychological research?
    a. Random sampling is used so that each member of the sample is equally likely to be chosen to represent the whole.
    b. Random sampling is used so members of the population can choose whether they want to be included in the sample.
    c. Random sampling is used so units can be selectively included in the sample because they are the easiest to access.
    d. Random sampling is used so that each member of the sample is not equally likely to be chosen to represent the whole.

175. Describing a client as "a person with schizophrenia" is an example of:
    a. Intellectualization
    b. Person-centered language
    c. Paraphrasing
    d. Inclusive language

176. Lionel practices therapy using the Gestalt model. One could assume that he views awareness as:
    a. Inconsequential because unconscious trauma is the direct focus of therapy
    b. A non-variable
    c. Being on a continuum
    d. Unrelated to a person's ability to self-regulate

177. Carl Rogers indicates three attributes that exemplify an impactful and effective counselor. Which of the following is NOT included?
    a. Congruence
    b. Unconditional positive regard
    c. Reflective listening
    d. Empathic understanding

178. Which of the following is the most common cause of addiction relapse?
    a. Lack of commitment to recovery
    b. Stress
    c. Poor confidence
    d. Genetics

179. Virginia Satir's "super-reasonable" communication style can be described as:
    a. Talkative, distrustful of confrontation, and uses evasive strategies to deflect stress
    b. Critical, aggressive, and has difficulty taking responsibility for one's own actions
    c. People-pleasing, timid demeanor, and derives value from external approval
    d. Calm, disconnected from emotional responses, and chooses words carefully

180. TJ's mom pours a few glasses of water for TJ and his sister. One of the glasses is tall and thin, while the other is short and wide. TJ demands the tall and thin glass because he believes that it has the most water, despite his mother's reassurance that both glasses contain equal amounts of water. TJ has not yet mastered:
    a. Conservation
    b. Object permanence
    c. Reciprocal socialization
    d. Abstract reasoning

181. What should a counselor do if they run into their client in public?
    a. The counselor should acknowledge the client with a friendly greeting.
    b. The counselor should ask how the client has been since their last session.
    c. The counselor should ignore the client unless the client addresses them first.
    d. The counselor should ignore the client even if the client chooses to initiate conversation.

182. Multicultural competence refers to the awareness of, responsiveness to, and respect for
_____.
    a. race, ethnicity, gender, spirituality, religion, sexual orientation, and social class
    b. race, ethnicity, spirituality, religion, sexual orientation, and social class
    c. race, ethnicity, religion, sexual orientation, and social class
    d. race and ethnicity when viewed from the racial ideology of colorblindness

183. What is the type of relationship described by the five correlation coefficients?
    a. The relationship described is nonlinear.
    b. The relationship described is linear.
    c. The relationship described can be linear or nonlinear.
    d. None of the above

184. What is the purpose of conducting a Z-test?
    a. A Z-test compares the means of two independent groups to determine if there is evidence that the means of the represented population are significantly different.
    b. A Z-test allows one to examine differences between one sample and a population.
    c. A Z-test compares the means of two related groups to determine whether the means differ in a manner that is statistically significant.
    d. A Z-test assesses the goodness of fit between observed values and those expected theoretically.

185. Emilio had an argument with his father prior to a therapy session with his client, Mark. During the session, Mark discussed a conflict that arose with his own father. Emilio took the opportunity to talk about the recent fight he had with his father and how it made him feel. This is an example of which of the following?
    a. Transference
    b. Empathetic response
    c. Countertransference
    d. Congruence

186. Vera took a test in class earlier in the day. She has been going over the last two questions in detail with her roommates, convinced she got them wrong. Even though they've moved on to discussing different topics, Vera continues to return to those two questions. What is this an example of?
    a. Intrusive thoughts
    b. Rumination
    c. Overgeneralization
    d. Introspection

187. Which of the following are true regarding electronic communication between a counselor and a client?
    a. A client must give consent to electronic communication.
    b. A client must be made aware of the risks of electronic communication.
    c. All electronic communication between a client and therapist is automatically forwarded to the client's insurance company.
    d. Both A and B

188. In a couples therapy session, you decide to use the role reversal technique. Which of the following best describes the intention behind this?
    a. To help them see the error of their ways
    b. To encourage a permanent behavior change
    c. To shift perspective and cultivate empathy
    d. To bring conflict to the forefront

189. Chrissy has always been close with her mom. She watches her mom's daily routine in the morning, including her exercise routine. Each morning, Chrissy will follow her mom into the living room and imitate the yoga moves that her mom does. In Freudian terms, this would be:
    a. Introjection
    b. Initialization
    c. Identification
    d. Intellectualization

190. A counselor is working with a client who is their own legal guardian. To assess the client's ability to provide informed consent, a counselor should consider which of the following?
    a. The client's ability to understand presented information
    b. The opinion of the client's parent
    c. Whether or not informed consent is being given voluntarily
    d. Both A and C

191. In a family session, the dad, Mark, is talking about an incident that happened yesterday with his daughter, Marisol. "She didn't put away her shoes and backpack when she came home," Mark shares, "She just threw them on the floor and went to her room. Obviously, she is lazy and undisciplined." Mark is using _____ attribution to explain Marisol's behavior.
   a. situational
   b. defensive
   c. dispositional
   d. self-serving

192. Amanda is a young adult and just took a survey in class about Adverse Childhood Experiences (ACEs). She learned that her score is significantly higher than those of her peers. Research has shown that she might be at a higher risk of developing anxiety and depression, misusing alcohol and drugs, and developing chronic health issues. What might Amanda do to mitigate this risk?
   a. Maintain complete sobriety.
   b. Go to the emergency room when any health concern arises.
   c. Avoid therapy so that she is not triggered by reliving the past.
   d. Build healthy, sustainable relationships.

193. Which clinical situation would warrant a counselor referring their client to another professional for concurrent treatment?
   a. A client discloses that their mother is the counselor's close friend.
   b. A client is admitted to psychiatric inpatient care.
   c. A client with an anxiety disorder seeks to add psychiatric medication to their treatment regimen.
   d. A client is discharged from their rehabilitation program into outpatient care.

194. An infant's rooting reflex is an example of a _____ reflex.
   a. Moro
   b. locomotor
   c. primitive
   d. postural

195. A white counselor is engaging with a client for the first time. Statistically speaking, which client is least likely to divulge information to this counselor?
   a. Tracy, a 43-year-old black female
   b. Ray, a 23-year-old black male
   c. Jill, a 16-year-old Hispanic female
   d. Frank, a 34-year-old white male

196. In the _____ stage of group therapy, group members have become more in tune with their fellow group members' strengths and weaknesses and generally possess more insight into group processes.
   a. norming
   b. performing
   c. storming
   d. adjourning

197. Which of the following is NOT a useful element of a diagnostic interview?
   a. A mental status exam
   b. Only open-ended questions
   c. The DSM-5
   d. Developmental history

198. Aside from substance abuse disorders, which mental illness has the highest mortality rate?
   a. Anxiety
   b. Schizophrenia
   c. Anorexia nervosa
   d. Depression

199. Bowlby theorizes that bonding plays a pivotal role in emotional development. He theorizes that children are born with an innate need to attach to a primary caregiver and need continuous care from them, particularly in the first two and a half years of life. What term best describes this phenomenon?
   a. Monotropy
   b. Maternal deprivation
   c. Monogamy
   d. Attachment theory

200. Gregory is talking about his anger in therapy. He shares, "It's like you black out in the moment, you know? You just react out of pure rage." As a Gestalt therapist, how might you respond?
   a. "That is a great description. Let's try that again using 'I' statements."
   b. "I wonder what may have triggered that reaction."
   c. "If you got to wave a wand and choose your reaction, what might that look like?"
   d. "This seems similar to how you've described your dad's reactions when you were younger."

Answer Explanations #2

1. D: The correct answer is that trauma can manifest in children as somatic complaints, dissociation, and difficult sleeping. Choice *A* is incorrect, as pushing Sadie to talk about her experiences is not the best step, particularly if she has experienced trauma and may not feel safe. Choice *B* is incorrect, as the need for consistency and stability is high for children, especially for children who have experienced trauma. Choice *C* is incorrect, as it is still incredibly important for the foster parents to normalize talking about Sadie's family and her previous home and make sure that Sadie knows the topic is safe, even if she is not ready to talk about it yet.

2. D: Choice *D* is correct. The counselor should ask more about the client's ADHD symptoms and offer methods of reducing their intensity and duration by providing mindfulness techniques. The counselor can also refer the client to an assessment center that can evaluate them for ADHD and provide them with a formal diagnosis. Choice *A* is incorrect because Choice *C* is also correct. Choice *B* is incorrect. The counselor should not offer to write a note regarding the diagnosis in this case, even if a formal evaluation will not be covered by insurance. Choice *C* is incorrect because Choice *A* is also correct.

3. D: Choice *D* is correct. The independent ANOVA, also known as the simple analysis of variance or one-way analysis of variance, is used to find statistically significant differences in the means of two or more independent groups. The dependent ANOVA, also known as the repeated measures ANOVA or within-subjects ANOVA, is the same as the independent ANOVA, but it is for dependent groups instead of independent groups.

4. B: The correct answer is, "We are diverse, but they are all alike." Out-group homogeneity describes the phenomenon in which one group believes that its members are very diverse while viewing other groups as being all the same. Choice *A* is incorrect because this describes egocentrism. Choice *C* is incorrect because this is an example of a racial microaggression. Choice *D* is incorrect because this describes normopathy, which deals with seeking to conform to societal standards.

5. A: The correct answer is Choice *A* because initiating conversations about treatment plan compliance helps the client understand why compliance is important to their overall well-being. Choice *B* is incorrect; it is often essential that counselors integrate this conversation into sessions. Choice *C* is incorrect because intimidation should never be utilized in counseling. Choice *D* is incorrect because the counselor's personal feelings about the plan are not relevant.

6. B: The correct answer is positive punishment because something unpleasant or unwanted (i.e., the chore) is added to help modify behavior (i.e., test performance). Choice *A* is incorrect because negative punishment involves taking away something pleasant in response to an unwanted behavior. Choice *C* is incorrect because systematic desensitization refers to a type of exposure therapy that attempts to treat an extreme aversion to something. Choice *D* is incorrect because extinction involves gradually lessening an already conditioned response so that it eventually ceases to occur.

7. B: Choice *B* is correct. A counselor demonstrates self-awareness and emotional stability through congruence between both their mood and affect. Choices *A*, *C*, and *D* are incorrect because a counselor does not demonstrate self-awareness and emotional stability through immediate self-disclosure of their own biases and faults when meeting with a new client, by explaining any incongruence between their mood and affect, nor through explaining how they maintain both self-awareness and emotional stability to clients.

8. C: Choice C is correct. Motivational interviewing is not especially useful when conducting an initial interview for a highly motivated, help-seeking client; rather, motivational interviewing should be used with clients who are apathetic or irresolute regarding making changes. Choices A, B, and D are incorrect. Rapport-building, gentle redirection, and open-ended questions are all especially useful when conducting an initial interview for a highly motivated, help-seeking client.

9. A: The correct answer is psychosis, as mood changes, confused speech, social withdrawal, and delusions are majorly symptomatic of this. Choices B and C are incorrect. Although Hank may be experiencing anxious and depressive moods, his overall symptomology indicates psychosis. Choice D is incorrect, as this describes a symptom rather than an overall explanation.

10. D: The correct answer is that the development of personal fables can lead to an increase in risk-taking behaviors. When adolescents develop personal fables, they begin to believe they are unique and somewhat "invincible" to the point where they are not likely to be affected by the consequences of their actions. Choice A is incorrect, as dreaming about future endeavors is one of the benefits of personal fables. Choice B is incorrect, as this describes the *imaginary audience*, which is another facet of adolescent development. Choice C is incorrect, as egocentrism is a healthy and normal part of development.

11. A: The correct answer is an Adlerian perspective, which is based on the belief that a person's behavior is purposeful and geared toward accomplishing a life goal. Choice B is incorrect because a cognitive behavioral approach would help a person struggling with addiction to understand and harness the connections between their thoughts, feelings, and behaviors. Choice C is incorrect because a dialectical behavioral approach might involve treating relapse as a problem to solve and helping a person analyze the events that led up to the relapse. Choice D is incorrect because a psychoanalytical approach views addiction as a way to manage feelings or thoughts that are unbearable to experience in a sober state. A therapist with this perspective might support the client through processing unconscious feelings and thoughts.

12. D: The correct answer is dereflection, which is a process by which a therapist may encourage the client to redirect their attention from themselves to the broader picture. Choice A is incorrect because, although this is also a technique rooted in logotherapy, paradoxical intention refers to the process by which the client is encouraged to hope and wish for the very thing they fear or dread the most. Choice B is incorrect because attitude modification involves helping a client adjust their perspective of a situation rather than changing their actions. Choice C is incorrect because Socratic dialogue refers to when the therapist uses the client's own words to encourage self-discovery.

13. B: Choice B is correct. Since these results are statistically significant, we can reject the null hypothesis. Choice A is incorrect. We can reject the null hypothesis. Choice C is incorrect. This tells us we can reject the null hypothesis. Choice D is incorrect. The p-value only gives us information about the null hypothesis.

14. A: Choice A is correct. The most ethical way for the counselor to proceed is to suggest individual counseling to complete risk assessments with both clients, as couples counseling puts the potentially abused client at greater risk. Choice B is incorrect. The most ethical way for the counselor to proceed is not to accuse the potentially abusive client of being abusive since defending the potentially abused client could put them at greater risk once the couple leaves the session. Choice C is incorrect. Immediately declining to see either client again and referring the potential abuser to a domestic violence treatment program is not the most ethical way for the counselor to proceed. This could also trigger an intense reaction from the potential abuser and put the potentially abused client at greater risk. Choice *D* is incorrect. The most ethical way for the counselor to proceed is not to offer the potential victim of abuse information regarding the National Domestic Violence Hotline and cancel all future appointments. Doing so in front of the potential abuser could also put the potentially abused client at greater risk.

15. D: The correct answer is cognitive dissonance, as this describes the mental toll of having to behave in a way that contradicts one's beliefs or values. Choice *A* is incorrect, as rationalization instead describes a psychological tactic one might use to help resolve cognitive dissonance. Choice *B* is incorrect, as conformity might involve Tegan completely changing her belief system to match the practices of her company. Choice *C* is incorrect, as there is not enough information here to indicate clinical anxiety.

16. C: The correct answer is the stages of change model, otherwise known as the transtheoretical model, which combines a behavioral and person-centered approach to provide a supportive environment in which a person can explore and move through their decision-making abilities to pursue intentional change. Choice *A* is incorrect because the Freudian model is purely psychoanalytic in nature. Choices *B* and *D* are incorrect because, although they are each part of the transtheoretical approach, they do not encompass the entire model.

17. B: Choice *B* is correct. The counselor should wait to do the assessment until a room becomes available. Choices *A* and *C* are incorrect. The counselor should not complete the assessment in the hallway, even if the hallway becomes less crowded, because this presents a confidentiality issue. Choice *D* is incorrect. The counselor should not complete the assessment in the hallway's storage closet, as this is not an appropriate space for the assessment to occur either.

18. C: The correct answer is investigative, given Seth's analytic, observational, self-directed, and independent nature. Choice *A* is incorrect, as an enterprising career type fits someone who is outgoing, energetic, and likes to work with people. Choice *C* is incorrect, as a conventional career type is theorized to work best for someone who is careful and conforming and prefers to work under someone else's directive. Choice *D* is incorrect, as a realistic career type might be best suited for someone who is hands-on, practical, and adept with mechanics.

19. A: The correct answer is person-centered therapy, which places the onus on the client to lead the way in their treatment. Choice *B* is incorrect because Gestalt therapy is best encapsulated by the notion that one only needs to focus on their present environment and their own self-awareness. Choice *C* is incorrect because cognitive behavioral therapy seeks to identify negative thought patterns that are influencing unwanted behaviors. Choice *D* is incorrect because solution-focused therapy emphasizes solutions rather than problems.

20. B: Choice *B* is correct; Harold's focus for therapy will be identified in his treatment goals and objectives. Choice *A* is incorrect, as diagnostic criteria are a set of standards that need to be met to make a diagnosis. Choice *C* is incorrect because coping skills are skills someone can use when they are experiencing a difficult situation. Choice *D* is incorrect because triggering circumstances are those that the client identifies as evoking challenging emotions.

21. A: Choice *A* is correct. The counselor should refer the client to a provider who specializes in treatment for clients with postpartum depression and seek training in this area to broaden their scope. They could also consult with another professional who specializes in postpartum depression. Choice *B* is incorrect. The counselor should not move forward with the client's care if they have experience treating clients with major depressive disorder but not postpartum depression. Choice *C* is incorrect.

The counselor should not move forward with the client's care and seek training in this area at the same time. Choice *D* is incorrect. The counselor should not continue to meet with the client, regardless of whether the client expresses concern regarding the counselor's ability to treat them appropriately.

22. D: Choice *D* exemplifies the best use of empathy because it withholds judgment and simply reflects upon how Trey appears to be feeling. Choice *A* is incorrect because even though it contains empathy, it is paired with a judgment statement. Choice *B* is incorrect because it involves disclosure of personal information on the counselor's part and presumes to know how Trey is feeling. Choice *C* does not contain an empathetic response; instead, it generalizes and invalidates Trey's experience.

23. C: The correct answer is economic control. Choice *A* is incorrect, as emotional abuse would be things like humiliating Susie or using guilt to manipulate her. Choice *B* is incorrect, as intimidation might include using behaviors, such as looks, gestures, or actions, to scare or manipulate Susie into doing something. Choice *D* is incorrect, as coercion and threats are things like her husband indicating he would end his life if Susie left him or making threats against her safety.

24. B: The correct answer is sublimation, as Wren is using her yoga at the park as a constructive means to lessen her need to isolate at home. Choice *A* is incorrect. This might be the case if Wren were only isolating and unable to use her impulse constructively. Choice *C* is incorrect. This could be the case if Wren continued to isolate and explained away this behavior as appropriate because she was feeling drained. Choice *D* is incorrect. This would be the case if Wren refused to acknowledge that she was feeling drained and that her self-isolating behaviors were a result of that.

25. B: The correct answer is racial microaggression, as Tracy's colleague is communicating that because she is close with someone black, she is immune to engaging in any racist behaviors. Choice *A* is incorrect, as objectivity refers to someone being without bias or prejudice. Choice *C* is incorrect, as transference is instead the redirection of someone's feelings about one person onto someone else. Choice *D* is incorrect, as egotism refers to a person's complete focus on themselves because of an inflated sense of self-value.

26. B: The correct answer is self-directed search, which includes the six themes established by Holland: realistic, investigative, artistic, social, enterprising, and conventional. Choice *A* is incorrect because the Myers-Briggs assessment instead categorizes people into "four-letter types." Choice *C* is incorrect, as Keirsey's test sorts people into one of four temperament types. Choice *D* is incorrect, as the Vanderbilt scale is not a career test but instead an assessment to help determine an ADHD diagnosis in children.

27. A: Choice *A* is correct because the PHQ-9 assesses depression. Choices *B*, *C*, and *D* are incorrect because those conditions are not assessed by the PHQ-9.

28. D: The correct answer is that they are most often in the age range of adolescent girls to young adult women, as this accurately depicts typical patients with anorexia nervosa. Choice *A* is incorrect, as these patients often display a significant preoccupation with food. Choice *B* is incorrect, as there is often immense guilt associated with any caloric intake. Choice *C* is incorrect because "binge-purge" is only one subtype of anorexia nervosa, with the second being "restrictive."

29. A: Choice *A* is correct. The biopsychosocial interview is typically conducted at the beginning of counseling as part of the intake process. Choices *B* and *C* are incorrect. The biopsychosocial interview is not conducted two or six months into counseling. Choice *D* is incorrect. The biopsychosocial

226

interview is not typically conducted upon the discontinuation of counseling as part of the termination process.

30. D: Choice *D* is correct. *A*, *B*, and *C* are all correct. A counselor is required to break client confidentiality when a client is a danger to themselves, when a client is a danger to others, and when they suspect a child is being abused or neglected.

31. D: The correct answer is, "You value sobriety, but surrounding yourself with people who are still using doesn't seem to support that value." This statement is well-structured because it gently points out incongruencies between the client's values and actions without placing judgement. Choice *A* is incorrect since it is both judgement-based and unhelpful. Choice *B* is incorrect because it is permissive and includes an unhelpful, vague warning. Choice *C* is incorrect because it is not an example of confrontation but rather a poor use of self-disclosure.

32. C: Choice *C* is correct. The counseling skills utilized in a counseling consultation remain the same as in traditional counseling. Choice *A* is incorrect. The function of a counseling consultation is different from that of traditional counseling because the consultant is providing assistance to a counselor so they can better assist their clients. Choice *B* is incorrect. The role of a counseling consultant is different from that of a traditional counselor because the consultant focuses on technical and practical strategies, which provide the counselor with actionable solutions. Choice *D* is incorrect. The context of a counseling consultation is different from that of traditional counseling because the consultant is assisting a counselor or other professional so that they can better assist their own clients.

33. A: The correct answer is blocking, which is a technique that a group therapist can use when they need to redirect counterproductive behavior for the group's benefit. Choice *B* is incorrect because linking refers to the process of encouraging interaction and connection between group therapy members by actively identifying common themes. Choice *C* is incorrect because confronting occurs when the therapist challenges one or more group members on contradictions or inconsistencies in thought or behavior patterns. Choice *D* is incorrect because active listening occurs when the therapist engages in focused and alert listening to pick up on all forms of communication occurring within the session, whether direct or subtle.

34. D: The correct answer is moving toward people, which indicates an intense desire to be needed or liked and to avoid conflict or criticism. Choice *A* is incorrect because moving against people is an approach in which a person can be domineering and/or unable to admit fault or powerlessness. Choice *B* is incorrect because moving with people is not an established interpersonal coping style. Choice *C* is incorrect because moving away from people looks like emotionally detaching from others, having a strong need for privacy, and generally keeping relationships at a superficial level.

35. C: The correct answer is 25, which is the age that 79.6% of rape victims who are female experienced rape. Choice *A*, though also a high statistic, is incorrect, as 42.2% of rape victims who are female experienced rape before the age of 18. Choices *B* and *D* are incorrect, as they are much higher than the previously stated correct age of 25.

36. C: The correct answer is school age, as this is the age in which a child's mortality becomes of greater understanding. Choice *A* is incorrect, as an adolescent might have a greater grasp on mortality and what could impact one's mortality. Choice *B* is incorrect, as preschool-aged children tend to believe that death is temporary and reversible. Choice *D* is incorrect, as toddlers generally have limited understanding of time or none of death at all.

37. D: Choice *D* is correct. The initial goal for inpatient treatment is for this client to stop losing weight. Choices *A* and *B* are incorrect. The initial goal for inpatient treatment is not for this client to verbalize self-acceptance or to participate in groups regularly because the client's physical safety is the initial goal in inpatient treatment. Choice *C* is incorrect. The initial goal for inpatient treatment is not for this client to be on bedrest. Though excessive exercise will be discouraged, and the client's physical safety is the first priority, the initial goal of maintaining weight is not contingent on bedrest.

38. A: The correct answer is amphetamines, as the side effects that Chloe is exhibiting appear to be similar to someone who is abusing stimulants. Choices *B* and *D* are incorrect, as these are opioids and tend to manifest more as sleepiness, euphoria, and impaired concentration. Choice *C* is incorrect, as alcohol is classified as a depressant, and its impact would generally not be characterized by high energy.

39. C: Choice *C* is correct. The counselor should be building rapport with the client from the first time they meet and continue to do so throughout the therapeutic relationship. Choices *A* and *D* are incorrect. The counselor should not wait three or five sessions into the therapeutic relationship to begin establishing a rapport with the client. Choice *B* is incorrect. Rapport-building should not begin whenever the client and counselor cross paths in public spaces. The counselor should only address the client in public if the client first addresses the counselor.

40. C: The correct answer is an insecure-ambivalent attachment style, which is characterized by difficulty accepting comfort from a primary caregiver despite seeking their presence or attention. Choice *A* is incorrect, as this might have been the case if Jane refused to look at or go to Fredricka in times of distress or when exploring a new environment. Choice *B* is incorrect, as this would have looked like Jane comfortably and easily going to Fredricka for comfort and reassurance. Choice *D* is incorrect, as this is often characterized by violent, frightening behaviors and/or dazed, confused demeanor. Jane might have lashed out at Fredricka, or vice versa.

41. B: The correct answer is humanistic theory, which is founded on the idea that people have all they need within themselves to succeed, but problematic thoughts and behaviors can be caused by a lack of problem-solving resources. Choice *A* is incorrect because psychoanalytic theory states that behavioral issues are driven by unconscious motivations. Choice *C* is incorrect because behavioral theory states that unwanted behavior only occurs when one's environment reinforces it. Choice *D* is incorrect because cognitive theory is founded on the belief that difficulties arise when one's thought processes are out of sync with reality.

42. C: Choice *C* is correct. The counselor should refer the client elsewhere. The referral should be made to a counselor who can focus on the client's feelings regarding the abortion without passing judgement. Choice *A* is incorrect. The counselor should not ignore the appointment request. Choice *B* is incorrect. The counselor should not respond with their opinion on the matter. Choice *D* is incorrect. The counselor should not ignore their feelings on the matter and move forward with scheduling the appointment. The counselor should move forward with a treatment plan for the client only if they can retain a neutral stance on the subject without imposing personal bias.

43. A: Choice *A* is correct. It should take around two and a half hours to conduct a diagnostic interview. Choice *B* is incorrect. It should take less than five hours to conduct a diagnostic interview. Choice *C* is incorrect. It should take more than 30 minutes to conduct a diagnostic interview. Choice *D* is incorrect. It should take much less than seven hours, even including breaks, to conduct a diagnostic interview.

228

44. B: The correct answer is that when Molly is hallucinating, Molly's family should empathize with the feelings the voices can elicit, such as fear and anxiety, and avoid challenging the validity of her experience. Choice A is incorrect, as this approach can be condescending and disingenuous. Choice C is incorrect, as challenging a person's hallucinations or delusions can be dangerous, potentially leading to or increasing feelings of defensiveness, isolation, and fear. Choice D is incorrect, as experiencing and interacting with hallucinations is not necessarily a reason for someone to be hospitalized, unless there are other specific factors indicating one is at risk of harm to oneself or others.

45. B: The correct answer is dialectal behavioral therapy (DBT), which focuses on acceptance, mindfulness, and the regulation of intense emotions that have led to destructive behaviors. Choice A is incorrect because, while DBT developed from cognitive behavioral therapy (CBT), DBT focuses on the impact of acceptance on ability to change, whereas CBT primarily focuses on redirecting thought patterns. Choice C is incorrect because psychoanalysis delves into the client's past experiences, both conscious and unconscious. Choice D is incorrect because Gestalt therapy involves a client's personal responsibility as well as significant concentration on the impact of their current environment on overall wellness.

46. C: The correct answer is prescription pain medications, which account for 9.3 million of those people reported to be misusing opioids. Choice A is incorrect, as heroin accounts for approximately 902,000 of the people misusing opioids. Choice B is incorrect, as cocaine is considered a stimulant drug rather than an opioid. Choice D is incorrect, as ketamine is considered a dissociative drug rather than an opioid.

47. A: The usual age range for the industry vs. inferiority stage is 5–12 years. Choice B is incorrect, as this is the age group for initiative vs. guilt stage. Choice C is incorrect, as this is the age group for identity vs. role confusion stage. Choice D is incorrect, as this is the age group for autonomy vs. shame stage.

48. B: Rational emotive behavior therapy uses the framework of the ABC model to support treatment. This model involves an activating event, or adversity faced, the beliefs involved, and the consequences received. Therefore, Choice B is correct.

49. A: The correct answer is that teens present as sleepier in the morning and more awake at night. Choice B is incorrect, as studies show that teens are more likely to be up later in the night. Choice C is incorrect, as studies show that teens are more likely to be drowsy in the morning. Choice D is incorrect, as teens need eight to ten hours of sleep to function at their best.

50. A: Rescuers are constantly vying to be viewed as "good." Choice B is incorrect because the victim ultimately wants others to love them unconditionally. Choice C is incorrect because the persecutor's goal is to be "right." Choice D is incorrect because *observer* is not a role in Karpman's triangle.

51. B: The correct answer is stonewalling, in which one or both partners are unable or unwilling to continue a discussion, often due to overwhelming emotions at the prospect of discussing something challenging or emotionally charged. Choice A is incorrect, as criticism refers to the act of noticing something one is displeased with and turning it into comments about their partner's character flaws. Choice C is incorrect, as defensiveness describes a reaction to an apparent criticism. Choice D is incorrect, as contempt refers to the escalation of criticism into emotional abuse, such as using harsh sarcasm or shame to put someone down or express one's feelings.

52. A: The correct answer is vicarious learning, as Christopher is learning from Regina's consequences. Choice B is incorrect, as this would be if Christopher were learning from Regina modeling behavior that led to a reward or preferable result. Choice *C* is incorrect, as this refers to being rewarded by internal feelings, such as satisfaction or pride. Choice *D* is incorrect, as this is not part of Bandura's social learning theory and refers to the subconscious process of being influenced by external stimuli; Christopher is being influenced consciously.

53. D: The correct answer is operant conditioning because the music is being used as a reward for the child's behavior. Choice *A* is incorrect because modeling is when someone learns by observation or imitation. Choice *B* is incorrect because classical conditioning refers to the process in which involuntary responses are elicited. Choice *C* is incorrect because praise involves actively expressing admiration or recognition.

54. B: The correct answer is person-centered therapy, which is founded on the concept that people are fundamentally motivated to work toward a positive framework and are experts on their own lives. Choice *A* is incorrect because psychodynamic therapy focuses on the unconscious happenings occurring in one's brain that drive everyday actions and emotions. Choice *C* is incorrect because Adlerian therapy takes a psychoeducational approach in which the counselor plays a teaching role. Choice *D* is incorrect because the Gestalt model focuses on increasing clients' awareness of self and of the present time with limited exploration of the past.

55. A: The correct answer is self-disclosure, which involves sharing a personal experience directly related to the client with the intent of validating their feelings. Choice *B* is incorrect because reflective listening involves reflecting back what the client said to demonstrate understanding; this example takes it a step further using self-disclosure. Choice *C* is incorrect because you are not disclosing this information to serve your own psychological needs but to appropriately advance the therapeutic purpose. Choice *D* is incorrect because transference refers to a situation in which the client unconsciously transfers thoughts and feelings they have had about another person onto the therapist.

56. D: The ABC model refers to the cycle in which a negative event occurs, we explain why it occurred, and we respond with feelings and behaviors (**A**ctivating events, **B**eliefs, and **C**onsequences). Choice *A* is incorrect because it refers to the core techniques of DBT therapy. Choice *B* is incorrect because it refers to the stages of change model. Choice *C* is incorrect because the ABC model does not refer to a set of breathing and relaxation techniques.

57. D: Choice *D* is correct because universalism is the concept that one is not alone in facing a specific problem and that one's problem is not unique. Choice *A* is incorrect because catharsis is the release of emotional tension. Choice *B* is incorrect as congruence is a therapeutic practice in which the counselor is authentic with their client. Choice *C* is incorrect because altruism is the practice of helping others.

58. B: The correct answer is solution-focused therapy because the miracle question technique is a tool that solution-focused counselors use when trying to help a client get "unstuck" in terms of identifying and solving their current problem. Choice *A* is incorrect because psychoanalysis focuses much more on trying to understand and analyze the past rather than delving into future planning. Choice *C* is incorrect because REBT (rational emotive behavior therapy) seeks to help clients achieve radical acceptance of themselves and their life circumstances while working to identify irrational thoughts or behavioral patterns. Choice *D* is incorrect because structural family therapy is grounded in understanding family members' roles and behaviors within a family unit.

59. C: Choice *C* is correct. *Mixed diagnostic category* is not a term a counselor could use to define this client's presentation since this would indicate the client does not meet the diagnostic criteria for both individual diagnoses. Choices *A*, *B*, and *D* are incorrect. *Dual disorders, co-occurring disorders,* and *comorbid disorders* are all terms a counselor could use to define this client's presentation.

60. D: Choice *D* is correct because associating with a close member of his family could inadvertently lead to contact with the former partner. Choices *A* and *B* are incorrect and are examples of healthy self-care activities. Choice *C* is incorrect because it is a preventative measure to support the client's goal.

61. D: The correct answer is a safety plan because suicidal ideation and self-harm present such high risk that clients can benefit from having a go-to plan for when these thoughts and behaviors come to a head. Choice *A* is incorrect because it refers to legally assigning someone to be temporarily responsible for another adult, which is not necessarily required in self-injurious or suicidal cases. Choice *B* is incorrect because, although it may be helpful for some clients to have a sponsor to call in times of crisis, this is a specific intervention that would be included in the general safety plan. Choice *C* is incorrect because a person with self-injurious behaviors or suicidal ideation does not necessarily need a hospital bed, though hospitalization can indeed be an element of their overall safety plan.

62. C: Choice *C* is the initial stage of the group process, which includes establishing rules. Choices *A*, *B*, and *D* refer to later stages of the group process.

63. A: The correct answer is self-disclosure, which happens when a therapist reveals personal information about themselves. "Why Am I Telling?" is a method that involves "waiting" and reflecting on the purpose for disclosing personal information. Is it in service of the client? Does it serve their best interests? If not, it shouldn't be shared. Choice *B* is incorrect because WAIT is not a tactic that a therapist would use when deciding whether to confront a client regarding inconsistencies. Choice *C* is incorrect because WAIT is also not a technique that a therapist would use when deciding whether to use therapeutic silence with a client. Choice *D* is incorrect because treatment planning is a required part of therapy and would not necessitate use of the WAIT technique.

64. B: The correct answer is inferential reasoning, as Reid can elicit understanding or meaning from something that was not explicitly stated. Choice *A* is incorrect, as this situation does not have to do with morality, and thus this term does not apply. Choice *C* is incorrect, as theory of mind instead refers to the ability to think about how someone else is thinking, which is inapplicable here. Choice *D* is incorrect, as this instead refers to a child's ability to know that an object or person exists, even outside of their immediate view.

65. D: The correct answer is Choice *D*, "Tell me more about what you think the best approach is here." This avoids giving advice, is open-ended, and encourages the client to share further, revealing more about her thought patterns. Choice *A* is unhelpful and would stop the conversation, which wouldn't help elicit further conversation. Choices *B* and *C* are opinion-based statements, and Choice *B* also gives advice. These approaches are unprofessional for a counselor.

66. D: Soft determinism is the belief that although genetic and social factors influence a person's behaviors, there is still an element of free will. Choice *A* is incorrect because environmental determinism focuses primarily on socialization and reinforcement that shape a person's behaviors. Choice *B* is incorrect because biological determinism involves influence from factors outside of one's control, such as genetics. Choice *C* is incorrect because hard determinism denies the concept of free will and states that there is a cause for every action, whether biological or environmental.

67. C: A crossed transaction involves one person engaging from an adult ego state and expecting the other person to respond from that state as well, but the other person is triggered in some way and

231

responds from a child or parent ego state. Choice *A* is incorrect because this describes two people responding from appropriate ego states and having a smooth, appropriate conversational transaction. Choices *B* and *D* are incorrect because duplex and angular transactions are subtypes of ulterior transactions in which there is subtle subtext behind seemingly normal transactions. There is nothing in this example to suggest a subtle subtext; your client indicates genuine surprise at her mother's reaction.

68. D: Choice *D* is the most appropriate answer, as it best reflects Wendy's assessment and interpretation of Xu's behavior through her cultural lens. Choice *A* is incorrect because countertransference occurs when a therapist projects her own feelings and experiences onto a client. Choice *B* is incorrect because Wendy's approach does not appear to be free of bias. Choice *C* is incorrect because individualism refers to the value system in which the individual is favored over the community or society itself.

69. D: Choice *D* is correct. This is the common factors hypothesis. Choice *A* is incorrect. This is not the direct causal hypothesis, which suggests that one diagnosis is the direct cause of another. Choice *B* is incorrect. This is not the indirect causal hypothesis, which suggests that one diagnosis is the indirect cause of another. Choice *C* is incorrect. This is not the genetic vulnerability hypothesis; rather, genetic vulnerability is a risk factor within the common factors hypothesis.

70. C: The correct answer is moving away from people, which can be healthy when one is able to develop characteristics like taking the time to care for oneself, cultivating healthy levels of independence, and learning to contain one's emotional responses to express them in a helpful manner. Choice *A* is incorrect because the healthy version of moving toward people might include caring for and empathizing with others and being vulnerable and open in a relationship. Choice *B* is incorrect because a healthy version of moving against people may include setting strong boundaries and respectfully challenging others' ideas. Choice *D* is incorrect because moving with people is not an established interpersonal coping skill.

71. A: Choice *A* is correct because attention-deficit/hyperactivity disorder can be characterized by impulsivity. It would be more unlikely to have improved impulse control as a treatment goal for Choices *B, C,* and *D*.

72. B: Choice *B* is correct because these factors (in addition to self-awareness and self-care) are five important components of resiliency. Choice *A* is incorrect, as these factors are unrelated to Sev's DSM-5 diagnosis. Choice *C* is incorrect because it refers to factors that make a negative outcome more likely. Choice *D* is incorrect because although the identified factors could be components of treatment goals for Sev, this is not the most intuitive answer.

73. B: Choice *B* is correct. The underlying issue stems from the client's social history. Choice *A* is incorrect. The underlying issue does not stem from the client's biological history. Choice *C* is incorrect. The underlying issue does not stem from the client's psychological history. Choice *D* is incorrect because Choice *B* is correct.

74. C: Choice *C* is the best answer because it is specific, measurable, attainable, realistic, and time-bound. Choice *A* is not the best answer because it is not as specific as Choice *C*. Choice *B* is incorrect since it is not realistic or attainable given that Ren just sustained an injury. Choice *D* is incorrect because it is vague.

75. C: Choice *C* is correct. It would be best if the counselor allows the client to determine their own goals for counseling and listens while the client presents issues which arise throughout treatment, encouraging self-discovery without inserting their own ideas of right or wrong outcomes. Choices *A*, *B*, and *D* are incorrect. Giving the client an outline of what their goals for counseling should be, offering solutions to problems, and redirecting the client to issues that really matter are not the best ways for the counselor to encourage autonomy.

76. D: The correct answer is token economy, which is a system that uses rewards in exchange for desired behaviors. Choice *A* is incorrect because positive punishment adds something unwanted or unpleasant to influence behavior. Choice *B* is incorrect because praise involves actively expressing recognition or admiration. Choice *C* is incorrect because shaping involves taking approximate steps to help a client get closer to their goal behavior.

77. A: Choice *A* is correct. The counselor should recommend partial hospitalization programming or intensive outpatient programming next, as a higher level of care may be beneficial for the client. Choice *B* is incorrect. The counselor should not recommend the client continue to come to outpatient counseling without recommending alternatives. Choice *C* is incorrect. Given that the client's psychiatric condition is unclear, the counselor should not necessarily recommend that the client explore alternatives to traditional counseling, such as ketamine therapy. Choice *D* is incorrect. The counselor should not recommend the client find a new psychiatrist since nothing has indicated the current psychiatrist is providing improper medication management.

78. D: The correct answer is falsifiability, which is the ability of a theory to be proven wrong. Because Freud's theories are so intangible, and thus unmeasurable, there is technically no way to prove them wrong. Choice *A* is incorrect because, although replication is a process used to test a theory, it refers to the ability to duplicate an existing experiment's result using similar methods or circumstances. Choice *B* is incorrect because Occam's razor refers to the idea that the simplest explanation is typically the correct one. Choice *C* is incorrect because, although Freud was criticized for how he projected his personality onto his theories, this criticism is not applicable to this example.

79. C: The correct answer is selective abstraction, which is a cognitive distortion in which someone takes one detail out of context and lets that detail describe the entire experience. Choice *A* is incorrect because overgeneralization would have occurred if your client insisted that all parties henceforth would be failures based on that one awkward moment. Choice *B* is incorrect because personalization is a cognitive distortion in which a person believes that anything someone else says or does is a personal reaction to them. Choice *D* is incorrect because labeling is a distortion that singles out one behavior and applies it to the whole person. For example, "I had an awkward encounter, so I am an awkward person."

80. D: Choice *D* is correct. The most appropriate modality for treatment would be dialectical behavior therapy (DBT), as research has shown this approach to be the most effective treatment for BPD. Choices *A*, *B*, and *C* are incorrect because humanistic therapy, cognitive behavioral therapy (CBT), and rational emotive behavior therapy (REBT) are not the most appropriate modalities for treatment.

81. B: The correct answer is fictional finalism, which is Alfred Alder's theory that children have a conscious drive to overcome feelings of inferiority and achieve individually set goals. Choice *A* is incorrect, as Albert Bandura's social learning theory instead focused on the importance of conditioning and reinforcement by one's environment. Choice *C* is incorrect, as Sigmund Freud's theory was in sharp contrast to Alder's theory in that it focused primarily on a child's past experiences shaping them as a human being. Choice *D* is incorrect, as John Bowlby's attachment theory primarily focused on a child's innate need to attach to a caregiver.

82. B: The correct answer is solution-focused therapy, which involves eliciting the solutions that worked well for the client in the past, searching for "exceptions" (times in the client's life when things may not have felt this poor), and avoiding use of past-focused dialogue. Choice *A* is incorrect because this model delves more deeply into understanding the presenting problem rather than primarily focusing on solutions. Choice *C* is incorrect because psychoanalysis focuses on exploring the past. Choice *D* is incorrect because REBT makes space to incorporate and understand a person's deficits rather than being primarily strengths-based.

83. D: The correct answer is triangulation, which is a dysfunctional family communication pattern in which one person is placed in the middle of a conflict between two other people. The middleperson is often used to carry messages back and forth. Choice *A* is incorrect because Regina's dad is not being defensive; in other words, he is not demonstrating sensitivity to criticism or an inability to tolerate another's emotions or words. Choice *B* is incorrect because reality shifting occurs when what is said directly contradicts what is really happening. Choice *C* is incorrect because stonewalling occurs when someone refuses to communicate at all, particularly during a conflict. Regina's dad *is* communicating here, but he is doing it through Regina.

84. B: The correct answer is schema, as this refers to the mental model a person uses to organize their current fund of knowledge and prepare for future understanding. Choice *A* is incorrect, as bias is the act of distorting perception of current events based on previous experiences. Choice *C* is incorrect, as cognition more broadly refers to all types of thought. Choice *D* is incorrect, as a phobia refers to an irrational fear.

85. D: The correct answer is "That is unusual." This statement gently voices doubt in response to something a client said. Choice *A* is an example of a close-ended question. Choice *B* is incorrect because it is an example of a clarifying question. Choice *C* is incorrect because it is an example of reflective listening.

86. C: The correct answer is dopamine, as it is the chemical that is released in response to the addictive behavior/process. Choice *A* is incorrect, as neurons are not a chemical released by the brain but rather signals sent throughout the brain. Choice *B* is incorrect, as serotonin acts more as a chemical that mediates the responses to the behavior/process. Choice *D* is incorrect, as there is limited research to support that the brain's release of oxytocin is tied to addiction. There is, however, research to suggest that it can sometimes mitigate the impacts of addiction-seeking behaviors.

87. D: Choice *D* is the best answer because it is a specific and manageable short-term objective. Choices *A*, *B*, and *C* are excellent goals, but they are examples of long-term goals that can guide overall treatment.

88. C: Choice *C* is correct. This counselor is utilizing a psychoanalytic or psychodynamic therapeutic approach. Choice *A* is incorrect. This counselor is not utilizing a cognitive behavioral therapy (CBT) approach, which is a more collaborative orientation. Choice *B* is incorrect. This counselor is not utilizing a rational emotive behavior therapy (REBT) approach, which is a more directive orientation. Choice *D* is incorrect. This counselor is not utilizing a dialectical behavior therapy (DBT) approach, which is a more directive orientation.

89. D: The correct answer is unoccupied play, which is the first stage of play that children engage in as babies when they are learning how their body moves. Choice *A* is incorrect, as this refers to when a child observes another child playing but does not engage with them. Choice *B* is incorrect, as this refers to children interacting with other children in play but without much cooperation required to engage. Choice *C* is incorrect, as this is when a child is engaging with play alone and is not interested in playing with others. Although Kiki is playing alone in this example, the fact that she is engaging in learning how her body moves is best described by Choice *D*.

90. D: The correct answer is generativity, which focuses on the legacy and care one pours into the next generation. Choice *A* is incorrect, as initiative refers to Erikson's third stage when children in earlier development develop the ability to assert themselves. Choice *B* is incorrect, as stagnation refers to the reverse of generativity when one might reach middle adulthood having felt unproductive and disconnected. Choice *C* is incorrect, as industry in this context refers to Erikson's fourth stage, which encompasses an adolescent's developing ability to manage social and academic expectations.

91. C: The correct answer is groupthink, which is when members of a group are unwilling to express a dissenting opinion and emphasis is placed on unanimity. Choice *A* is incorrect because this describes the process in which members of a group lean more toward extreme decision making than they would individually. Choice *B* is incorrect because deindividuation occurs when a person loses their sense of self in a group and acts in an unsocialized or anti-social manner. Choice *D* is incorrect because the inoculation effect is a communication theory stating that a belief or attitude can be protected from influence.

92. B: Choice *B* is correct. The counselor should explain that they are not able to provide any additional information regarding their counseling sessions. The client is his own legal guardian, and legally nothing else can be disclosed even though the father is paying for the sessions. Choice *A* is incorrect. Even though the father is paying for the sessions, the counselor cannot provide him with information regarding his son's progress in therapy. Choice *C* is incorrect. The counselor cannot provide the father with even a brief update. Choice *D* is incorrect. The counselor does not need to hang up the phone immediately and block the father's number since it is not a conflict of interest that the father has called to inquire into his son's counseling.

93. C: Choice *C* is correct because it reflects the counselor's initiative to learn more about an important situation in their client's life. Having knowledge of hormone therapy's mental and emotional impacts can help them provide proper empathy and support. Choices *A* and *B* are incorrect because they describe actions that are outside the counselor's scope of practice. Choice *D* is incorrect because it is dismissive and creates unhelpful barriers in therapy.

94. B: In a complementary transaction, a person receives a response that aligns with what they've said. Choice *A* is incorrect because in an angular transaction, someone communicates openly but with a "hidden message" that they want the respondent to pick up on and respond to in a certain way. Choice *C* is incorrect because a crossed transaction occurs when one person engages from an adult ego state and expects the other person to respond from that state as well; however, the other person is triggered in some way and responds from a child or parent ego state. Choice *D* is incorrect because a duplex transaction occurs when a person masks a "hidden message" with an open message, and the other person responds with an open message that includes the "hidden response."

95. D: The career development theorist who focused on the correlation between individual personality traits and knowledge of the labor market is Frank Parsons. Choice *A* is incorrect, as Holland's theory is founded on the categorization of six personality types. Choice *B* is incorrect, as Bandura focuses on how an individual's past experiences might influence their career development. Choice *C* is incorrect, as Gottfredson primarily studies the developmental stages of children and how their understanding of the world at a certain stage might influence their career decisions.

96. C: The correct answer is that Kris will help identify and reframe Betty's negative thought patterns regarding her loss, which is a common approach in cognitive behavioral therapy. Choice *A* is incorrect, as it is an example of acceptance and commitment therapy. Choice *B* is incorrect, as it is an example of art therapy. Choice *D* is incorrect, as it is an example of a group therapy approach.

97. C: Choice *C* is correct because the Vanderbilt Assessment Scales are used to assess and diagnose ADHD. Choices *A* and *B* are tools that measure intelligence. Choice *D* is used to diagnose and assess severity of depression.

98. C: The correct answer is transitive inference, which is the ability to understand social relationships between people. Choice *A* is incorrect, as this only refers to the ability to understand specific objects/concepts, not the relationship between them. Choice *B* is incorrect, as this is the ability to know when an object or person still exists, even if they are out of sight. Choice *D* is incorrect. Although this does refer to a logical thinking skill, it describes the ability to understand that a certain quantity is the same despite being in a differently sized or shaped container.

99. B: The correct answer is parental generativity, as Jorge is passing down family traditions. Choice *A* is incorrect because biological generativity refers to conceiving, bearing, and raising children. Choice *C* is incorrect, as technical generativity is focused on teaching skills. Choice *D* is incorrect, as cultural generativity refers to folks within a certain culture preserving and passing down cultural knowledge and traditions.

100. A: Choice *A* is correct. An achievement test measures maximum performance. Choice *B* is incorrect. An achievement test measures maximum performance, not minimum performance. Choice *C* is incorrect. An inventory test, rather than an achievement test, measures typical performance. Choice *D* is incorrect. A projective test, rather than an achievement test, measures unconscious traits.

101. A: The correct answer is exploring, as this is the stage in which the counselor helps the client to identify thoughts, feelings, and primary concerns. Choice *B* is incorrect because reflecting involves mirroring back what a client just shared with you. Choice *C* is incorrect because clarifying is a tool that counselors use to help the client specify or explain vague or ambiguous thoughts or feelings. Choice *D* is incorrect because empathizing involves helping the client feel understood and seen in their own world.

102. A: Choice *A* is correct because the counselor is demonstrating awareness of Erica's current emotional needs and responding appropriately. Choice *D*, unconditional positive regard, is the demonstration of complete support and acceptance of a client; while that may be happening in this situation, Choice *A* is a better answer because the counselor's actions are actively demonstrating attunement to Erica's needs. Choice *B* is incorrect because the counselor isn't using listening as a tactic for empathizing. Choice *C* is incorrect because while the counselor's actions do reflect congruence, empathic attunement is a more specific description of those actions.

103. A: Choice *A* is correct because collectivism refers to a system in which the larger group (family, in this instance) is valued above all. Choice *B* is incorrect, as individualism focuses on the importance of the individual above all. Choice *C* is incorrect because a low context culture describes an individualistic culture in which explicit verbal communication is essential, leaving little to be implied. Choice *D* is incorrect, as acculturation refers to the process of someone acclimating to a new culture while still retaining important elements of their own culture.

104. D: The correct answer is environmental factor, as Yara's immediate environment has changed, causing her to change in response. Choice *A* is incorrect, as emotional factors are not part of the

236

triadic model. Choice *B* is incorrect, as an individual factor instead refers to personality traits, beliefs, etc. Choice *C* is incorrect, as a behavioral factor refers to when person's behaviors cause something to change.

105. C: Choice *C* is correct because acculturation refers to the process in which a minority culture adjusts to the majority culture while maintaining elements of their own culture. Choice *A* is incorrect because assimilation reflects a two-way process in which the majority and minority cultures change. Choice *B* is incorrect because congruence is a therapeutic practice in which the counselor is authentic with their client. Choice *D* is incorrect because immigration is the process by which someone comes to live permanently in a country other than their home country.

106. A: The correct answer is a primary circular reaction, as Kirk is at the stage in which he can intentionally engage in behaviors with his body that bring pleasure. Choice *B* is incorrect, as reflex acts refer to the first month of a child's life, during which they are engaging in certain behaviors innately. Choice *C* is incorrect, as this is a more advanced reaction that involves intentionally manipulating an object to do different things that bring pleasure or engaging in trial-and-error behavior to elicit reactions from their environment. Choice *D* is incorrect, as this refers to the reaction in which babies learn that they can not only do things with their body intentionally, but they can also repeatedly engage in actions that trigger a response in their environment as well.

107. A: The correct answer is egocentrism, which at this age can manifest as the idea that there is an "imaginary audience" that cares deeply about what the child looks like or how they behave. Choice *B* is incorrect, as sublimation is the process in which a generally unacceptable impulse is channeled into a socially acceptable action or behavior. Choice *C* is incorrect, as this describes the process of creating a reasonable explanation for an unreasonable behavior or event. Choice *D* is incorrect because assimilation refers to fitting a new experience into an existing schema.

108. D: The correct answer is authoritarian, which is a parenting style that is highly demanding but less responsive. Choice *A* is incorrect. Although authoritative parents are demanding, they are also generally warm and responsive. Choice *B* is incorrect, as permissive parents tend to be much less demanding and very responsive. Choice *C* is incorrect, as a neglectful parenting style is absent of both demands of the child and responsiveness to their child's needs.

109. B: Makala can let her clients know that gender and sexuality are safe topics to address and that she will keep their identities in mind during treatment, but she must allow the client to guide their own treatment. Therefore, the topic of gender and/or sexuality should only become a focus if the client desires. Choices *A*, *C*, and *D* can enhance Makala's practice.

110. D: Choice *D* is correct. The counselor should ultimately determine the client's diagnosis by consulting the DSM-5. Choice *A* is incorrect. Though it may be useful to obtain documentation from the previous counselor for continuity of care, the counselor should not ultimately determine the client's diagnosis by consulting the client's previous counselor. Choice *B* is incorrect. The counselor should not ultimately determine the client's diagnosis by allowing the client to decide, as self-diagnosing can be more harmful than beneficial. Choice *C* is incorrect. The counselor should not ultimately determine the client's diagnosis by consulting the client's family members, but it may be beneficial to obtain collateral information from these individuals.

111. A: The correct answer is "Did you engage in binging/purging last night?" because this is a question that can be answered by a "yes" or "no." Choices *B*, *C*, and *D* are incorrect because they are open-ended questions that are more complex and require a bit more information in response.

237

112. D: The correct answer is positive reinforcement, which is the use of a positive stimulus in response to a desirable behavior. Choice *A* is incorrect, as this refers to an agreement between two individuals that when one person does something agreed upon, the other gives them something of value. There is nothing here that indicates this was an agreement between Lena and her parents. Choice *B* is incorrect, as this refers to removing something negative to increase a specific behavior. Choice *C* is incorrect, as this refers to the act of demonstrating a specific behavior that one is hoping another person will begin imitating.

113. B: The correct answer is that mutual support can help encourage healthy behaviors; fellow group members who are also seeking continued sobriety can offer a positive support network. Choice *A* is incorrect because 12-step group settings can be structurally rigid with requirements that can limit personal choice. Choice *C* is incorrect because 12-step programs can be very helpful to newly and longtime sober people alike. Choice *D* is incorrect because group settings are not void of triggers for relapse; in fact, for some addicts, being in social settings that expose them to other addicts' journeys can be triggering.

114. A: The correct answer is autoplastic adaptation, which occurs when an individual adjusts their own behaviors to better survive in their environment. Choice *B* is incorrect because alloplastic adaptation involves changing one's environment to better suit their needs. Choice *C* is incorrect because individualism involves putting one's own interests ahead of the collective group's needs. Choice *D* is incorrect because collectivism involves putting the group's interests ahead of one's own needs.

115. C: Choice *C* is correct. There are 16 questions in the cultural formulation interview. Choices *A*, *B*, and *D* are incorrect because they list the incorrect number of questions for a cultural formulation interview.

116. C: The correct answer is victim because Ricky is dismissing his potential by believing that he is incapable. Choice *A* is incorrect because a rescuer dismisses others' potential and believes they are capable of solving problems that others are incapable of solving for themselves. Choice *B* is incorrect because *observer* is not a role in Karpman's triangle. Choice *D* is incorrect because a persecutor dismisses the feelings of others.

117. D: Choice *D* is correct. The counselor should disagree because this would be a dual relationship and an unethical way to practice. Choices *A*, *B*, and *C* are all incorrect. The counselor should not agree to this arrangement under any of these terms because of the dual relationship that exists.

118. D: The correct answer is that there is often difficulty separating physical symptoms related to terminal illness from those secondary to depression. Choice *A* is incorrect. Although this might be an issue in some cases, this has not been statistically identified as the prevalent issue here. Choice *B* is incorrect, as the symptoms are not often hidden but rather misattributed to the terminal illness. Choice *C* is incorrect, as identifying and treating depression in patients boosts quality of life and creates increased resilience, which are vital for living with a terminal illness.

119. A: The correct answer is Choice *A* because bipolar disorder primarily involves noticeable patterns of mood and energy shifts. Choice *B* is incorrect because this method of psychoeducation is a better fit for a client coping with generalized anxiety disorder. Choice *C* is incorrect because this method of psychoeducation applies to a client diagnosed with obsessive-compulsive disorder. Choice *D* is incorrect, as it would be more appropriate for a client with schizophrenia.

120. B: The correct answer is Karen Horney, who believed that challenging parent-child relationships lead to basic anxiety in children. To ease some of that anxiety that will inevitably affect their other relationships, they develop specific interpersonal coping skills. Choice *A* is incorrect because Freud's perspective on healthy parent-child relationships is centered around heavy maternal involvement early on as well as the child's development of a healthy id, ego, and superego. Choice *C* is incorrect because Erikson focuses on developmental stages of a child's life; although a child's development is highly impacted by their parents, their personality is not fixed in early life, and there is space for evolution. Choice *D* is incorrect because Jung's theories delve more into the impact of a parent's "unlived life" on their child.

121. A: The correct answer is hypoarousal, which is a stress response that can make a person "freeze" and want to withdraw from the cause of stress. Choice *B* is incorrect, as hyperarousal refers to the other side of the stress response spectrum in which a person is incredibly triggered by a stressful stimulus and may present as hypervigilant, aggressive, or irritable. Choice *C* is incorrect, as there is not enough information here to indicate that Trent is experiencing trauma. Choice *D* is incorrect, as grounding is a coping strategy that a person can use in response to stress.

122. A: The correct answer is that they will follow societal rules to maintain law and order, as this is typical of the conventional morality stage. Choices *B* and *C* are incorrect, as these reflect the postconventional morality stage. Choice *D* is incorrect, as it reflects the preconventional morality stage.

123. D: Choice *D* is correct. The counselor should refer the client to a provider who offers counseling services on a sliding scale fee basis. This way the client can continue to receive the support they need without the same degree of financial burden. Choice *A* is incorrect. The counselor should not request that the client see them more often since there are more affordable services available, and the financial strain could outweigh the added support the counselor could provide. Choice *B* is incorrect. The counselor should not suggest they meet less often so the client is able to afford their services. It would be more ethical and beneficial for the client if the counselor refers them elsewhere. Choice *C* is incorrect for the same reason that Choice *B* is incorrect. The counselor should not recommend that the client take a break from counseling and return once they have regained employment because it would be more ethical and beneficial for the client if the counselor refers them elsewhere.

124. D: Choice *D* is correct because inpatient hospitalization reflects the most intensive level of care. The remaining choices do not include 24/7 monitoring and psychiatric treatment, which would be the safest option for someone with intent to act on suicidal ideation.

125. C: The correct answer is a delayed nonevent, as this refers to anticipating a transition that still may happen. Choice *A* is incorrect, as this refers to a transition not happening due to a specific event's causation. Choice *B* is incorrect, as this is instead describing someone else's experience of a person's transition not occurring. Choice *D* is incorrect, as this is referring to when an unexpected transition occurrs (i.e., a loved one's sudden death or divorce).

126. C: Choice *C* is correct. This example can be best identified as implicit cultural bias. Choice *A* is incorrect. This example cannot be best identified as explicit racial bias since the counselor is unaware of their own prejudice and how it affects their actions. Choice *B* is incorrect. This example cannot be best identified as social comparison bias since the counselor knows nothing about the clients' social, physical, or mental attributes. Choice *D* is incorrect. This example cannot be best identified as affinity bias since the counselor does not know how the clients appear physically.

239

127. C: The correct answer is shaping, which uses approximate steps to help a client get closer to the goal behavior. Choice *A* is incorrect because operant conditioning is the process of using rewards and/or punishments to achieve goal behavior. Choice *B* is incorrect because modeling involves using observation and imitation to learn a behavior. Choice *D* is incorrect because chaining involves connecting previously conditioned behaviors to end up with the goal behavior.

128. B: Choice *B* is correct. The counselor does not need to provide the client with their website address or business card as a way for the client to contact them with any additional questions. This is not a requirement to obtain valid informed consent. Choices *A, C,* and *D* are incorrect. Disclosing any risks involved for the client throughout the counseling process, providing information regarding their credentials and experience, and disclosing any other professionals involved in the client's care, including a supervisor or consulting provider, are all requirements for obtaining valid informed consent.

129. D: The correct answer is the adult ego state, which is theorized to be rooted firmly in the present and appears to be the most rational part of one's personality. Choice *A* is incorrect because the parent ego state is rooted in the past and describes thoughts and behaviors derived from influential people in one's life, including one's parents and/or caregivers. Choice *B* is incorrect because the unconscious ego state is not an established ego state. Choice *C* is incorrect because the child ego state is rooted in the past and includes behaviors and feelings developed in one's childhood.

130. B: The correct answer is that children who have been bullied are at a higher risk for sleep issues, anxiety, and struggles with their academics. Choice *A* is incorrect, as studies show that 49.8% of children this age indicated experiencing bullying in school versus the 14.5% who did online. Choice *C* is incorrect, as studies have shown that children who have been bullied are more likely to struggle with trust and self-esteem concerns in adulthood. Choice *D* is incorrect, as LGBTQ students are far more likely to experience bullying, particularly focused on their sexual orientation and gender expressions, than their peers.

131. B: Choice *B* is correct. The Davidson Trauma Scale measures the frequency and severity of post-traumatic stress disorder symptoms. Choices *A, C,* and *D* are incorrect. The Davidson Scale does not measure suicidality or self-esteem, nor does it assess for self-harm.

132. D: The correct answer is establishment, as Helena is working to establish herself in her chosen field. Choice *A* is incorrect, as this refers to a later stage in which a person is continuing to maintain the status they have gained in their field of work. Choice *B* is incorrect, as this refers to the stage in which one is just exploring different classes or topics of interest. Choice *C* is incorrect, as this refers to the very early stage of development in which children are just learning their sense of self and developing their own attitude and perspective.

133. A: The correct answer is catastrophizing, as this refers to a person magnifying a negative experience into something bigger than it really is. Choice *B* is incorrect, as emotional reasoning instead focuses on a person taking their feeling in the moment and applying it to be true in all cases (i.e., "I am failing in school, thus I am a failure in all facets of my life."). Choice *C* is incorrect given that fallacy of change refers to the belief that others should change to suit one's own interests. Choice *D* is incorrect, as personalization is taking whatever someone else says or does personally, assuming it is an intentional slight.

134. B: Choice *B* reflects the concept of helping others, which can increase group members' self-esteem. Choice *A* is incorrect because instillation of hope describes the concept of showing that recovery is possible. Choice C is incorrect; development of social skills reflects the idea that group members are learning new ways to talk about their experiences, feelings, and observations. Choice D is incorrect because group cohesiveness describes the concept of group members finding belonging within their group of peers.

135. B: Choice B is correct because counselors have a legal and ethical duty to warn and protect in cases where there is potential and imminent risk of harm. Choice A is incorrect, as the right to privacy becomes secondary in cases of imminent risk. Choices C and D are incorrect because there is always an ethical obligation to warn and protect in these situations, and most often there is a legal obligation as well.

136. C: The correct answer is linking, which is the process of encouraging interaction and connection between group therapy members by actively identifying common themes. Choice A is incorrect because blocking is the process of stopping counterproductive behaviors during a group session, either to protect the established ground rules or another group member. Choice B is incorrect because interpreting involves explaining a behavior, thought process, or phenomenon for the group through the lens of a theoretical framework. Choice D is incorrect because supporting involves providing positive reinforcement to encourage a specific behavior.

137. D: Choice D is correct. The Rosenberg Self-Esteem Scale measures positive and negative feelings about oneself. Choices A, B, and C are incorrect. The Rosenberg Scale does not measure suicidality or symptoms of trauma, nor does it assess for self-harm.

138. C: The correct answer is, "You have a few friends, but you'd like to make more," because it reframes Emily's original statement and takes on a more positive perspective. Choice A is incorrect because it is an example of reflective listening. Choice B is incorrect because it is an example of clarification. Choice D is incorrect because it is an example of normalization.

139. C: The correct answer is reflective listening, which demonstrates that the counselor both hears and understands what the client is communicating. Choice A is incorrect because clarification happens when a therapist asks a client to specify something they've communicated that came across as vague or ambiguous. Choice B is incorrect because it describes a state of cognitive/emotional discomfort that occurs when opposing beliefs are simultaneously held. Choice D is incorrect because psychoanalysis is a therapeutic modality that focuses on the client's past experiences, both conscious and unconscious.

140. C: Choice C is correct because objectives are smaller, short-term goals that support a larger, overarching goal. Choices A and D are incorrect, as outcomes and therapeutic progress refer to regular components that the counselor and client will use to measure progress and plan effectiveness. Choice B is incorrect, as barriers are factors that may impact a client's ability to reach their goals.

141. C: Choice C is correct. Rapport-building is not necessarily an aspect of conducting an MSE. Choices A, B, and D are incorrect because assessing behavior, appearance, and cognitive functions and thought processes are all aspects of conducting an MSE.

142. A: Choice A would be the best option here because DBT therapy is an intensive method that has been proven to be highly effective for patients struggling with chronic self-injurious behaviors. Choice B is incorrect, as a provider within the same scope of practice is not likely to be any more impactful. Given the chronic and long-lasting nature of Haley's symptoms, Choices C and D are incorrect since they only offer a short period of intensive care.

143. A: Compliance is to explicit (i.e., following explicit instructions or direction) as conformity is to implicit (i.e., adherence to "unspoken rules"). Choice *B* is incorrect because both fear and agreeability can be factors in both compliance and conformity; they are not mutually exclusive. Choice *C* is incorrect because social norms are more related to conformity, and a direct request describes what can initiate compliance. Choice *D* is incorrect because rejection is a potential outcome of lack of conformity, while legal consequence is a potential outcome of lack of compliance.

144. C: Choice *C* is correct. SDQ stands for Strengths and Difficulties Questionnaire. This questionnaire is used for children and young people as a measure of the following areas: emotional issues, conduct issues, hyperactivity, peer issues, and prosocial behavior. Choices *A, B* and *D* are incorrect. SDQ does not stand for Suicide and Depression Questionnaire, Symptoms of Depression Questionnaire, or Similarities and Differences Questionnaire.

145. D: Choice *D* is correct. Positive Z-scores are above the mean, and negative Z-scores are below the mean, making Choice *A* incorrect. Choices *B* and *C* are incorrect because positive Z-scores do indicate that they are above the mean, while negative Z-scores do indicate that they are below the mean.

146. C: The correct answer is a fixed ratio reinforcement pattern, which includes an established number of times a behavior must be conducted before moving to the next task. Choices *A* and *B* are incorrect because *interval* refers to a period of time rather than a certain number of behaviors or responses that must occur before moving to the next task. Choice *D* is incorrect because a variable ratio suggests that the number of behaviors or responses could change each time, which is not the case in this example.

147. B: The correct answer is tuning into physical symptoms, as Heather is working to regulate her breathing so that her mind can think clearly. Choice *A* is incorrect, as distraction might include listening to music, watching TV, or using something else to distract from the overwhelming feelings in the moment. Choice *C* is incorrect, as seeking emotional support may look like calling a friend or loved one for advice and support. Choice *D* is incorrect, as cognitive reappraisal involves trying to think about or see the situation in a new or different way.

148. A: A non-judgmental stance exemplifies that the therapist is reserving both positive and negative judgement for their client's thoughts and feelings; they are simply allowing them to share freely. Choice *C* is incorrect because a non-judgmental stance withholds even positive judgement. Choices *B* and *D* refer to different concepts.

149. C: The correct answer is that genetic traits relate to "nature," and environmental influences refer to "nurture." Choice *A* is incorrect, as both terms described here refer to elements of one's nurturing. Choice *B* is incorrect, as they are listed in the reverse order of what would be correct. Choice *D* is incorrect, as both elements here refer to the impact of one's natural influence.

150. B: Choice *B* is correct. The Brief Symptom Inventory (BSI) would be most helpful for the counselor to assess both the client's presenting problem and their current level of psychological distress during intake. Without an identified presenting problem, the BSI will be most useful, as it covers a wide range of symptom dimensions and will allow the counselor to appropriately identify any psychiatric conditions as well as the client's level of distress in relation to each. Choice *A* is incorrect. The Generalized Anxiety Disorder Scale (GAD-7) and the Mood and Feeling Questionnaire (MFQ) would be most helpful for the counselor to assess the client's symptoms of anxiety and depression. If it is discovered from the BSI that these are the presenting problems, these would be useful tools moving forward. Choices *C* and *D* are incorrect because the Emotional Avoidance Strategy Inventory for

Adolescents (EASI-A) and Adverse Childhood Experiences (ACES) Questionnaire would not be the most helpful options for the counselor to assess both the client's presenting problem and their current level of psychological distress.

151. B: Choice *B* is correct; in the contemplation stage, clients often consider change and focus on its potential barriers and/or benefits. Choice *A* is incorrect, as clients in the precontemplation stage are not yet considering change as an option. Choice *C* is incorrect because the client has not yet engaged in the program. Choice *D* is incorrect, as relapse reflects the stage in which someone has achieved change and then relapsed back into problematic behavior.

152. B: Choice *B* is correct. The best way to proceed is for the counselor to block the client and address the matter with them during their next session. Choice *A* is incorrect. The counselor should not ignore that this has occurred without mentioning it at their next appointment. Choice *C* is incorrect. If the counselor is concerned that the client may follow through with their threats or in some way harm them, the best way to proceed is to terminate the counseling relationship. Choice *D* is incorrect. The best way to proceed is not for the counselor to laugh it off and send the client a funny message, letting them know it's no big deal, as this does not set clear boundaries.

153. B: The correct answer is bibliotherapy, which is a therapeutic approach that uses reading materials to guide growth and change. Choice *A* is incorrect because mindfulness refers to bringing intentional awareness to thoughts, feelings, and actions. Choice *C* is incorrect because art therapy specifically refers to the use of art modalities in session to help clients express their thoughts and feelings and process their experiences. Choice *D* is incorrect because visualization generally refers to a relaxation technique in which the therapist guides their client through imagery or something similar.

154. A: The correct answer is age 25. At this age, the frontal lobe, which is responsible for reasoning and planning, is thought to be fully developed. Choices *B*, *C*, and *D* are incorrect because they are much younger than the proper age of frontal lobe development.

155. B: The correct answer is Alfred Adler, who theorized that everyone is born with the notion that they are inferior to other people. He coined the term *inferiority complex*. Choice *A* is incorrect because Adler developed his work after Freud, who focused more intently on unconscious desires and how they can develop into personal feelings of inferiority within parent-child relationships. Choice *C* is incorrect because Perls founded Gestalt therapy, which focuses on the present rather than delving into the impact of past experiences. Choice *D* is incorrect because Bandura believed that people are not born with specific personality attributes; instead, they are shaped and developed by the people they encounter throughout their lives.

156. A: Choice *A* is the correct answer because Frida does not need to relate to Bee's experience before empathizing and providing appropriate treatment and support. Choices *B*, *C*, and *D* are examples of appropriate approaches.

157. D: The correct answer is structural family therapy, which views the family as one unit made up of individuals who each serve unique roles and/or functions within the unit. Choice *A* is incorrect because transgenerational therapy typically serves to clarify and resolve conflict amidst multiple generations within a family, which is not necessarily what is being reflected in this example. Choice *B* is incorrect because strategic family therapy does not typically involve the therapist spending time observing the family's home environment. Choice *C* is incorrect because narrative therapy takes a deeper dive into understanding the underlying stories and stigmatization that arises within families, including what is considered "normal" or "acceptable" within that narrative.

158. C: The correct answer is muscle aches and tension, cardiovascular concerns, headaches, and digestion issues because these are all symptoms closely associated with anxiety. Choice *A* is incorrect, as this better describes symptoms of attention-deficit/hyperactivity disorder. Choice *B* is incorrect, as it characterizes symptoms of depression. Choice *D* is incorrect, as this instead details symptoms of autism spectrum disorder.

159. D: The correct answer is safe haven, as Amber is returning to a familiar, comforting presence in the face of something unfamiliar and scary. Choice *A* is incorrect, as this does not appear to represent an insecure attachment style. Choice *B* is incorrect, as Amber is not being separated from her caregiver. Choice *C* is incorrect, as Amber was near her mother; the act of returning to her mother for comfort is more accurately described as safe haven.

160. D: Choice *D* is correct because you need signed informed consent from this client to be legally and ethically able continue the conversation. Choice *A* is incorrect, as engaging in care coordination without consent from the patient violates HIPAA. Choice *B* is incorrect because it is more than appropriate to engage in care coordination in this case; in fact, it would increase the patient's ability to acclimate successfully post-hospitalization. Choice *C* is incorrect, as this way of asking for informed consent is informal and unethical.

161. B: The correct answer is the preoperational stage, which is most closely associated with the development tasks listed. Choices *A* and *C* are incorrect, as both the formal and concrete operational stages would see a more advanced ability to distinguish an object from the category in which it belongs. Choice *D* is incorrect, as the sensorimotor stage is too early for pretend play and is more characterized by parallel play.

162. A: The correct answer is post-traumatic stress disorder (PTSD) because EMDR is designed to support clients in processing past experiences that have led to unresolved distressing thoughts, feelings, and behaviors. Choices *B*, *C*, and *D* are incorrect because these are examples of diagnoses for which EMDR is not a recommended treatment.

163. A: The correct answer is tension reliver because he helped to reduce the formality and/or seriousness of a situation, therefore allowing group members to relax. Choice *B* is incorrect because a harmonizer helps to mediate disagreements and reconcile differences. Choice *C* is incorrect because an energizer specifically serves to push the group toward action, whereas the tension reliver simply creates the situation that makes action possible. Choice *D* is incorrect because a supporter or encourager utilizes active praise and encouragement of group members' feelings, contributions, and growth.

164. D: The correct answer is suppression, which refers to the conscious stopping of memories. Choice *A* is incorrect, as repression is rather the unconscious blocking of thoughts or memories. Choice *B* is incorrect, as there is not enough information here to dictate if Angie is regressing in her ability to cope with or process these memories. Choice *C* is incorrect, as displacement is when someone redirects their feelings or impulse onto something or someone else.

165. A: Choice *A* is correct. The counselor should recommend partial hospitalization, as this will provide the client with more structure at a higher level of care without requiring admission to inpatient care. Choice *B* is incorrect. The counselor should not recommend the client return to inpatient care. Another inpatient admission is unnecessary at this time given the client has a supportive network, is safe at home, and is not a danger to himself or others. Choice *C* is incorrect. The counselor should not recommend another chemical dependency assessment, as the client received

244

one prior to inpatient admission and has just left inpatient care after one month. It would be unnecessary to complete another assessment so soon, though it may be beneficial for the counselor to obtain a copy of the initial assessment. Choice *D* is incorrect. The counselor should not recommend a support group for addiction; though a support group may be beneficial, it would be better for the counselor to recommend partial hospitalization since this will ease the client's transition from inpatient to outpatient services.

166. C: Choice *C* is the most appropriate tool for this situation because this test is a behavior assessment. Choice *A* is incorrect because the DAST-10 is administered directly to clients, and it measures drug use. Choice *B* is often a helpful tool for parents and teachers to complete, but it is more appropriate for situations in which ADHD is the primary concern. Choice *D* is incorrect, as the GAD-7 is administered to the client to assess and diagnose anxiety.

167. B: The correct answer is the bargaining stage, in which patients may try to achieve some level of control over the meaning or outcome and may find themselves in a cycle of guilt (i.e., "If I could have done *this* differently, *that* wouldn't have happened."). Choice *A* is incorrect, as this stage is characterized by denial or avoidance of the entire event or topic. Choice *C* is incorrect because the depression stage is when the patient is deep into understanding the loss, and the emotional pain they've worked to avoid becomes evident. Choice *D* is incorrect, as this stage is when the reality is just beginning to set in, and the patient may lash out.

168. D: Choice *D* encompasses housing, which Maslow identified as a basic need that should be met before exploring other needs. Choices *A*, *B,* and *C* are levels in Maslow's hierarchy of needs, but they are ranked after physiological needs.

169. C: The correct answer is "I wonder if there are decisions coming up for you that you're worried about making." Jung believed that dreams prepare us for the future. Choice *A* is incorrect because this approach is past-focused, which is more reflective of Freud's interpretation of dreams. Choice *B* is incorrect because Jung theorized that our dreams compensate for and balance out what we present in everyday life. He would theorize that Gary typically has an easy time making decisions. Choice *D* is incorrect because Jung placed great importance on dreams and believed that important insights could be gleaned from them.

170. D: Choice *D* exemplifies unconditional positive regard. Choice *A* is incorrect; it is an example of an opinion or judgmental stance. Choice *B* is incorrect because it is an example of reflective listening. Choice *C* is incorrect because it uses a reflection of discrepancy/confrontation to respond.

171. A: Choice *A* is correct. Resolving conflict and altering unhelpful individual patterns for more fulfilling relationships are often the focus in couples counseling. Choices *B*, *C*, and *D* are incorrect because resolving conflict and altering unhelpful individual patterns for more fulfilling relationships are not the focus of guidance counseling, systemic counseling, or psychodynamic counseling.

172. A: The correct answer is depression, as these symptoms are most closely associated with this disorder. Choice *B* is incorrect. Although an individual with anxiety may display these symptoms, they are more likely to experience things like shortness of breath, a fast or irregular heartbeat, and muscle aches and tension. Choice *C* is incorrect. Although trauma can coexist with depression, much like anxiety, its symptoms often manifest as increased physical reactivity to stress, dissociation, and increased exhaustion. Choice *D* is incorrect, as oppositional defiant disorder typically manifests with primarily emotional or behavioral symptoms.

245

173. A: The correct answer is that the suicide rate is four times higher among adoptees than non-adopted people. Choice *B* is incorrect, as studies have reflected that adoptees have *higher* instances of disenfranchised grief, which is to say that grief associated with being adopted is not often recognized societally as a valid and supported type of grief. Choice *C* is incorrect, as it is a generalization and has not been proven to be accurate. Choice *D* is incorrect, as adoptees are shown to be twice as likely to be in therapy as non-adoptees.

174. A: Choice *A* is correct. Random sampling is used so that each member of the sample is equally likely to be chosen to represent the whole. This is intended to emulate the answer arrived at had the entire population been measured. Choice *B* is incorrect. Volunteer sampling, rather than random sampling, is used so members of the population can choose whether they want to be included in the sample. Choice *C* is incorrect. Convenience sampling, rather than random sampling, is used so units can be selectively included in the sample because they are the easiest to access. Choice *D* is incorrect. Random sampling is used so that each member of the sample *is* equally likely to be chosen to represent the whole.

175. B: The correct answer is person-centered language, which puts the person ahead of their diagnosis (for example, "a person with schizophrenia" instead of "a schizophrenic"). Choice *A* is incorrect because intellectualization is a defense mechanism in which someone uses reasoning and logic to mask an emotional response. Choice *C* is incorrect because paraphrasing is a way of briefly recounting what a person has just shared. Choice *D* is incorrect because inclusive language is a manner of speaking in which one avoids using language or expressions that are racist, sexist, or otherwise prejudicial against marginalized people.

176. C: The correct answer is Choice *C* because the Gestalt model identifies self-awareness as a vital component of self-growth and recognizes that there may be things "blocking" a person's self-awareness. Choice *A* is incorrect because it reflects a Freudian model; the Gestalt model primarily focuses on the "here and now." Choice *B* is incorrect because the hallmark belief of Gestalt therapy is that self-awareness is always varying. Choice *D* is incorrect because Gestalt clinicians believe that awareness is essential in a person's ability to self-regulate.

177. C: While reflective listening is a useful therapeutic technique, it is not one of the three primary attributes noted by Carl Rogers, which are correctly identified in Choices *A*, *B*, and *D* as congruence, unconditional positive regard, and empathic understanding.

178. B: The correct answer is Choice *B* because stress is intertwined with the most common stressors for relapsing: hunger, anger, loneliness, tiredness (HALT). This acronym is widely utilized in recovery programs. Choices *A* and *C* can certainly be predictors of recovery maintenance, but they are not the best answers. Choice *D* is irrelevant to recovery.

179. D: A person with a "super-reasonable" communication style is calm, disconnected from emotional responses, and chooses their words carefully. Choice *A* is incorrect because it describes a "distractor" stress communication style. Choice *B* is incorrect because it describes a "blamer" stress communication style. Choice *C* is incorrect because it describes a "placater" stress communication style.

180. A: The correct answer is conservation, which in this case is the understanding that the volume of water is equal in each glass despite the shapes of the glasses. Choice *B* is incorrect, as object permanence refers to understanding that an object or person is still there despite them not being in direct eyesight. Choice *C* is incorrect, as reciprocal socialization means being able to socialize

246

bidirectionally with another person. Choice *D* is incorrect, as abstract reasoning refers to a more advanced ability to logically solve problems and understand complex patterns.

181. C: Choice *C* is correct. The counselor should ignore the client unless the client addresses them first. Choice *A* is incorrect. The counselor should not acknowledge the client with a friendly greeting unless the client greets them first. Choice *B* is incorrect. The counselor should not ask how the client has been since their last session, as this puts the client's confidentiality at risk. Choice *D* is incorrect. The counselor should not ignore the client if the client chooses to initiate conversation; it is fine to speak with a client if they have chosen to say hello to the counselor while in public.

182. A: Choice *A* is correct. Awareness of, responsiveness to, and respect for race, ethnicity, gender, spirituality, religion, sexual orientation, and social class fall into the category of multicultural competence. Choices *B* is incorrect because it does not include gender as one of the cultural aspects. Choice *C* is incorrect because it does not include gender nor spirituality in the list of cultural aspects. Choice *D* is incorrect because colorblindness dismisses the lived experiences of people of color.

183. B: Choice *B* is correct. There are five types of correlation coefficients; each describes a linear relationship between two variables. It is a relationship between two variables, such that when one changes, so does the other. Choice *A* is incorrect. The relationship described is linear. Choice *C* is incorrect. The relationship described can only be linear. Choice *D* is incorrect because Choice *B* is true.

184. B: Choice *B* is correct. A Z-test allows one to examine differences between one sample and a population. When computing the Z-test statistic, one is testing whether a sample mean belongs to or represents a population mean. Choice *A* is incorrect because instead of a Z-test, an independent T-test looks at the means of two independent groups to find any evidence that the means of the population being represented may be significantly different. Choice *C* is incorrect. A dependent T-test, rather than a Z-test, compares the means of two related groups to determine whether the means differ in a manner which is statistically significant. Choice *D* is incorrect. A chi-squared test, rather than a Z-test, assesses the goodness of fit between observed values and those expected theoretically.

185. C: Choice *C* is correct because Emilio gave a personal reaction to his client's presenting issue. This is an example of countertransference, which is when a therapist projects their own emotions onto their client. Choice *A* is the opposite concept; transference refers to when the client projects their feelings about someone else onto their counselor. Choice *B* is incorrect; an empathetic response would have required Emilio to engage in reflective listening and empathize with his client's feelings. Choice *D* is incorrect because while Emilio is being open with Mark, he is doing so in a way that serves himself rather than Mark. This displays incongruence.

186. B: The correct answer is rumination, as Vera is engaging in a repetitive cycle of negative thinking. Choice *A* is incorrect, as intrusive thoughts are typically frightening in nature and are not necessarily repetitive. Choice *C* is incorrect, as overgeneralization refers to a cognitive distortion in which a person believes they can predict the outcome of something based on one instance. Choice *D* is incorrect, as introspection is typically a healthy process in which a person looks inward to reflect on their own thoughts and feelings.

187. D: Choice *D* is correct. Choice *A* and *B* are both true. A client must give consent to electronic communication, and a client must be made aware of the risks of electronic communication. Choice *A* is incorrect because Choice *B* is also true. Choice *B* is incorrect because Choice *A* is also true. Choice *C* is incorrect. Electronic communication between a client and therapist is not automatically forwarded to the client's insurance company.

188. C: The correct answer is to shift perspective and cultivate empathy; through role reversal, each member of the couple can see themselves through a "mirror" and understand how their partner might be feeling. Choice *A* is incorrect because role reversal is not about determining who is right or wrong. Choice *B* is incorrect because role reversal is not meant to elicit permanent behavior change, which might not even be necessary depending on the situation. Choice *D* is incorrect because role reversal is typically intended to help couples respond to conflict rather than elicit it.

189. C: The correct answer is identification, which is the process by which a child assumes the characteristics or behaviors of their parent. Choice *A* is incorrect. Although introjection is a Freudian term, it instead refers to the internalization of another person's values or beliefs (in other words, their "voice"). Choice *B* is incorrect, as *initialization* is not a Freudian term, and it refers to the process in which we internalize external values and are unaware of the origin of said values. Choice *D* is incorrect. Although intellectualization is a Freudian term, it refers to a defense mechanism in which one uses intellectual knowledge and processes to avoid emotional experiences or expression.

190. D: Choice *D* is correct. All of the above, except the opinion of the client's parent, must be considered when a counselor is assessing this client's ability to provide informed consent. Choice *A* is incorrect. This is only one factor a counselor must consider to assess the client's ability to provide informed consent. Choice *B* is incorrect. The opinion of the client's parent is irrelevant to the client's ability to provide informed consent when the client's parent is not their legal guardian. Choice *C* is incorrect. This is only one factor a counselor must consider while assessing the client's ability to provide informed consent.

191. C: The correct answer is dispositional (internal) attribution, which means that Mark is attributing Marisol's behavior to personal character traits and/or flaws. Choice *A* is incorrect because situational (external) attribution claims that a behavior results from some event or occurrence outside of the person's control. Choice *B* is incorrect because defensive attribution occurs when one blames outside forces for an event to minimize one's participation in the event. Choice *D* is incorrect because self-serving attribution attributes positive events to their own character or ability while attributing negative events to outside forces beyond their control.

192. D: The correct answer is to build healthy, sustainable relationships, as research demonstrates that along with reducing overall stress and strengthening life skills, this helps to counteract potential effects of ACEs. Choice *A* is incorrect, as one does not need to maintain complete sobriety if drug and alcohol use has not been identified as an issue. It is instead encouraged for someone to be aware of the biological and social elements at play with regard to one's alcohol and drug use. Choice *B* is incorrect, as engaging in regular preventative healthcare is the preferred approach for non-emergent health issues. Choice *C* is incorrect because, although therapy can indeed bring up stressful memories, engaging in true trauma-informed care can be an extremely useful tactic in mitigating future negative impacts of ACEs.

193. C: Choice *C* is correct because it describes a situation in which concurrent treatment can occur: counseling and psychiatric care. Choice *A* is incorrect; it describes a conflict of interest, and the counselor would need to refer the client to a new provider. Choice *B* is incorrect as this client is entering a more intensive level of care. Choice *D* is incorrect because it is an example of a client going into less intensive treatment.

194. C: The correct answer is a primitive reflex, as rooting is an innate reflex that normally-developed infants exhibit. Choice *A* is incorrect, as the Moro reflex refers to another primitive reflex in which infants startle in response to a stimulus. Choice *B* is incorrect, as locomotor reflexes include

248

swimming, crawling, and stepping, which do not appear until much later in child development. Choice D is incorrect, as postural reflexes do not appear until later in child development and are related to keeping the body aligned and upright.

195. B: The correct answer is Ray, a 23-year-old black male. Statistically speaking, both males and black people rank highest in hesitancy to share with a counselor, particularly one of a different race. Choices A and C are incorrect because female clients are statistically more likely to engage in therapy. Choice D is incorrect because Frank would be statistically more likely to engage with someone who is of the same race.

196. B: The correct answer is performing, a later stage in group therapy in which group members have become more in tune with their fellow group members' strengths and weaknesses and generally possess more insight into group processes. Choice A is incorrect because in the norming stage, group cohesion is still in early development. Choice C is incorrect because storming is a very early stage in which surface conflicts are still in the midst of being resolved. Choice D is incorrect because, although group cohesion is strongly developed by the adjourning stage, group members are more focused on grieving and processing the group's end.

197. B: Choice B is correct. Solely asking open-ended questions is not a useful element of a diagnostic interview. It is helpful to use both closed-ended or checklist questions as well as open-ended questions in a diagnostic interview. Choices A, C, and D are incorrect. A mental status exam, the DSM-5, and obtaining a developmental history are all useful elements of a diagnostic interview.

198. C: The correct answer is anorexia nervosa. Aside from substance abuse-related disorders, it holds the highest mortality rate. Choices A and D are incorrect, as neither are specifically associated with a particularly high mortality rate. Choice B, although also associated with a higher all-cause mortality rate, is incorrect, as the rate is significantly lower than Choice C.

199. A: The correct answer is monotropy, which is the innate need to attach to a primary caregiver and receive continuous care from them, particularly in the first two and a half years of life. Choice B is incorrect, as maternal deprivation instead refers to the process of a child being removed from their mother during the pivotal attachment period. Choice C is incorrect, as monogamy refers to a style of marriage. Choice D is incorrect. Although attachment theory describes the overarching theory that Bowlby subscribes to, it does not describe the specific phenomenon in question here.

200. A: The correct answer is, "That is a great description. Let's try that again using 'I' statements." Gestalt therapists are oriented to the present and encourage clients to own their thoughts and feelings rather than distancing themselves by using language like "it" or "you." Choices B and D are incorrect because they are past-oriented statements. Choice C is incorrect because it is future-oriented; this would be an appropriate response in solution-focused therapy.

NCE Practice Test #3, #4, & #5

To keep the size of this book manageable, save paper, and provide a digital test-taking experience, the 3rd – 5th practice test can be found online. Scan the QR code or go to this link to access it:

testprepbooks.com/bonus/nce

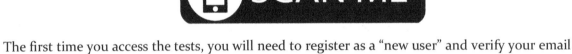

The first time you access the tests, you will need to register as a "new user" and verify your email address.

If you have any issues, please email support@testprepbooks.com.

Index

ACA Code of Ethics, 22, 23, 25, 35, 37, 152, 176

Achievable, 90

Action, 22, 27, 30, 31, 58, 72, 77, 81, 89, 96, 101, 102, 113, 114, 137, 141, 148, 154, 159, 166, 169, 170, 175, 178

Active Listening, 44, 134

Activity Theory, 63

Addiction, 79, 102

Addictions, 75, 87, 102

Adjourning, 123, 125

Adjustment (Separation), 83

Affectional Orientation, 106

Affirmations, 102

Aggressive Style of Communication, 85

Aging, 62, 63, 66

Albert Roberts, 114, 152

Alliances, 99

Alternative Family, 106

Alternative Hypothesis, 21

American Counseling Association (ACA), 32, 35

American Counseling Association (ACA) Code of Ethics, 32

Americans With Disabilities Act of 1990 (ADA), 34, 146

Analyses of Covariance (ANCOVA), 21

Analyses of Variance Tests, 21

Anxiety, 28, 41, 49, 54, 55, 62, 64, 66, 67, 68, 69, 70, 71, 72, 73, 75, 76, 77, 78, 80, 81, 82, 83, 84, 88, 90, 93, 102, 105, 112, 114, 122, 128, 131, 137, 148, 153, 158, 165, 168, 170, 177, 179, 187

Anxious Attachment Style, 69

Arousal and Reactivity Symptoms, 75

Asexual, 129

Assertive Communication Style, 84

Assessment Tools, 92

Attachment Style, 69, 77, 84, 138, 150, 168, 177

Attachment Theory, 69

Attending, 134

Attunement, 132

Atypical Depression, 71

Authoritarian Parenting Style, 85

Authoritative Parenting Style, 85, 152

Autocratic, 121, 182

Autonomy, 23, 149, 177

Avoidance Symptoms, 75

Avoidant, 69, 77, 138, 150, 168, 177

Avoiding Style, 113

Bad Transference, 115

Beck Depression Inventory (BDI), 69, 159

Beck Depression Inventory-II (BDI-II), 53

Beck Hopelessness Scale (BHS), 69

Behavioral Process Addictions, 75

Beneficence, 23

Bergen Shopping Addiction Scale, 75

Bi-Gender, 130

Biofeedback, 73

Biological Aging, 62

Biopsychosocial Framework, 39

Bio-Psychosocial Model of Addiction, 79

Bisexual, 129

Bivariate Tabular Analysis, 21

Blended Family, 82, 110

Blocking, 120, 146, 174

Boundaries, 99, 108, 109

Boundaries In Systems Theory, 108

Bricklin Perceptual Scales (BPS), 53

Bruce Tuckman's Four-Stage Model, 123

Bullying, 64

Business Associate Agreement (BAA), 32

CAGE Questionnaire, 55

CAGE-Adapted to Include Drugs (AID), 55

Career Counseling, 72

Carl Rogers, 119, 129, 133, 135, 136, 142, 151, 177

Case Studies, 16, 37, 38

Change Talk, 103

Chief Complaint, 39

Chi-Square Tests, 21

Chronological Aging, 62

Clarification Phase, 29

Clarifying, 43, 44, 93

Client Progress, 93

Closed Boundaries, 108

Closed Group, 92

Closed Groups, 100, 147, 175

Close-Ended Questions, 43

Code of Ethics, 23, 25, 26

Co-Dependents Anonymous (CoDA), 112

Cognition and Mood Symptoms, 75

Cognitive and Behavioral Aspects, 41

Cognitive Behavioral Groups, 126